Rune Magic

Figure 1 The most ancient forerunners of the runes: pre-alphabetic
symbols painted in Tiver on the skull of a mammoth from
Mezhirich, Ukraine, 14,000 years old.

Rune Magic

Nigel Pennick

Thorsons
An Imprint of HarperCollins*Publishers*

Thorsons
An Imprint of HarperCollins*Publishers*
77–85 Fulham Palace Road,
Hammersmith, London W6 8JB

First published by The Aquarian Press 1992
Thorsons edition 1995
5 7 9 10 8 6 4

A catalogue record for this book
is available from the British Library

ISBN 1 85538 105 2

Phototypeset by Harper Phototypesetters Limited
Northampton, England
Printed in Great Britain by
HarperCollinsManufacturing Glasgow

Contents

Acknowledgements

I would like to thank some people who have been helpful in various ways in the gestation of this book; either they have been with me at the right place and the right time, have taken me there, or have given information that has proved insightful. They are: Karl Aldinger, Freya Aswynn, Michael Behrend, the late John Blackthorn, Charla Devereux, Richard Dufton, Hermann Haindl, K. Frank Jensen, Rosemarie Kirschmann, Barbara Meyer, Barry Millard, Reinhart Mumm, Martin Pennick, Rupert Pennick and Robert J.M. Rickard.

All of the illustrations in this book were drawn by Nigel Pennick, except for Figures 15, 17, 18, 24 and 29, which are taken from the author's collection.

Introduction

Ebbing and flowing . . .
As it was,
As it is,
As it shall be, evermore –
The ebb and the flow
   Traditional Scottish adage

In many ways, modern society is in crisis. During the last century, industrial technology has transformed human life to the point of threatening its very existence. Human life, always precarious, has become even more unstable. Enormous changes have taken place in the world recently, and we can expect more surprises in the future. Unfortunately, modern society has no power to deal with the problems it has created. It is based on materialism, which has been tested and proven to be psychologically and spiritually bankrupt. The looming ecological crisis is just the outward expression of a human internal crisis: large numbers of people are cut off from their spiritual roots and cast adrift in a world which seems chaotic and meaningless.

In response to this, many people are now seeking a more natural, spiritual way of living, generally through 'New Age' thinking: the recognition that a change is due. Time passes in cycles, and has now reached the point where people are rediscovering the ancient skills and wisdom of their ancestors. No longer can traditional life-skills be ignored – they offer a way out of the dead-end of materialism. According to runic astrology, we are living at the beginning of the era of Peorth, the rune of creative opportunities. This is bringing us new possibilities that help us to live a life-affirming, holistic lifestyle, combining personal wholeness with the well-being of Planet Earth.

If we take time to listen to Mother Earth herself, she will speak to us in many ways. Personified as the goddess Erda, she uses the language of the runes. Historically, the runes come from the native spiritual path of Northern Europe – the Northern Tradition – but, like all true magical systems, they are universal. Rooted in shamanism, they are symbols of natural truth. Like any living system, the runes continue to adapt to new conditions, to grow and evolve to access the essence of being, creating new forms appropriate for new ages. Used carefully, they can raise our consciousness, giving us access to the inner knowledge of reality. With them we can explore the limitless possibilities of existence.

Using the runes today promises us a return to eternal values, balance within ourselves and harmony between human beings and Nature. Ultimately, rune magic is a means of self-transformation. It is not an end in itself: it is a means towards personal growth. If we use the runes respectfully, the way will be shown to us, step by step, revealing truths and potentials we could never have thought possible at the beginning of our journey.

Nigel Campbell Pennick
Bar Hill, Lammas 1991

1

The Runes in History

Attention, ye hearers, give ear to my words,
High-born and low-born of Heimdall's children,
You want me to word the works of Woden,
To recite the oldest rhymes I know.
The Chant of Wala

The Origin of Runes

Several ancient Western alphabets, not only the runes, have
strong magical content. These include Hebrew, Greek,
Glagolitic, Westphalian, Coelbren, Ogham, Gaelic and of
course, Runic. In each of these alphabets, every character
has a name which reflects its sound and has a series of
related meanings. Through these meanings, we can gain a
greater understanding of the world.

Of all the magical alphabets, runes are the most
developed. Technically, runic is not actually an 'alphabet'.
The word 'alphabet' really means a row of characters
beginning with *alpha* and *beta* – A, B, and so on. Other
letter-systems have other names. For example, the ancient
Welsh 'alphabet' is called the *Abcedilros* because this is the
order of the letters. Unlike most systems, the various runic
rows begin with the letters F, U, Th, A, R, K. So runic
'alphabets' are always known as the *Futhark*.

The actual word 'rune' denotes its secret and magical
uses. The old languages of northern Europe preserve this
meaning in several ways. One of the basic meanings of *rune*
is 'to whisper'. The Old English verb 'to rown' and the

modern German *raunen* have a similar meaning. In Anglo-Saxon times, legal and political discussions were called runes. At such meetings, actual runes were used for guidance. The confidentiality and secrecy of the ancient runes still persists in modern Irish. Here, *rún* means 'secret', 'intention', 'inclination' or 'resolution'. Scots Gaelic, too, has the word *rùn* which means 'secret', 'mystery', 'intention', 'purpose', 'wish', 'accord' and 'love'. The word 'rune' can also mean a 'lot' used in divination. The Scots word *run-rig* describes the old method of allocating 'rigs' or allotments of land, using runes in a lottery.

Basically, then, the word 'rune' refers to some aspect of the mysterious inner structure of existence. These are specifically described by the rune's name. Each rune has its own name which describes an object or quality from everyday life: ox, horse, bow, torch, etc. But the concept present in each rune name also contains the ideas and correspondences surrounding it. In this way, every runic letter is a storehouse of knowledge and meaning which can

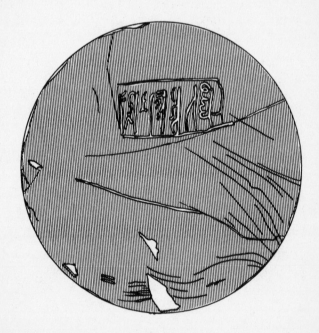

Figure 2 Pre-runic characters on a lignite disc found at Portpatrick, Galloway, Scotland, among the debris of an ancient workshop for lignite ornaments and talismans (*c*.1000 BCE).

only be understood fully by those who study runecraft. With the runes, we can examine and describe every aspect of life.

The magical power of the runes lies not only in their individual meanings, but also in the possibility of combining these meanings. Rune magic is also dynamic, flexible, creative and developing. In the nature of things, each day brings something new. Novel circumstances produce new experiences and new relationships. No time and no place can ever be exactly like any other, before or afterwards. Although these events are different from any that happened before, naturally they will still conform to the broader patterns of the way things happen – the process of transvolution. Correspondingly, the action of the runes must also be interpreted in new ways. If they are to have any value at all, both the meanings and the magical uses of the runes must relate to present conditions. Of course, whilst there are some meanings that will never be appropriate for certain runes, they must always be understood in terms of present conditions. This creative, non-dogmatic approach is a characteristic aspect of the Northern Tradition today, as it was in past times.

The Historical Origin of the Runes

The runes have no 'single source'. As a phonetic alphabet, most runic letters come from the North Italic script. This was the system used by the Etruscans. Before it was destroyed by Roman militarism, the Etruscan culture was very influential, and its magic lies at the roots of later European magic. Etruscan artistic influence can be seen in continental Celtic and Germanic metalwork of the first millennium BCE. The link between the Etruscan alphabet and the runes is known from 26 bronze helmets, dug up in 1812 at Negau in the Austrian Empire, and dating from the fourth century BCE. Engraved on the helmets were Germanic words, including an invocation of the war-god Harigast (*Harigasti teiva*) in Etruscan script. Also, around this period, seers in the Tyrol began to use these letters for divination, possibly following Etruscan practice. Some of the earliest runic divination-sticks were found at Kitzbühel.

These finds could, in theory, prove the Etruscan origin

of runes, but it is not that simple. Many of the characters that became runestaves already existed elsewhere. Pictographic symbols representing trees, tools and natural phenomena have been preserved in rock carvings and a few surviving wooden objects. During the late Bronze and early Iron Ages (1300 – 800 BCE), a large number of pictographic rock carvings, known as *Hällristningar*, were made in Scandinavia. It is possible that these carvings are part of a lost, ancient form of writing. Over the years, other strange carvings have come to light but they have been ignored because they cannot be deciphered. One example is the lignite disc, found at Portpatrick in Galloway, Scotland, illustrated here (Figure 2). Many of the individual carvings from this culture were almost identical in form to the letters of the Etruscan alphabet. The runes may well have come into being through a combination of the two systems.

It is certain that some of these symbols were used for divination before the creation of the Futhark. But the runes as such came into being when some of these symbols were identified with corresponding letters of the Etruscan alphabet. This act of creative insight is symbolised in the Norse legend of Odin. It seems that the runes as we know them were obtained through a precise ritual. His ordeal is recorded in *Hávamál* (stanzas 138 and 139):

> I know that I hung on the windswept tree,
> For nine days and nine nights,
> I was pierced with a spear, and given to Odin,
> Myself given to myself,
> On that tree, which no man knows,
> From which roots it arises.
> They helped me neither with bread,
> Nor with drinking horn.
> I took the runes.
> Screaming, I took them,
> Then I fell back from that place.

According to tradition, Odin is the god of magic, poetry, divination and inspiration. In ancient society, these abilities were associated with shamanism. The practice of shamanism gives direct access to the otherworld, which cannot be reached in a normal state of consciousness. To access the otherworld, shamans have undergone the experience of the primal being, Ymir, by which he or she experiences the psychic trauma of being dismembered, scattered through the worlds, and finally reassembled. The person who survives this ordeal transcends the horror, becoming reintegrated as a shaman. Sometimes this happens spontaneously, as the result of injury or illness. In order to achieve this artificially, shamanic techniques include dangerous, potentially lethal, practices. Often, they involve using natural hallucinogenic or trance-inducing roots, herbs, seeds, fruits and fungi, or some form of self-torture and mutilation. *Hávamál* tells of such a shamanic initiation. Odin's ordeal was to hang from a tree, enduring pain, hunger and thirst for nine days and nights, a magically powerful period of time. His torment was concluded by a flash of insight which allowed him to release the full potential of the runes for human use. It was a rare moment in history where the two sides of the brain, analytical and intuitive, were linked by a unified response. Ultimately, this magical overview of existence is at the root of the power of the runes.

The Elder Futhark

Today, most rune users work with a row of 24 runes. This is the oldest and most widespread runic system, known as the Common Germanic Futhark or the Elder Futhark, evidence of which dates back to the fifth century CE.

The rune rows are divided into three groups of eight runes which are as aettir (singular aett). This is a Norse word which, as well as describing a group of eight runes, denotes the eight directions, place, and family. The Scots word Airt has the same meaning. Magically, each of these three aettir is ruled over by a god and goddess. The first aett, which begins with the letter Feoh (F), is sacred to Frey and Freyja, the divinities of fertility. They are the main figures of the Vanir, the gods of the older Norse pantheon. The second aett begins with Hagal (H) and is ruled by the guardian god and goddess, Heimdall and Mordgud. The third begins with Tyr (T) and is ruled by Tyr and Zisa, god and goddess of law and justice.

Like the letters of the Roman alphabet, each of the runes has its own name, representing a sound. This is the basis of runic writing. But, because each runestave has a

Figure 3 Common variations on the rune-rows: Lines 1–3, the Elder Futhark and its extensions; Line 4, the Younger Futhark; Lines 5–6, medieval Scandinavian Dotted Runes; Line 7, Hälsinge Runes; Line 8, modern German Armanen runes after Guido von List.

meaning, anything written in runes is also a combination of the meanings present in those characters. These meanings are described in the three ancient rune poems from England, Norway and Iceland. The runes' names may vary, but the basic meanings do not.

In the Elder Futhark the runes are as follows:

First aett:

1	F	Feoh	cattle, wealth
2	U	Ur	ox (Aurochs), primal strength
3	Th	Thorn	thorn, giant, protection

4	A	As	god, divine power
5	R	Rad	riding, wheel, motion
6	K	Ken	pine, torch, knowledge
7	G	Gyfu	gift of the gods, talent/burden
8	W	Wyn	joy, prosperity

Second aett:

9	H	Hagal	hail, formation
10	N	Nyd	need, necessity
11	I	Is	ice, static force
12	J	Jera	season, year, completion
13	Z/Eo	Eoh	yew tree, bow, defence
14	P	Peorth	dice cup, womb, dance of fate
15	X	Elhaz	elk, defensive power
16	S	Sigel	sun, brightness, victory

Third aett:

17	T	Tyr	the god Tyr, sword, power
18	B	Beorc	birch tree, purification, regeneration
19	E	Ehwaz	horse, transformation
20	M	Man	human being
21	L	Lagu	water, life energy, flow
22	Ng	Ing	the god Ing, expansion and protection
23	O	Odal	homestead, possessions
24	D	Dag	day, the light of noontide

As with all alphabets, the order of letters in the Elder Futhark is fixed. But unlike the Roman alphabet, where the letters have little meaning, the whole Futhark is a symbol of progression. The order of its letters is a step-by-step development of meaning, creating a coherent whole. This is why those who have ignored its order through ignorance or perversity have only succeeded in destroying its overall meaning.

There is only one exception to this basic rune order. It is with the final two runes, Odal and Dag. In a few historic rune rows, these two are reversed, making the 'Od' of Odin but, more conventionally, Dag comes before Odal, which terminates the row. The symbolic reason for this is that standard runic order relates directly to the cycles of both the day and the year, each rune representing some quality of

its corresponding time. This is explained in detail in my
book *Runic Astrology* (Aquarian, 1990).

Later Developments

The Elder Futhark did not remain unchanged for long.
Unlike the Greek and Roman alphabets, the runes did not
become fixed. There was no Pagan church or state
institution to enforce standards. Instead, new forms came
into being when the need arose. In Frisia (Friesland), now
north-eastern Holland and north-western Germany,
around the fifth century, four new runes were added to the
existing 24. This formed the Futhark which migrants
brought to England. This 28-character Futhark is known
from a single-edged short sword found in the River Thames
in 1857. It has the complete rune row inlaid in silver as a
magic protection.

The extra letters in this rune row are:

25	A(short)	Ac	oak tree
26(4)	O	Os	mouth/speech
27	Y	Yr	a bow, yew tree
28	Io	Ior	a water-beast

In Britain, a further rune was added to this row. It is:

29	Ea	Ear	earth/grave

This created the 'Anglo-Saxon' Futhark of 29 runes. It seems
that this last rune was then reimported by Frisians to their
homeland and used there in magical inscriptions. At this
time, runic was the major form of writing in these
countries. Coins minted in the English kingdoms of East
Anglia and Mercia bear runic inscriptions. Among the
English kings whose names appeared in runes were
Beonna, Ethilberht, Peada and Aethelred.

Around the year 800, in the north of England and what
is now the south of Scotland, the Anglo-Saxon Futhark was
extended further. Another four runes appeared, creating
the 33-character Northumbrian Futhork, the longest rune
row of the Elder Futhark. This marked the end of Anglo-
Saxon runic development.

Although there are some variations, the Northumbrian rune row is divided into four aettir of eight staves, leaving one rune, Gar, which is placed in the centre. Some of the runes of the fourth aett have a Celtic influence. Their names and meanings are related to those of their corresponding Ogham letters. This is strong evidence of communication and interchange between Celtic and Germanic magicians, probably in what is now southern Scotland. The extra runes in the Northumbrian row are:

30 Q Cweorth apple tree, ceremonial fire
31 K Calc chalice, calculating-stone or chessman
32 St Stan a stone
33 G Gar a spear

The most remarkable surviving evidence of Northumbrian runes is the so-called 'Franks Casket' in the British Museum. It is carved from whale's bone, bearing scenes from Northern Tradition and Christian mythology, with the scenes described in decorative Northumbrian runes. Another notable relic of this period is the cross at Ruthwell in Scotland, which dates from the eighth century. It has a long runic inscription which is a passage from the Old English Christian poem, 'The Dream of the Rood'. The

Figure 4 'Hogsback' (house-shaped) tombstone from Falstone, Northumberland, England, with biliteral inscription in runes and Anglo-Saxon letters, 8th century CE.

Ruthwell Cross is an early example of runes used by the church, but it is not unique. Other runic crosses of the period still exist in northern England and southern Scotland although many were destroyed in the 1600s by religious fanatics. There are also many Christian runic monuments in Scandinavia.

When King Alfred the Great introduced Roman-style education to England the runes were no longer used for everyday writing and were reserved for magical use. Also, by then, another rune row was being used in Britain. These were the real 'Viking Runes', a version of the Younger Futhark, used by the invading Danes.

Runes in Scandinavia

As the rune row was expanding in England, it was being reduced in Scandinavia. Some time around the eighth century, eight of the original runes went out of use, reducing the row to sixteen characters. Two variants of this Younger Futhark emerged, the Danish and the Swedish-Norse Futharks. The Danish rune row is probably the older of the two. A complete example of it can be found on the Gørlev Stone in Zealand, Denmark, on a monument that dates from around 900 CE. The letters of both the Danish and Swedish-Norse Futharks are: F, U, Th, A, R, K, H, N, I, A, S, T, B, M, L, R. The earliest known list of the sixteen Danish runes comes from the *Abecedarium Nordmannicum*, a ninth century manuscript from St Gallen in Switzerland. It reads: 'Feu first, Ur thereafter, Thuris the third stave, Os thereabove, at the end write Rait; Chaion joins thereto, Hagal, Naut has Iss, Ar and Sol, T, Bria and Man in the middle, Lagu filled with light, Yr ends them all.' These names are very close to those of the Elder Futhark runes, from which they were derived. Like the Elder Futhark, both versions of the Younger Futhark were divided into three aettir. The first aett of the Younger Futhark has six runes, whilst the other two each have five. The aettir are named Frey, Hagal and Tyr, respectively.

The Swedish-Norse runes are simpler than the Danish runes. This indicates a slightly later origin. They also have slightly different names. They are:

First aett:

1	F	Fa	money, gold
2	U	Dr	drizzle, slag
3	Th	Thurs	giant
4	O	áss	a god, estuary
5	R	Reidh	a riding
6	K	Kaun	a sore, ulcer

Second aett:

7	H	Hagall	hail
8	N	Naudhr	need, distress
9	I	íss	ice
10	A	ár	good year, harvest
11	S	Sól	the goddess Sól, sun

Third aett:

12	T	Tyr	the god Tyr
13	B	Bjarkan	a birch twig
14	L	Laugur	water
15	M	Madur	a man
16	R/Y	Yr	a yew tree

As well as the Elder Futhark, the Anglo-Saxon Futhark and the Northumbrian Futhork, all of the Younger Futhark systems were used in Britain. During the tenth century, yet another version came into being. This was the Hälsinge rune row, even simpler in form. As far as possible, this Futhark removed all vertical strokes. Instead, letters were written between two lines, with a series of marks that resemble shorthand. Clearly, it was developed to assist rapid writing. But the Hälsinge rune row was never used widely. By the thirteenth century, Scandinavian runes were becoming standardised. In Sweden, the Danish Futhark became the norm, whilst in Norway, a new form arose. This was the so-called *mixed* rune row, which used letters from both the Danish and Swedish-Norse systems. A form of it was used in various parts of the British Isles. Finally, around 1200, this gave rise to yet another distinct runic alphabet, the *pointed* or *dotted* runes. This expanded the rune row once more, to 25 characters. The Futhark order was given up in favour of that of the Roman alphabet. There were a number of local versions, but a standard form was most widespread.

This version of runic was used for many years. In the thirteenth century, the Swedish *Codex Runicus*, recording the provincial law of the province of Skåne, was written in runes. Most runestones in Sweden have this script. There are also several notable inscriptions in Swedish churches. Good examples are the thirteenth-century font at Burserud, and the tombstone of Bishop Gisike at Lösen, which dates from 1311. A beautiful runic inscription also exists in the cathedral at Lund. Carved at the base of one of the pillars are the words 'Got Help' (God help us), in dotted runes. The inscription was made by the master mason Adam Van Düren in 1500.

A later variant of the dotted runes was known as the *Alphabeticum Gothicum* (literally, and incorrectly, the Gothic Alphabet), used in printed type-faces. People continued to use these runes in private correspondence and in calendars until the late eighteenth century. In the 1540s, Mogens Gyldenstjerne, admiral of the Danish Royal Navy, used runes to write his private journal. Later, in the Thirty Years' War (1618–48), the Swedish general, Jacob de la Gardie, wrote his secret military orders in runes. For calendars, new runes were developed. The traditional wooden almanacs known as *primestaves*, *clog almanacks* or *runestocks* used runes for numbers. To mark the number of years in the Sun and Moon cycles one needs nineteen numbers, so three others were added to the sixteen runes of Scandinavia. These were new runes, called Aurlaugr, Twimadur and Belgtzhor (17, 18 and 19 respectively).

Although the Irish Druids had their own alphabet, Ogham, they also used several runic systems. At one time, it seems that runic was the main form of writing in Ireland. This is apparent because all words related to writing in modern Irish have the element rún. Excavations in Dublin have revealed objects with Danish and Swedish-Norse runes, and in later times, local versions were used there. These are known from medieval manuscripts, where they are called *Gall Ogham* and *Lockland Ogham*. The name 'Ogham' identifies these alphabets as magical. They are scribes' versions of the mixed and dotted runes, with some extra characters necessary for writing in Irish.

Other Runes

Although they have never been included in any rune row, there are a number of other ancient runic characters. Compared with the Elder Futhark, they are less well known, and little used today. They are mainly the runes of some ancient gods. Along with Gar they form the nucleus of a developing fifth aett. They are:

34	Ai	Wolfsangel	wolf-hook
35	Oe	Erda	earth, garden
36	Ue	Ul	the god Waldh, turning-point
37	Zz	Ziu	the god Ziu, a thunderbolt
38	Ss	Sol	the goddess Sól, sun-disc

These runes were used in the middle ages for healing and magical protection.

Modern Runes

The twentieth century saw a renewal of rune use. From 1902, the Austrian occultist Guido von List, the father of nationalist-oriented Germanic magic, developed his own runic system. To the sixteen staves of the Norwegian mixed runes, he added two more, which he called Eh and Gibor. He called his new eighteen-letter system the Armanen Runes. He claimed it was the restoration of the 'true' runic system described in the eighteen spells of *Hávamál* (see pages 25–8). The meanings of von List's runes are virtually the same as those of the Scandinavian rows. Their names differ slightly:

1	F	Fa	10	A	Ar
2	U	Ursache	11	S	Sig
3	Th	Thor/Dorn	12	T	Tyr
4	O	Os	13	B	Bar
5	R	Rit	14	L	Laf
6	K	Ka	15	M	Man
7	H	Hagal	16	Y	Yr
8	N	Not	17	E	Eh
9	I	Is	18	G	Gibor

The Armanen runes are based upon the six-branches of the Hagal rune. This, in turn, came from the hexagonal lattice which underlies the structure of matter. The most striking natural example of this form can be seen in clear quartz crystals which have many magical uses, being extremely popular in New Age circles today. In the Northern Tradition, the hexagonal system of crystals corresponds with the powers of the Moon. These crystals are 'frozen light' in which the Armanen runes are encoded. The different runes can be produced by shining light through a hexagonal crystal in certain ways. For example, when light is shone vertically through the crystal, Hagal is projected. When it is shone at right angles to the crystal, Is is projected. This means that the special orientation which produces each rune also describes its magical relationship to the cosmos. Looked at in this way, each rune is a form of spatial energy-mathematics.

During the 1920s and 1930s, runes became part of the decorative repertoire of architects. Runes and related craftsmen's marks from the tradition of the carpenters' guild were carved visibly to symbolise continuity with old times. For example, the Zipfer Bierhaus in Salzburg, Austria, built in 1931, is a good example. It has a series of these carved on the ceiling-rafters (Figure 6). But perhaps the most remarkable of all runic ornament of this time was in the Haus Atlantis in Bremen. Designed by the pioneering architect Bernhard Hötger, it was built in 1928. The Haus Atlantis was totally modern, and was the first building ever to use rolled steel in its construction. Inside, the decor used metal runes and tree-of-life motifs, but its most notable feature was the wood-carving on the facade. This was a representation of Odin's revelation, showing the god crucified on a wheel around which were carved the runes. Unfortunately, this Pagan sacred icon was destroyed in the 1930s for political reasons.

The Armanen runes have been very influential in German-speaking countries, where they are better known than the Elder Futhark. Many authors have written in the German language about all aspects of the Armanen runes, including the so-called 'runic yoga' of posture-magic. Further work continues today. But, in the main, this is happening independently of other rune work.

During the 1960s, outside the Germanic lands, there was

a renewal of interest in runes for divination and magic. This interest had no connection with the Armanen runes. It came from other roots, mainly scholarly research into historic rune use, and a general feeling that the time had come to re-examine the indigenous spiritual traditions of the West. The rune system which came to the fore was the oldest one, the Elder Futhark. Since then, most rune work has been done with the Elder Futhark, which remains the most popular today, even when wrongly described as 'Viking'.

Gothic Runes and the Gothic Alphabet

Another ancient version of the runes is the alphabet of the Goths. Originally, the Goths were the tribe of the Baltic island of Gotland, now part of Sweden. From there, they spread through east Prussia, Lithuania and Poland, to the northern shores of the Black Sea. There they grew in numbers, power and prosperity. Later, the Goths marched westwards to challenge the Roman Empire, eventually conquering Italy, southern France and Spain.

Before leaving Gotland, the Goths were Pagan and used the runes. On Gotland, the Kylver Stone, with the oldest complete rune row, was carved by a Gothic runester. When the Goths migrated, they converted to Arian Christianity.

Figure 5 The Gothic alphabet, in the runic letter order. Most of the letters have the same meaning as their corresponding runes.

Then, their Bishop, Ulfilas, created a new alphabet, based on the runes. He took some letters from Greek, and modified other runes. But every letter of the Gothic alphabet still had the same meaning as its runic counterpart. Like runes, they were used in magic and divination. For many years, the Goths used both the new alphabet and the runes in parallel. Gradually, the runes went out of use, but the Gothic alphabet was used by the Visigoths in Spain and the south of France until 1018. Then a church council at Toledo condemned the Gothic alphabet as heretical, and most of the books written in Gothic were burnt.

The Goths had their own names for the runes, and similar names for the letters of their alphabet. The Gothic alphabet shows its runic origin by having the same order as the runes. The first aett begins with Fe, corresponding with the Gothic rune Fahu. Next comes Uraz (Urus); then Thyth (Thauris); Aza (Ansus); Reda (Raida); Chozma (Kusma); Gewa (Giba) and Winne (Winja). The second aett is: Haal (Hagl); Noicz (Nauths); Iiz (Eis); Gaar (Jer), Waer (Aihus); Pertra (Pairthra); Ezec (Algs) and Sugil (Sadil). The last aett is: Tyz (Teiws); Bercna (Babrkan); Eyz (Egeis); Manna (Manna); Laaz,(Lagus); Enguz (Iggws); Utal (Othal) and Daaz (Dags). There is also the letter Quairtra (Cweorth).

The Gothic alphabet uses eleven Greek-style letters in place of the original runic shapes. These are Aza, Bercna, Gewa, Daaz, Eyz, Ezec, Chozma, Laaz, Noicz, Pertra and Tyz. Gothic magic integrates the magic meanings of the Greek letters with the runic ones. In this way, the Gothic alphabet continues and expands the runic tradition.

The Gothic letters have the following meaning:

1	F	Fe	bull, phallus
2	U	Uraz	primal strength, flow
3	Th	Thyth	crystal sphere
4	A	Aza	god, wealth
5	R	Reda	fruitfulness
6	K	Chozma	illness/illumination
7	G	Gewa	gift, divinity
8	W	Winne	joy
9	H	Haal	transformation
10	N	Noicz	need, old woman archetype

11	I	Iiz	ice, destiny
12	J	Gaar	year, season
13	Z	Waer	defence, sacrifice
14	P	Pertra	solar halo
15	X	Ezec	the fifteen stars
16	S	Sugil	sun, light, willpower
17	T	Tyz	human power
18	B	Bercna	birch tree, feminine power
19	W	Eyz	partnership, the aether
20	M	Manna	human being, tree
21	L	Laaz	growth, flowingness
22	Ng	Enguz	becoming
23	O	Utal	riches, abundance
24	D	Daaz	day, fourfold
25	Q	Quairtra	ceremonial fire

Historic rune magic

Northern Tradition scripture tells us of the wonderful scope of rune magic. The words of Odin, recorded in *Hávamál*, speak of 18 different power spells:

Nine power-spells I learned from the noted son
Of Bestla's father, Bolthorn: And a drink I took
Of the precious mead poured out of Othrerir.

Then I became fruitful; to grow and thrive.
Word sought word after word in me:
Spell sought spell after spell in me.

Runes you will find, and skilful characters;
Very great characters, very strong characters;
That a mighty thule painted, and great gods made,
Carved by the prophet of the gods.

Odin among Æsir, but Dain for elves
And Dvalin for dwarves,
Asviðr for giants:
Some I carved myself.

Do you know how to carve them?
Do you know how to read them?
Do you know how to paint them?
Do you know how to prove them?
Do you know how to pray with them?
Do you know how to sacrifice with them?

Do you know how to send with them?
Do you know how to offer with them?

It is better not to pray at all than to sacrifice too much:
a gift always demands a repayment.
It is better not to send at all than to offer too much:
Thus Thundr carved before the birth of nations
At that point he began when he came back.

I know those spells which no lord's wife knows,
Nor any man's son.

One is called Help, and it will help you
Against sorrows and ordeals and every grief there is.

I know the second, which those sons of men need
Who wish to live as healers.

I know the third:
If my need grows dire
For binding my deadly enemies, I dull the blades
Of my foes – neither weapon nor deception will bite for them.

I know this, the fourth:
If warriors tie up
My arms, I call this,
And I can go free: the shackles break from my feet,
And the handcuffs from my hands.

I know this, the fifth:
If I see an arrow shot in combat,
Shot deadly straight,
None flies so hard that I cannot stop it
If I catch sight of it.

I know this, the sixth;
If a lord curses me by the roots of a fresh young tree,
The man who calls down curses on me
Misfortunes will destroy him, rather than me.

I know this, the seventh:
If I see a high hall on fire around my comrades,
None burns so fiercely that I cannot rescue them;
I know the spell to chant.

I know this, the eighth:
Which is useful for everyone to learn,
Whose hatred grows for a war-king's sons:
I can soon alter that.

I know this, the ninth:
If I need to keep my ship afloat,
I can calm the wind, smooth the waves,
And lull the sea to sleep.

I know this, the tenth:
If I see the hedge-riders magically flying high,
I can make it so that they go astray
Of their own skins, and of their own souls.

I know this, the eleventh:
If I must lead old friends to battle,
I call under their shields, and they go empowered,
Safe to war, safe from war, safe wherever they are.

I know this, the twelfth:
If I see a corpse swinging from a noose high in a tree,
Then I carve and I paint the runes,
So that the man comes down and speaks with me.

I know this the thirteenth:
If I should sprinkle water on a young lord,
He will not fall, no matter if he goes to war –
The hero will not go down beneath the swords.

I know this, the fourteenth:
If I should preach of the gods at a moot,
I will know how to distinguish between all gods and elves:
Few of the unwise know this.

I know this, the fifteenth,
Which the dwarf Thjothrerir
Called before Delling's doors.
He chanted power to the gods and strength to elves,
And foresight to Hropta-Tyr.

I know this, the sixteenth:
If I want to have the wise woman's spirited games,
I steal the heart of a white-armed wench
And I turn all her thoughts.

I know this, the seventeenth:
So that the young woman will not want to avoid me.
Loddfafnir, you will be long in learning these lays,
Though they will do you good if you get them,
Be usable if you can grasp them,
Handy if you have them.

I know this, the eighteenth,
Which never will I teach Maid or Man's wife
(It is better to understand it alone – the end of the poem follows),

Except that woman who folds me in her arms,
Or perhaps my sister.

Now are the Hávamál sung in Hávi's Hall,
Essential to the sons of men, useless to the son's of giants.
Hale he sang, hale he who understands.
May he use them well who has grasped them,
Hale those who have listened.

This list of runic spells covers all possibilities: there are binding spells, love spells, battle-magic, protection against harmful magic, and the means to distinguish beneficial gods from harmful spirits. They are the basis for all modern rune magic.

The Norse sagas also give us a first-hand account of rune magic in action. *The Saga of Egill-Skallagrimsson* tells of how the hero used runes to detect poison in a drink. To do this, he cut runes onto the drinking-horn. Then, as he coloured the runes, he recited a spell. 'The horn burst asunder, spilling the drink down into the straw.' At Thorfinnr's house, Egill looked at some runes carved on a whale bone in the bed of a very ill woman. He discovered that the runester who wrote them was incompetent. Taking away the useless runes, Egill said, 'A man should not cut runes unless he can read them well. Many men can stumble on a dark stave. I saw ten dark letters scored on a scraped whale-bone: they have brought an over-long sickness to the leek-linden.' Then he cut some appropriate runes on a new tine, and laid them under the bolster of the woman's bed. Soon she awoke, as if from a sleep, and said that she was healed. This story warns us to remember that some magic was done badly in ancient times, as well as now.

Not every ancient runic inscription is necessarily good or effective rune magic. The past had errors as well as wisdom. To be successful, we must develop the understanding to distinguish the good from the bad.

Figure 6 Carved bind runes and runic sigils in the Zipfer Bierhaus, Salzburg, Austria, 1931.

Ancient Runic Amulets

Many ancient objects still exist to show us the techniques of historic rune magic. In ancient times, as now, rune magic used wood extensively, for it contains the önd (vital qualities) of the tree from which it comes (see trees, pages 145–59, for individual details). But because of their perishable nature, relatively few ancient wooden items still exist. Most of these have been discovered in waterlogged ground, which has preserved them. In Holland the remains of terpen, artificial mounds on which people once lived to avoid flooding, have revealed many wooden runic objects. They have also come to light in the old harbour districts of Bergen and Dublin, and in Danish bogs. A good example of such an object is the wooden sword discovered at Arum, near Harlingen in West Friesland, in the Netherlands. Dating from around the year 650, it bears the runic inscription *edaeboda*, interpreted as 'return', 'messenger'. It is a magical amulet intended to protect a traveller on his or her missions. Another wooden amulet, found at Britsum, Frisia, dating from the sixth or seventh century, has a runic inscription that translates: 'always carry this Yew in the battle-host'. This is warrior-magic. Yet another Frisian yew wand, found at Westeremden, has a reference to Amluth, Shakespeare's Hamlet. This amulet promises magical power over the waves of the sea and dates from around 800 CE.

Another remarkable survival from the earlier times of rune magic is the Ribe Healing Stick, a pine-wood stave, 30 centimetres in length, carrying a runic spell to exorcise the disease called The Trembler, which is thought to be the old name for malaria. Cut around the year 1300, its inscription uses both Pagan and Christian words of power: 'I pray, guard Earth and Heaven above; Sól and St Mary; and Himself the Lord God; that he grant me the hands to make whole, and words of remedy, to heal The Trembler, when treatment is necessary . . . A stone is called *Swart* [black]: it stands out to sea. On it are nine *Needs*. Neither shall they sleep nor warmly awaken until you have recovered from it.' The spell also has the words *Thoet Se* – 'so be it' – the equivalent of the magical phrases 'So mote it be' and 'Ka!'.

Grettirs Saga tells of the use of a runestaff as a means of

leaving a record of an event. The hero, Gretti the Strong,
hunted a giantess who had killed men. He set off with a
priest, who took fright and abandoned him. Gretti found
and slew the giantess, then discovered the remains of the
men. He took the bones to the priest's church, and left them
there with a runestaff on which he carved a poem
describing the events at the giantess's cave. When the priest
came to the church the next morning, he found the
runestaff which told him what had happened. This story
dates from around the year 1023.

Several amulets are shaped like tusks. This shape appears
to be a continuation of the very ancient cult of the
mammoth tusk, whose ivory had magical properties. This
cult continued into the middle ages, 10,000 years after the
last mammoth died. A mammoth tusk still hangs in a
church at Swabisch Hall in Germany, where it was believed
to be the horn of a unicorn.

Like wood, bone contains the magical essence of the
being from which it was taken. A sixth century bone amulet
from Lindholm, Sweden bears the runic formula, 'ek erilaz
sa wilagaz hateka', which translates as 'I am Erilaz, I am the
cunning one'. This is the earliest known object which bears
the runemaster's title, Erilaz. Originally, this seems to have
come from the personal name Herulian, one of the nation
of the Heruli. But whatever its origin, Erilaz later became
the title for any runemaster, which it remains today.

So as not to attract attention, many runic formulae were
written very small, often in an invisible place. They are
found on the backs of brooches, inside the bosses of
shields, and on the underside of stones. Because of this, it
is possible that many objects in museums might bear runes,
yet undiscovered. Runes were inscribed on any object that
came to hand and had the power of transforming it. A good
example is a Cufic coin minted in Samarkand, found in an
eleventh century burial place in Denmark. This bore
inscriptions in runic which were Christian prayers for
eternal life. By any account, it is a remarkable magic object,
for it combines in one small place the Islamic, Pagan and
Christian talismanic traditions. To the magicians of old,
there were no conceptual boundaries.

Runestones

Magic has always been used to protect the dead. Before runes were introduced, Scandinavian burials were marked with megalithic, unworked boulders known as bauta-stones. They can be anything between one and six metres in height. Erected from the Bronze Age onwards, these bauta-stones protected the dead from evil spirits. At a later date, runemasters began to write magical formulae upon them. Many name the runemaster rather than the dead person. Because of this, we know the names of several runemasters: Soti, Asmund Karason, Gaut Björnsson, Öpir, Toki, Lifstein and Balli. Often, the inscriptions were hidden beneath the stone for the benefit of the dead. This parallels the ancient Egyptian tradition of magical paintings inside the coffin-lid. An eighth century gravestone inscription from Eggjum, in Sogndal, Norway, describes the details of this darkness magic. It states that neither stone nor runes have seen sunlight, and that the runes were not carved with iron. It says that the stone must never be brought into the light of day. This magical procedure is identical with that of the Moonstones used by British wise women in more modern times.

Other stones were memorials, with inscriptions commemorating the dead person. Not all of them were erected over the grave. Most of them have a formula like: 'Ragnhild erected this stone in memory of Alli Sölvi, priest of the Vé, most worthy captain of the Housecarls (militia). The sons made this monument in memory of their father, and his wife in memory of her husband. Soti carved these runes in memory of his lord. May Thor consecrate them . . .' This example comes from a runestone at Glavendrup, Denmark. Sometimes, a genealogy was written, such as 'Freymund erected this stone in memory of Fe-Gylfi, son of Bresi. And Bresi was the son of Linin. And Linin was the son of Aun. And Aun the son of Ofeig. And Ofeig the son of Thori'. This is carved on a runestone at Malsta in Sweden.

As well as being memorials for the dead, runestones were put up to commemorate landowners' good works done for the benefit of the community. Road-making and bridge-building are recorded by formulae such as 'Sazur raised this stone and made the bridge', or 'Thririk's daughter made this

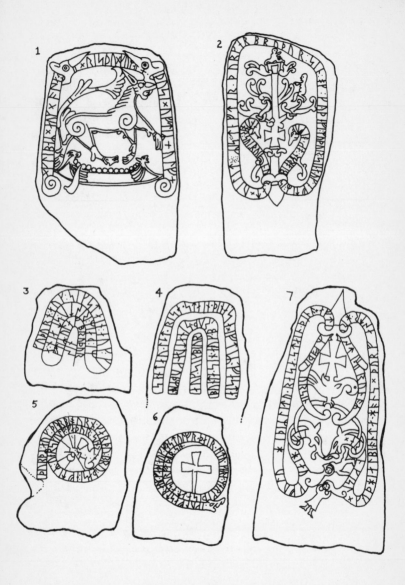

Figure 7 Medieval Swedish runestones. 1, Tulstorp, Vemenhög; 2,
Årsunda parish, Gestrike; 3, Mödisgård, Linköping; 4, Linköping
city; 5, near Glömsiö bridge, Börke, Småland; 6, Hesle, Eggeby,
Upland; 7, Grynsta Backe, Tible, Upland. These stones all have their
runes written inside the *lindwurm* pattern, which takes spiral, world-
tree and labyrinth forms.

Figure 8 Runic font, *c.*1280, at Burserud, Småland, Sweden. The inscription reads 'Arinbjorn made me, the priest Vitkundr wrote me, and here I shall stand for a while'.

bridge after Astrid, her daughter. She was the most skilful woman in Hadeland'. Two runestones at Taby in Uppland, Sweden, tell of Jarlabanki who '. . . erected these stones in his own honour, while he was still alive, and made this bridge for the good of his soul . . .'.

The later runestones have their inscriptions written between parallel lines. Often, this took the form of a serpent, the Lindorm. These often snake all over the stone in a decorative pattern. Another, more formal, layout was the Irminsul or Yggdrasil pattern. This reproduces the northern Tree of Life at the centre of the inscription. The first line of runic words begin at the bottom of the tree, written from left to right. When they reach the top, they make another line on the right of the first one. These are read from top to bottom. The next line (if there is one) starts at the left of the tree. It is read from bottom to top. Any additional lines follow on in the same sequence. The whole inscription thus forms a deosil (sunwise) spiral.

Sometimes there were magical formulae and sigils accompanying the commemorative text. These are complementary to one another, combining the pictographic and phonetic traditions. A runestone from Snoldelev in Denmark, commemorating a Thule (shaman), has a fylfot, triskele and sunwheel. Its inscription reads: 'The stone of Gunnvald, son of Hroald, Thule in Salløv'. Sometimes, inscriptions ended with a curse. One on a runestone at Tryggvaelde in Zealand, Denmark, ends with '. . . A *rati* be he who destroys this stone or drags it from here'. (A *rati* is a cursed person, whose soul is taken away by the Wild Hunt.) Another Danish runestone inscription ends '. . . a *rati* be he who destroys this stone or drags it for another'. Other people taking away memorial stones for re-use have always been a problem. Cursing them in advance is a practical way of preventing it. The tradition of memorial runestones flourished for many centuries in every place with a Scandinavian presence, from Ireland to Russia. They were made in large numbers, though many have been destroyed over the years. Nonetheless, there are still over 2500 runestones known from Sweden alone.

The Geomythics of Runamo

One of the most famous and enigmatic runic inscriptions is at Runamo, close to Brakne-Hoby, in Blekinge, Sweden. The bizarre history of this place is a valuable teaching about the nature of the runes. In former times, Runamo was a notable site. A remarkable line of runes ran along veins of quartz that stood out from Granite rock-faces. These veins were followed by a path. In the thirteenth century, Saxo Grammaticus described the scene as 'a ridge with a path . . . dotted over with peculiar written characters. This path can be seen all the way from the sea into the wilderness of Varend, along which two lines extend for a long way, one line being on each side of the path. The space between is narrow, and its surface is followed by runic inscriptions. Even though the path sometimes leads across the mountains and sometimes leads through the valleys, traces of runic writing can be seen along the entire path.'

Even in the twelfth century, when rune knowledge was

commonplace, the meaning of these runes was puzzling. But, whatever the meaning of the inscription, the ribbon-like quartz outcrop was recognised as the *Lindorm* – the Earth Dragon – bearer of the runes. Then, the Danish king, Valdemar the Great, ordered his academics to investigate the runes at Runamo. A scholarly expedition was arranged. The professors visited the site and recorded the enigmatic markings on wooden tablets but, recalls Saxo, 'they could make no sense out of it'. According to local tradition, the runes in some way recorded the Battle of Bravoll, fought between the armies of Harald Hilditonn and Sigurd Hring, around the year 700.

In later times, other scholars also failed to make sense of the runes until, in 1833, the Royal Society of Denmark set up a committee to investigate the Runamo inscription. An expedition, led by Finnur Magnusson of Copenhagen University, visited the site and recorded runes from 22 metres (72 feet) of rock-face. Magnusson then spent ten months attempting to decipher the runes. It seemed as if there was no solution. He was almost at the point of giving up, when he noticed a what he thought was a wend-rune. This triggered a sudden recognition of the principles behind the inscription. In what he described as an 'ecstasy' or 'trance', he wrote down the translation. In this flash of insight, Magnusson had broken the rune code, which he saw as a combination of complex bind-runes. What he wrote down was a fine metrical poem in Old Norse in the classical form known as *fornyrdislag*. It referred to the Bravoll battle:

Hildekind captured the kingdom
Gardar carved the runes
Ola took the oath
May Odin hallow the magic
May King Hring
Fall in dust
The Elves, the Love-Gods
Must leave Ola
Odin and Frey
And the race of Aesir
Must destroy,
Destroy,
Our enemies
Give Harald
Great victory.

For a while, Magnusson's translation was hailed as a great breakthrough – until geologists decided to examine the site for themselves. Shortly afterwards, they announced that the Runamo runes were not deliberate carvings at all, but only natural cracks in the quartz vein. Magnusson suffered a storm of criticism. Suddenly, his Runamo interpretation, once hailed as brilliant, was seen as nothing more than a monumental mistake. This criticism did not deter Magnusson, who continued to defend his discovery and, in 1841, his book, *Runamo og Runerne*, was published. However, despite his protests, it is clear that the geologists were right – the runes are natural, not carved by a human runemaster. But this is not the end of the matter. How such a fine piece of Old Norse poetry could come out of natural rock-patterns is also important. It cannot be dismissed as some sort of elaborate hoax. Magnusson was highly respected, his ability and honesty were never questioned, and it was clear to all that he was sincere, having had a real insight into the message of the rocks.

Finally, the matter was left to rest, unresolved. The materialist science of the 1830s had no time for shamanic psychology and non-material psychic links. Nobody pointed out that even when the geologists had proved conclusively that the markings were natural, this did not mean that they could not still be interpreted as runes! But there were indications, even at the time, that something else might be happening – a 'third way'. An interesting anecdote was told by the Swedish geologist Berzelius: when he visited Runamo in 1836, he was told that there was only one man in the district who could interpret the runes. This man did so by standing on his head. It is likely that he was a local cunning man who had inherited the ancient magical practices of communicating with other states of consciousness through these natural runes. Perhaps Magnusson also came into contact with this current.

This shamanic communion with patterns in the earth is little understood in the West today. But as a technique, it is not lost. The visionary author Antonin Artaud recounted in his book, *Journey to the Land of Tarahumara*, how he first saw certain alchemical symbols in the Mexican mountains. Then he saw them repeated in the designs and artwork of the local inhabitants. To Artaud, this close contact with the innate nature of a place was at the roots of a 'Universal

Esotericism', a technique suppressed by the modern Western world-view. In Artaud's 'Universal Esotericism', people read and utilise their local natural symbols, which express eternal realities. Later, the earth mysteries writer Anthony Roberts described it as 'geomythics', where symbolic truths are contained within physical realities, usually of a topographical nature. Artaud wrote that when one comes into contact with this reality, it is as if one has arrived at the source of a mystery.

From the Runamo experience, as with earlier traditions, it is clear that natural runic patterns have a great deal to tell us. They have their own geomythic content, from which we can learn. Also, in rune magic, our recognition of runic patterns depends on the conditions present when we see the patterns. These conditions are both external and internal. They include the weather, time of day and year, light direction, and our own internal state. The runes we read at such places tell us as much about our own state of consciousness as they do about themselves. At places like Runamo, strange things can happen. If we return at another time, we may not see the same runes that we did on our first visit. This is puzzling when we experience it for the first time, but it is the very essence of shamanic insight that lies at the core of the runic mysteries.

American Runic Inscriptions

By their very nature, rune stones in North America are controversial. Courageous Norse navigators such as Erik the Red and Thorfinn Karlsefni are known to have reached the mainland of North America, which they called Vinland, around the year 1000. They travelled by way of Greenland, upon which was based the Norse colony known as the Westvikings. This colony lasted for almost 500 years, being in its heyday around 1100–1200. By the middle 1300s, the colony was in decline, owing to climatic changes. The last Bishop of Greenland died in 1378, but there was constant contact until 1408. Occasionally, sailors put into Greenland in later years, until the last inhabitants succumbed to the steadily-worsening climate around 1500.

So regular Norse visits to Vinland during this period are not at all unlikely. Unfortunately, due to the fact that it literally died out, the Westvikings' colony on Greenland is so badly documented that almost nothing is known of their expeditions into mainland America. Discoveries of runic artefacts there ask important questions about the extent and duration of Norse exploration in North America. Of these, the Kensington Runestone is the most controversial. This stone was discovered in 1898 near Kensington, Minnesota, by Olaf Ohman, a farmer. Pulling up a tree stump, he unearthed the stone, a slab of Greywacke weighing about 100 kilos. Ohman showed the stone to his friends and neighbours, who were amazed. Soon, academics were asked about it. Naturally, they denounced it as a fraud. Their opinion was that there were 'anomalies' in the text and, anyway, such a stone was very unlikely in North America. But, despite this dismissal, this remarkable runestone was exhibited in the museum at Alexandria, Maine.

Translated, the inscription on the Kensington Stone reads:

8 Goths and 22 Norsemen on an exploration-tour from Vinland of West. We had camp on 2 skerries, one day's journey north from this stone.

We went and fished one day.

After we came home found 10 men red of blood and dead. Ave Virgo Maria. Save from ill.

Have 10 men at sea to look after our ship 14 days' journey from this island. Year 1362.

The numerical figures are written in stave-numbers. When the Norse scholar Hjalmar Holand deciphered the text, he showed that the anomalies in the text, cited as evidence of fraud, were compatible with its fourteenth century dating. Then, in the 1960s, the Danish cryptographer Alf Monge analysed the runes, and found the date 24 April, 1362, encoded in them. But most academic runic scholars still consider this runestone to be a fake, i.e. that it does not date from 1362, but is from the later European settlements after Columbus. The date of 1362 for a Norse expedition to Minnesota does not correspond with known historical records of visits from Europe, and so this, rather than other evidence, is held to be conclusive proof that it is a fake. Unfortunately, one piece of crucial evidence is now lost.

Figure 9 Horn found at Winnetka, Illinois, showing Vidar with his boot, killing the Fenris Wolf, panel with runic inscription below.

The root of a tree, which had grown in contact with the runes, and contained their imprint, hung on the wall of the farm's granary for years, but finally disappeared. Tree-ring analysis of the root could have provided valuable evidence of dating. Tragically, it seems to have been burnt as firewood.

From time to time, other runestones have turned up in north America, but they, like the Kensington Runestone, have been dismissed as fakes. They include stones from Poteau, Heavener and Shawnee, all in Oklahoma; from Rushville, Ohio and Spirit Pond, Maine. The Heavener inscription, on rockface, reads *gaomedat*, an undeciphered reading. Apart from the Kensington stone, the most remarkable runic artefact from north America is a horn found in 1952 by a milkman, Ronald Mason, near Winnetka, Illinois, near Chicago. He found it protruding from the earth of a freshly-cut bank by the roadside. On one side, it bears a carving of a man pointing to the Sun. He is standing amid vegetation next to the World Ash Tree, Yggdrasil. On the other side is Vidar, Odin's son, fighting the Fenris Wolf on the day of Ragnarsk, the Twilight of the Gods. His magic boot is in the wolf's mouth, while he pulls at its upper jaw with his gloved hands. Beneath the carving is a two-winged panel with runes. These read *grundu; smidar; helgur; har; himin; skidi; breka; mundu; vidar; klifur; knar; kiaftin; stridani; freka*. These words translate as: 'Ground'; 'build'; 'holy'; 'hair'; 'heaven' (new-born Sun); 'shine'; 'billowing'; 'fist'; 'vidar'; 'lift up'; 'strength'; 'jaw'; 'struggle'; 'freka'. The arrangement of the runes was analysed by Alf Monge, who found the runemaster's name, Audin, and the date, 15 December 1317, encoded there. But although its age and origin are still a matter of opinion among runic commentators, the Winnetka Horn is a most remarkable artefact. It celebrates the rising of the new sacred order after the destruction of the old, the spirit of eternal return present in the runes.

2

Practical and Secret Runes

Runes of War know thou,
If great thou wilt be!
Cut them into the hilt of hardened sword,
Some into the brand's back,
Some into its shining side,
Twice the name Tyr therein.

Völsunga Saga

The Runic Warriors

Rune magic was born in harsh conditions. For isolated communities, life was a continuous struggle against hostile conditions. People who lived in these conditions had a culture of self-reliance and effective ways of calling upon those reserves of enormous human strength which usually remain untapped today. Northern Tradition spirituality preserves this knowledge, and so it is present in runelore.

In the past, if someone wanted to be successful in the arts of hunting or fighting, then he or she had to undertake strict training in all aspects of self-control. Today, these techniques are known both in modern shamanry and the martial arts, combining physical development with magic and psychology. Many examples are recorded in the hero-traditions of the Irish and Teutonic Sagas and the Arthurian cycle. Ancient tales of warrior-craft show that the feats of these martial artists were far more than just the uncontrolled acts of enraged maniacs. They tell us that these men were experts who had been through sophisticated physical, spiritual and magical training. In this, they are comparable with modern exponents of the oriental martial arts. Like them, the masters of the arts were capable of extraordinary feats of strength and endurance.

Our best records of these techniques come from Viking times. This was the age of high rune magic. At that time, the warrior tradition was divided into three main 'clans' or cults, each named after a strong animal: the wolf, the bear, and the wild boar. The wolf-cult warriors were known as Ûlfhednar, and they wore wolf-skins over their chain mail, fighting singly as guerrillas, ambushing their enemies. The bear warrior-cult – the Berserkers – is the best known today. 'They . . . went without mailcoats, were frantic as dogs or wolves', says the *Ynglinga Saga*, 'they bit their shields and were as strong as bears or boars; they slew men, but neither fire nor iron could hurt them. This is called "running berserk" . . .'. The phrase 'going berserk' is still used to describe frenzied behaviour accompanied by almost superhuman strength. This was the manner of the Berserk warrior, who went into battle fearlessly, wearing a bear-skin 'shirt' in place of the usual chain mail armour. Berserkers were known for their enormous strength and ferocity, like that of an enraged bear. Through his shamanic connection with the bear, the warrior drew magically upon Bear's Strength. As a demonstration of prowess, the Berserker could sit scantily clothed or naked in the winter snow, not feeling the cold or suffering ill effects. This was Bear's Warmth. Bear's Strength was gained at the Berserker's initiation, an example of which is described in *Hrolfs Saga Kraki*. During this ceremony, the would-be Berserker had to 'kill' ritually the image of a bear. If successful, the warrior then drank its blood. At this moment, the power of the beast flowed into the warrior, who then became a Berserker. Other magical powers gained by the Berserker at his initiation included *Hamrammr* (shape-shifting). *Hamrammr* took two forms – first, by acting upon and altering the perception of others, and secondly, as an out-of-body experience. Naturally, these powers were of great use in combat. The third cult was that of Svínfylking, the Boar-Warriors. In combat, they used the formation known as Svínfylking, (the Boar's Head). This was a wedge-shaped squad, led by two champions known as the Rani (snout). The Boar-Warrior was a master of disguise and escape. Detailed knowledge of the landscape was second nature to him.

Until the late middle ages, there was no professional warrior who did not use some form of magic. His training, weapons and techniques were assisted by magic. Several Norse sagas tell us of this magic. For example, the *Hardar Saga* describes the use of the magic Herfjotturr (war fetter), a binding spell which caused the enemy to lose their strength and be immobilised (for further details, see page 49). The *Flateyjarbók* tells of the magic used in the Battle of Fyrisvellir, fought in Iceland in the year 960 CE. Eric, king of Sweden, had called upon Odin to help him and soon afterwards, he met a tall man with a hood over his face. He gave Eric a thin runic stick, which he told him to shoot over the enemy when the battle began. 'When he had shot it', tells the *Flateyjarbók*, 'it appeared to him like an airborne javelin, and it flew over Styrbiorn's army. Immediately this was done, blindness fell upon Styrbiorn's men and then upon Styrbiorn himself. Next, a great wonder came to pass, for an avalanche came from the mountainside, and fell upon Styrbiorn's army, killing all his people.'

Once guns came into use, however, the martial arts and their magic lost their former importance, although they were not forgotten. They were practised for self-defence in seventeenth-century Holland, and survived until recent times in France in the techniques of kick-fighting and staff-combat. But, with the decline of the martial arts, many magical techniques faded from memory and are only now being reconstructed. The related techniques of shooting-magic, however, have continued into recent times.

Equal Rights in Battle

The Northern Tradition, of which the runes are an important part, has never distinguished between man and woman, able-bodied and disabled: all are equal. Women and men, able and disabled, are considered equal. In the old Pagan era, there was equality of opportunity for men and women, evidenced in documents and artefacts. For example, a fragment of loom found in 1979 at Neudingen in Germany has the inscription in runes, 'Blithgund wrait runa'. The name of the woman runester Blithgund is one of the earliest known. Runestones in Sweden tell us that women landowners built bridges and roads. In later times, by contrast, women were not even taught to read or write, as a deliberate policy to keep women from developing their true human potential. The imposition of patriarchal religion and the feudal system transformed women into 'second-class citizens'. This state of affairs lasted formally until the twentieth century, and is still not abolished completely.

Another striking example of equality in Pagan times comes from the records of a battle fought at Bravoll in eastern Jutland (Denmark) in about the year 700 CE. This was between the armies of Harald Hilditonn (Wartooth) and Sigurd Hring, his nephew. This is the battle of the Runamo 'inscription'. Harald's army contained women warriors: the Shield-Maidens. Among them were Visma and Heid 'each of whom had come with a numerous host'. Visma was one of the most important fighters in the army, being Harald's standard-bearer. 'Another Shield-Maiden was Vébjorg, who came from the south of Gotland, and many champions followed her . . . she attacked the champion Soknarskoti; she had trained herself so well in the use of the helmet, mail-shirt and sword, that she was one of the most distinguished people in knighthood . . . she dealt the champion heavy blows and attacked him for a long time . . . finally, with great courage, she fell, covered with wounds.' The account of this battle also shows that disability did not make a person a second-class citizen,

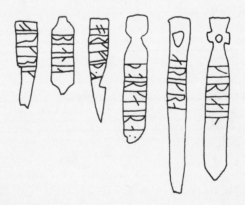

Figure 10 Merkelapper, wooden marking-tags with names in runes, found in Bryggen, the harbour trading district of Bergen, Norway.

either. The aged and disabled king Harald, fought bravely from a wagon until, finally, he was slain and the battle was lost.

The humane words of Odin in *Hávamál* speak of the practical rights of all people, regardless of their physical condition: 'The lame can ride, those without hands can herd, a deaf person can fight with spirit. A blind man is better than a corpse on a pyre: a corpse is no good to anybody'.

Some runic authors place great importance on the warrior tradition, but the received image of the bloodstained, pillaging Viking rapist sometimes obscures the more civilised aspects of their tradition. The fine sensibilities of artists, craftsmen and poets belies the image of complete savagery. In any case, in modern terms, even their warriors' ferocity in battle pales into insignificance when compared with the continuous mechanised warfare that has raged across the globe throughout most of the twentieth century. After all, the words of Odin tell us: 'A wise man will often refrain from fighting, but a fool will fight without cause or reason'. This is as relevant today as it ever was.

Weapon Magic and the Runes

In the warrior era, swords and other weapons were given names which names described their magical 'personality'. Some had descriptive names, whilst others were more personal. For example, *Magnus Barefoot's Saga* tells us that King Magnus 'was girt with a sword called *Leggbitr* (Leg-Biter). Its guards were made of walrus tusk, and its hilt was covered with gold. It was one of the best of weapons'. The sword owned by the two Saxon kings named Offa was *Skrep*, whilst that belonging to Sigurd Fafnir's-Bane was *Rotti*. Other names include: 'Odin's Flame', 'The Ice of Battle', 'The Fire of the Shields', 'The Sea-King's Fire', 'The Battle-Fire', 'Torch of the Blood', 'Serpent of the Wound', 'Snake of the Byrnie', 'The Byrnie's Fear', 'Harmer of War-Knittings', 'The Dog of the Helmet' and 'Tongue of the Scabbard'. Some of these weapons had their names written upon them in runes. Others had magical formulae, such as

'May *Márr* spare nobody'. These were either engraved in the metal, or written with *tiver*, a magically-prepared colouring material. This runic tradition survived the arrival of the Christian religion and continued well into the 'Age of Chivalry'. Since the nineteenth century, runic-inscribed swords have been made once more, generally for use in ceremony and magic. Today, there are fine modern armourers who produce wonderful new examples of the swordsmith's craft.

As well as swords, the warriors of old used several different types of staff-weapons. These are known both from the sagas and from archaeological finds. *Beowulf* tells us: 'Their stout spears stood stacked together, shod with iron and shaped of ash'. The most common types of staff-weapons were the Geflak, (javelin); the Höggspjøt (hewing spear); the Pal-staf, (pole staff), a pole with a spike at the end; the Atgeir (halbard); and the Snoeris-Spjøt (string spear). This was provided with a loop of cord on the shaft which gave additional power to the throw. String spears have been found in Danish bogs, sometimes with the string still in place after 1500 years. Another version of this was the Skepti-Fretta, (cord-shaft). Some spears had their centre of gravity marked with a ring of nails or a cord binding, to help the thrower to locate it quickly. All show their makers' sophisticated understanding of materials and techniques.

Like swords, spears were also named with magical titles engraved upon them in runes. Several names are known from ancient spears bearing runic inscriptions which have been found in warriors' graves. They include *Raunijar* ('The Tester'), from Øvre-Stabu in Denmark (150 CE); and *Rannja* ('The Assailer') from a grave at Dahmsdorf, Brandenburg, Germany (*c*. 250 CE). Other known runic names are *Gaois*, meaning 'The Barker' or 'The Roarer', and *Dorih* (from Thor-rih, 'Powerful in Courage'). Sometimes, single runes were used: a sixth-century Anglo-Saxon spearhead found in England at Holborough, Kent, has the Tyr rune engraved upon it.

These finds, and ancient literature, show us that rune magic was part of the craft of the weapon-maker. Ideally, a warrior's weapon should be made for his or her use, and for no-one else; a general principle with magic paraphernalia and weapons. Partly because of this, swords were buried with warriors in their graves. This had a double function, one sacred and the other practical. According to religious belief, the departed warrior, going to Valhalla to join the Einherjar, needed his weapon in the next world. But also, by taking the weapon away from the world of humans, it also prevented a fine and famous weapon from passing on to those who might not be worthy to bear it. There was a tradition that, if a person who was not entitled to it took a sword, it would serve him ill. Also, if the master's sword were not buried with him, then his ghost might come back from the next world to reclaim it. But the sword was not lost for ever if it was buried with its user. The best swords were wrapped carefully and coated in preservative materials before burial, so that they could be recovered at a time of trouble when only a special weapon, sanctified by a hero, would be able to accomplish a particular task.

Recovery of swords buried with heroes is recorded historically. *The Saga of Hrolf Kraki* tells of the sword called Sköfnung, 'the best of all swords which have been carried in the Northern Lands'. Sköfnung was buried with the famous Berserker, Hrolf Kraki. About two centuries after the burial, a man called Skeggi was sailing near Hrolf's burial mound at Roskilde in Denmark. He went ashore, 'broke into the home of Hrolf Kraki and removed Sköfnung, the royal sword'. If Sköfnung had not been prepared for preservation in some way before burial, certainly it would not have been usable as a weapon two centuries later. This exceptional weapon had a 'life stone' attached to it. A wound inflicted by Sköfnung could only be cured by rubbing it with this magic holed stone.

Sir Thomas Malory's account of the life and death of King Arthur, *Le Morte D'Arthur*, tells of the recovery of the magic sword *Excalibur* from a lake. At the time of the historic King Arthur (c.500 CE), throwing weapons into rivers and lakes was a ceremonial rite. So that Arthur could obtain *Excalibur*, Merlin had to take him to the Lady of the Lake, the female guardian of the sacred waters and its contents. Arthur had to give her a gift in exchange for the wondrous weapon. Having been thrown ceremonially into the lake at an earlier time, the sword had been taken to the otherworld. When Arthur recovered it miraculously, the sword became a symbol of the rebirth of the old power. On a more practical level, this weapon would have been one of the finest of its age, giving a physical as well as a spiritual advantage to anyone who bore it.

It is likely that *Excalibur* was preserved in the mud at the bottom of the lake, its location marked by the ceremonial poles or fence of spears there. In Denmark at the time of King Arthur, weapons were similarly deposited in lakes. These are bogs now, which have proved to be remarkable archaeological sites. One at Thorsbjerg, south of Flensburg (now Germany), excavated between 1856 and 1862, yielded many double-edged swords with wooden hilts mounted in bronze and silver. The hoard included wooden scabbards covered with metal, one with a runic inscription. Excavations at Vimose, near Odense, revealed 67 swords and more than 1000 spears with ash shafts, some of which had spearheads inlaid with threads of gold or silver. The Nydam bog had four ships buried in it. One large boat contained 106 double-edged swords, 93 of which were pattern-welded. The swords' hilts were of wood, covered with silver, bronze or bone. In addition to these, 552 spearheads, shafts and arrows were found. Some arrow-shafts bore runic inscriptions, including the runes Tyr and Elhaz, both militarily effective. The probable date of these was 200–350 CE.

Although some weapons were carefully preserved, many of the objects found in these places were damaged on purpose. Spears, arrows and bows were snapped, mail-shirts and fabric clothes torn up. But all were wrapped together carefully in votive bundles before being thrown into the sacred lake. Skulls and bones of sacrificed horses were cut and cleft, and large ceramic pots were weighted with stones so that they would sink. Some items were even fastened to the bottom by large wooden hooks. Magically, these iron artefacts were returned to the water from which came the metal in the first place.

Binding and Niding Magic in Viking Times

In the Viking age, magicians had various ways of binding and cursing people. In battle, runic binding magic was used in the shape of the War Fetter (Herfjotturr), magic sacred to Odin. This is recorded in *Hávamál*, the words of Odin.

The eighteen charms or spells in *Hávamál* give us the means of achieving many things magically, among them battlefield magic. In the third charm of *Hávamál*, Odin speaks of 'shackles on my deadly foes'. The effects of the War Fetter spell are described in *Ynglinga Saga*: 'Odin knew how to behave so that his enemies in battle went blind or deaf or were stricken by panic, and their weapons pierced no more than could wands'. Battlefield binding magic was effective. The *Hardar Saga* records how the warrior Hord was fleeing his enemies when they put the War Fetter on him: 'The War Fetter came upon Hord. He cut himself free once, and then twice. The War Fetter came upon him a third time. Then the men succeeded in trapping him, surrounding him with a ring of enemies . . .' Despite this, the hero Hord fought his way out. But a fourth application of the War Fetter was successful, and he was killed. This aggressive binding magic disorientates its victim, rendering him helpless. The runes Thorn, Is and Nyd are used in this War Fetter. The fourth charm of *Hávamál* also contains battlefield magic. This is the counter-magic we can use against fetters; material and psychic. The noted Dutch runemistress Freya Aswynn recommends a bind rune of Feoh, As and Ing to facilitate this charm. An ancient Germanic spell, the first *Merseburg Charm*, also tells of this power of binding and loosing:

> Once noble ladies were sitting,
> Here and there they sat,
> Some tied knots,
> Some hemmed in the warrior bands,
> Some picked at the fetters,
> So the padlocks broke,
> And the warriors went free.

The fifth charm in *Hávamál*, by contrast, is a different version of the War Fetter which allows the user to stop an arrow in flight. This ability is still demonstrated in the oriental martial arts today. As a runic spell, it is the binding of incoming attack, using the runes Rad, Is and Ken.

The most spectacular way of cursing an enemy was by the Niding Pole (the *Nithstong* or Scorn-Post). They were poles about nine feet (2.75 metres) long upon which insults and curses were carved in runes. Ceremonies were performed to activate the destructive magic of the pole. A horse's skull

Figure 11 Swedish horse offering to a sacred lake.

was fixed to the top of the pole, and it was stuck into the ground with the skull facing towards the house of the accursed person. The pole channelled the destructive forces of Hela, goddess of death. These forces were carried up the pole and projected through the horse skull. The runes carved on the pole defined the character and target of the destructive forces. Among others, triple Thorn runes, 'the three Thurses', and triple Is runes, were used to smite the enemy. When used maliciously, these had the effect of disempowering the accursed's will and delivering him or her to the forces of destruction. Here, the Thorn rune invokes the power of Thurs, the demonic earth-giant sometimes called Moldthurs. An example of this comes from *Skírnismál*, where the spell used by Skírnir against Frey's reluctant lover, Gerdhr invokes harm using the Thorn rune. This provides the power for three other runestaves: 'I shall inscribe Thurs for you, and three rune staves: lewdness, and rage and impotence'.

Magically, the Niding Pole was intended to disrupt and anger the earth sprites (Landvaettir, Land-Wights or earth-spirits) inhabiting the ground where the accursed's house was. These sprites would then vent their anger upon the person, whose livelihood and life would be destroyed. Niding Poles were also used to desecrate areas of ground. This technique is called álfreka, literally the 'driving away of the elves', by which the earth sprites of a place were banished, leaving the ground spiritually dead. In earlier times, these earth sprites were respected. The *Landnámabók* records that when Iceland was first settled, it was law that no one should have a ship at sea with a head carved on it unless they took it off before they came in sight of land. Under no circumstances were mariners to sail to land with 'gaping heads' or 'yawning mouths', lest the land-sprites might be frightened, and the land be rendered álfreka.

On the Niding Pole, the horse skull invokes the horse rune Ehwaz, using the linking and transmissive power of the rune for the magical working. The horse is sacred to Odin, god of runes and magic. In this context, there have been many archaeological finds of horse skulls buried for magical reasons. For example, at Galley Hill near Luton, a horse's skull was found buried with some bone dice. As a gallows hill, this is a place sacred to Odin, god of hanged men. Dice were also sacred to Odin, their inventor. Horse skulls have also been found in many old houses in England and Wales, where they had a magically-protective function. As well as being in foundations, they were placed in chimney breasts and under threshing floors. In 1895, one was buried ceremonially in the foundation of a chapel at Black Horse Drove, Cambridgeshire. The parading of the Mari Llwyd – a horse's skull on a post – is a Welsh New Year folk tradition. It prevents the evil spirits of the old year past from entering into the new year.

Niding Poles were the destructive side of pole and post magic. Fences or rings of sacred Hazel posts (the Vébond) defined holy ground, enclosing and protecting it. Poles or spears rammed into the mud at the bottom of sacred lakes defined the holy areas where offerings lay. In Pagan times in Sweden, protective poles stood over sacred water. As with Niding Poles, each post had a horse's skull at the end. The skin of the horse was draped over the post, which leant protectively over the sacred lake (Figure 11). Even today, in many parts of Europe, Maypoles and other marker-posts are set up ceremonially at places of power for beneficial purposes.

Magical Rings

Every ring, no matter how large or small, is a circle of power. Symbolically, the ring represents eternity, the circle that has no beginning and no end. Every smith-made metal ring echoes the shape of the Worm Ouroboros, the alchemical serpent that bites its own tail, symbolising eternal, enclosed power. Even before the invention of metal rings, natural rings were honoured. Holed stones known as hagstones or holeystones have been magical protectors since time immemorial. Today, as ever, it is customary to hang them up by a string made of flax (the sacred plant of Frigg). You can hang them above your bed to prevent nightmares and psychic attack. They are also hung in stables and byres to protect livestock. Especially powerful are protective chains made up of holed stones; rings of rings. On a larger scale, there are still a number of surviving megalithic standing stones with holes, although formerly, there were many more. The great holed stone of Men-an-Tol in Cornwall is

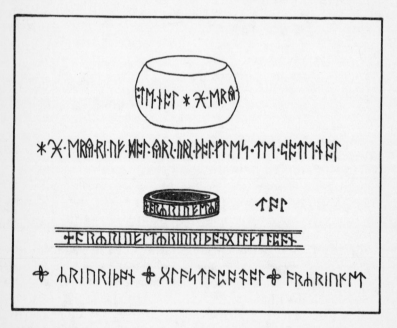

Figure 12 Anglo-Saxon runic rings. Top to bottom: Agate ring (full inscription below); Gold ring, Kingmoor, Cumbria, England; gold ring inscription, Bramham Moor, Yorkshire, England.

the most evocative of all. Folk-tradition holds them in great reverence as places of healing and foresight. Although they are not holes, ancient cup and ring marks carved on rockfaces are markers of sacred power. Stone circles are another form of magical ring. They are places of power at which human consciousness is altered in subtle ways.

In former times, it was traditional to gather together bystanders to witness a legal act, such as paying a debt. They would form a ring, at the middle of which the act was done. The *Saga of Howard the Halt* recounts such a debt-paying ring: 'Then Guest called to him many men, and they stood round about . . .'. In Viking times, this was called *Hringr* or *Hvirfing*. A ring was also formed to witness a ritual battle, such as trial by combat. The name of the modern boxing 'ring' (which is square) is a reminder of the magic circle formed around ritual combat.

The ring was also the form for discussions. The *Saga of the Banded Men* tells 'so they sat down in a ring in a certain place . . .'. This is a secular version of the magic circle cast by all magicians to enclose the power of their workings, and to exclude unwanted influences. On a much more cosmic scale, the Arctic Circle (Hjol-Gadds-Ringr) is a sacred enclosure, inside which the phenomenon of the Midnight Sun can be witnessed. The actual name of this circle is a word of power in rune magic.

Finger-rings are most associated with rune magic. Their magical power was popularised by J.R.R. Tolkien in his fantasy trilogy, *The Lord of the Rings*. Tolkien took as his model for these fantastic rings the ancient runic rings that are known from the Anglo-Saxon and Viking periods. Like Tolkien's master ring, many of the real rings bore magical as well as other inscriptions. Surviving rings are of several types, not only metallic. It is possible that there were wooden rings, but these are unlikely to have survived. Sometimes inscriptions record the names of the ring's maker and owner. An Anglo-Saxon example, found in Lancashire, has 'Æthred mec an Eanred mec agrof' (Aethred owns me, Eanred made me) written in a mixture of runes and Anglo-Saxon letters. Three Anglo-Saxon rings in the British Museum collection have magical runic inscriptions which have defied translation. One, found in 1817 on Greymoor Hill, Kingmoor, near Carlisle, is made of gold. It has the runes 'Æruriuflturiurithonglæstæpon' inscribed on the outside, and 'Tol' on the inside. Another ring of unknown origin, but with a known history since 1745, also in the British Museum collection, has an identical inscription. This ring is made of bronze. The third example is a ring made of agate. It, too, has an undeciphered magical inscription: 'Eruriufdol uriurithol wlestepotenol'. These are finger-rings of power, intended to be worn to bring magical fortune the way of the wearer.

Sacred arm-rings also played an important role in Norse religion and law. Several Norse sagas tell of the silver or gold rings, kept in temples dedicated to Thor, on which oaths were sworn. There are many historical records of these rings. For example, in the year 994, the Irish King Maelseachlainn looted the ring of Thor and other treasures from the temple of Thor in Dublin. This was a rich shrine which held a magnificent black image of the god. In the *Eyrbyggja Saga*, a priest called Snorri was saved from a swordblow by his golden arm ring which weighed 20 ounces. Generally, magical rings are sacred to Thor. They are magically linked to the ring attached to his sacred hammer, Mjöllnir.

Sometimes, magic rings were attached to other objects of power. A ring-sword is mentioned in *Beowulf*. This was a special type of sword which had a talismanic ring attached to the pommel. Also, cunning men and wise women sometimes carried ring-staves, where a magic ring was attached to a ceremonial staff.

Cryptic Runes

Many ancient runic inscriptions are in code, for the runes have the most complex cryptic lore of any alphabet. Putting a magical formula in code is very practical. It prevents others reading the meaning and also stops other rune users from altering the magic. The most basic runic 'code' uses runes written in the 'wrong' direction, that is, from right to left. These are called Wend Runes. In the days of semi-literacy, just doing this was enough to prevent many people from understanding them. A notable example of Wend Runes is on the standing stone at Moybro Stenen, near Uppsala in Sweden which shows a drawing of a horseman holding a wand or lance. Above him are two lines of Wend

Figure 13 Wend runes, horesman and dog carved on a megalith at
Moybro Stenen, Upland, Sweden.

Runes (Figure 13). This inscription contains all 24 letters of
the Elder Futhark, a magical formula in its own right, for
it dates from the time when the 16-character Younger
Futhark was in everyday use.

Most runemasters went further than just writing
backwards. A popular method substituted one letter for
another. The simplest form of this moved the whole
alphabet one letter in either direction. Thus, the name Nigel
will be written Hnibm if the preceding letter is substituted,
or Igzmng if the following letter replaces each one. Either
way, an apparently meaningless 'word' is created. This
method was often used to encode individual names. A
good example is on the church font at Kareby, in Bohuslan,
Sweden. This has an inscription in Norwegian runes,
which reads: 'Rathe Sa er kan namn orklaski' (Read who
can the name Orlaski). The final 'Orlaski' is a code. This
is decoded as the name Thorbjørn, by moving the whole
alphabet back one letter.

Another variety of magical code substitutes one character
for another. This can be done either letter-by-letter or in

groups. There are many ways of doing this. One ancient method is known from the runic code-stick found in the Bryggen excavations at Bergen in Norway. This stick is the key to a code which uses multiple letters to represent individual ones.

Code sticks such as this allowed runemasters to write messages that only they, or others with the key to the code, could read. They are related to the similar code sticks of the Celtic Druids, and the sett sticks of Scottish plaid weavers which encode the colours for the clan's tartan.

Another form of encryption is *Lonnrunor*. This technique uses number symbols that indicate the position of a letter in a pre-arranged group. There are several ways of doing this. It can be done simply by indicating the number of the letter from the beginning of the alphabet (for example, in the Roman alphabet, the number 13 represents 'M'). But, unlike the Roman alphabet, the Elder Futhark is divided into three aettir, and the number-symbols are based upon

Figure 14 Cryptic rune systems: Line 1, Buslubaen, Sweden, with Iis runes and Lagu runes; 2, baptismal font in Norum church, Sweden; 3, the Narssaq code stick, Eiriksfjord, Greenland; 4 and 5, Norse crusaders' runic graffiti in the megalithic chambered cairn at Maeshowe, Orkney; 6, fragment of high cross in Hackness church, Scarborough, Yorkshire, England.

this. The rune row is divided into its three aettir, which are numbered 1, 2 and 3. Inside each aett, each rune is given a number. In this way, two numbers are needed to denote each letter. First comes the aett number, and then the rune's number within the aett. The most common way of writing this code is as an upright stave bearing side branches which point upwards. On one side, the number of branches represent the number of the aett from which the rune comes. On the other side, the number of branches represent the number of the letter in that aett. For example, a Branch Rune that bears three strokes to the left and two to the right represents the second rune of the third aett. Thus, for example, the name Nigel would be denoted by the numbers 2,2; 2,3; 2,4; 3,3; 3,5. Also, because the numbers show the position of a specific rune, there is the possibility of 'scrambling' the letters, making the code even more difficult to crack. The numbers 1–3 can be given to any of the three aettir, and within the aettir, the order of the letters can be changed. This can be done in a number of ways.

Historically, this type of code includes the Branch Runes (Kvistrúnar), the Tree Runes (Hahalruna) and the Tent Runes (Tjaldrúnar). The side-branches on Tree Runes point upwards, whilst those of Hahalruna point downwards. But whichever way they are written, the principle is the same, representing aett number on one side and letter number on the other. Tent Runes are based on X-shaped forms. They are usually read clockwise, beginning at the left, using the same principle as the others.

Another related form are the Iis runes. They also use numbers to denote individual runes. But unlike the Branch, Tree and Tent Runes, the Iis Runes use collections of single strokes that are not connected to one another. To represent the number of the aett, the Iis Runes use short strokes. Longer strokes denote the number of each character within the aett. Similar codes using other runes are known, though these are uncommon. An example is the runic code stick found at Narssaq in Greenland, which used a version of the later K rune. Other systems use groups of dots or lines, combinations of dots and lines, and alternate short and long lines attached to an upright. Today, we can see yet-to-be-decoded examples on the fragment of stone cross kept in the church at Hackness, near Scarborough, Yorkshire. All of these rune codes are related closely to the Celtic

Ogham system of writing, which uses similar number-strokes to denote letters. This principle was even extended to the Klop Runes, which used sound to transmit messages.

This was the ancient forerunner of the Morse Code. Runic letters were 'sent' locally by clapping and knocking, and over longer distances by drums, horns and bells. Another type of rune code is the magical Bindruna – 'bind runes'. This uses a different method from the Lonnrunor codes. Bind runes are made by superimposing a number of runes upon one another. This creates dense but often very beautiful sigils, whose meaning is only truly known to their creator.

The final type of rune code works in reverse. The basic meanings of individual runes are used to spell out their corresponding letters. These are then put together to spell out a hidden word. An example of this is in the text 'Elene', written by the Anglo-Saxon author Cynewulf in the eighth century:

> Until then, the man had always been attacked by waves of sadness: he was a burning *torch* [Ken, C], though in the Mead-Hall he was given treasures, apple-shaped gold. He lamented the *evil* [Yr, Y], he the brother of *sorrow* [Nyd, N]; he suffered affliction, cruel secret thoughts, though for him the *horse* [Ehwaz, E], measured the mile-paths, ran proudly, adorned with ornaments. *Joy* [Wyn, W] diminishes, and pleasure too, as the years pass by; youth has gone and former pride. Once, the glory of youth was *ours* [Ur, U]. Now, with time, the old days have passed away, life's joys have slipped away, even as *water* [Lagu, L] drains away, the flowing floods. *Wealth* [Feoh, F] is transitory for all people under heaven: the Earth's ornaments disappear beneath clouds like the wind when it blows loudly . . .
>
> (my italics and interpretation).

This Anglo-Saxon poem is a fine example of this type of code. By this, and more complex, methods, the ancient northern skalds and runemasters were able to hide messages for those who could decode them. Sometimes, where the rune words spell out the author's name, this was done for artistic reasons. However, magic was the usual purpose.

Figure 15 Dragon door guardians on the medieval timber-frame stave church at Lomen, Norway. These carvings are protective, invoking the binding power of Iormungand against evil spirits.

Cryptic Runestone Dates

The Danish cryptographer, Alf Monge, deciphered many coded runic inscriptions. He showed that some of them contained encoded dates. Date encryption works on an ingenious principle. It is based upon the Julian Calendar, the standard calendar from Roman times until the period 1559–1752. Within the Julian Calendar are a number of cycles which are only used now by Churchmen for the calculation of Easter Sunday, the old Pagan festival of Ostara. This festival is defined by the correspondences between the Spring Equinox, the day of the week, and the phase of the Moon. To work out such complex cycles, Imperial Roman occultists worked out a system of notation using the *Golden Number* and the *Dominical Letter.*

In 325 CE, a Church conference at Niceaea ruled that Easter Day should be celebrated on the first Sunday after the Full Moon following the Vernal Equinox. If the Full Moon falls on a Sunday, however, then Easter must be celebrated a week later. A further complication is the stipulation that Easter must not coincide with the Jewish Passover. So an 'imaginary' Moon is used by the Church to obviate this 'problem'. Generally, this 'Moon' becomes full one or two days later than the authentic Moon we can see! Of course, whilst this is magically ineffective, it does not make the calendar useless as a means of recording time passed.

The calendar codes are based on the interaction between two sequences of numbers. Firstly, there is the sun-moon period of 19 years. It covers all of the phases of the moon, after which the new moons fall on the same cycle of dates as defined by the Sun. It is named the Metonic Cycle, after the fifth-century BCE Greek sage Meton, who first described it. Each year in the cycle is given a number from 1 to 19. It can be found by adding 1 to the year date, and then dividing it by 19. The remainder is the Golden Number. If there is no remainder, then the Golden Number is 19. The Golden Number sequence then consists of an 'endless chain' of the numbers 1 to 19. These are not in the normal sequence, however. Eight is added to the preceding number. The sequence is thus: 1, 9, 17, 6, 14, 3, 11, 19, 8, 16, 5, 13, 2, 10, 18, 7, 15, 4, 12, 1, 9, and so on. In runic almanacs (the carved wooden staves known as Clog

Figure 16 Irish runic systems. Top: Gall Ogham; Below: Lockland Ogham.

Almanacks, Primestaves and Rimstocks), they are represented by the 16 letters of the Younger Futhark with three other new runes: Fé, Iss, Aurlaugr, Kaun, Laugr, Thurs, Sól, Belgtzhor, Naudhr, Yr, Reidh, Bjarkan, úr, Ar, Twimadur, Hagall, Madhr, Os, Tyr, Fé, etc.

The Julian Calendar cycle also contains the Dominical Letters. They tell us when Sundays fall in any given year. This is calculated by adding to the year date a quarter of it, omitting remainders, and also the number six. Then, divide the sum by seven. If there is no remainder, the Dominical letter is A. If there is a remainder, then there is another Dominical Letter that year. The remainders from one to six define the other days, thus: 1, G; 2, F; 3, E; 4, D; 5, C; and 6, B. In the Church calendar, these seven possibilities are represented by the Roman letters A, B, C, D, E, F, G. On the Norse wooden almanacs, the Dominical Letters were represented by their corresponding runes in sequence: Fé, A; úr, B; Thurs, C; áss, D; Reidh, E; Kaun, F; and Hagall, G. The whole sequence of letters and numbers makes a 532-year cycle, composed of 28 x 19 years. Within this cycle, one can define any day by means of the

Golden Number, the Dominical Letter, and a number which corresponded with the number of days remaining in that year.

Runemasters used these sequences to record dates. Sometimes, they gave numbers which corresponded with a position on the Perpetual Easter Table, a list of Golden Numbers and Dominical Letters used by priests. These were encoded in runic inscriptions. As well as recording dates, these number sequences were used to find the magical, numerological, qualities of days. But during the eighteenth century, printed calendars and almanacs became available everywhere. The wooden almanacs went out of use, and runes ceased being used for Golden Numbers and Dominical Letters.

Rune Magic and Games

We are fortunate that a number of Icelandic runic formulae and their derivations have survived. Many of these spells and diagrams were collected in the nineteenth century, when they were still in everyday use. Icelandic magic contains runic diagrams for use in almost every area of life. Especially important among these are those used by contestants in sports and games. The folklorist, Bishop Jón Árnason recorded two magical symbols called Gapaldur and Ginfaxi, which were used in wrestling magic (Glímagaldur). The wrestler had to write the Gapaldur sigil under his right heel and the Ginfaxi under his left big toe, then recite a spell which invoked the power of the sigils and of a guardian spirit. This was supposed to make him unbeatable.

Board games, too, had their magic. In his monumental book, *Chess in Iceland* (1865), Daniel Willard Fiske, the authority on Icelandic board games, tells of the spells used there to win at games:

There still exist in Icelandic old magical formulas to enable one to win at Kotra (Backgammon), just as there are others applicable to chess. One of them runs thus: 'If thou wishest to win at Backgammon, take a raven's heart, dry it in a spot on which the sun does not shine, crush it, then rub it on the dice.'

The power of the raven, magic bird of Odin, is used here. Sometimes, words of power, such as royal names, were also used. Jón Árnason wrote of one in which 'the Backgammon player should cry "Olave, Olave, Harold, Harold, Erik, Erik" before the game. These royal names or other spells were also written in runes and hidden beneath the backgammon board or on the player. Another popular trick was to hold a runic parchment between the knees during the game. Árnason also described another magical operation for backgammon players:

> In order to win at Kotra, take the tongue of a wagtail and dry it in the sun; crush and mix it afterwards with communion-wine, and apply it to the points of the dice, then you are sure of the game.

Many of these talismans, known as Kotruvers, used bind runes and diagrams containing runes. They were a continuation of the runic folk-magic of pre-Christian times. The spell cited by Willard Fiske using the heart of a raven, the oracular bird of Odin, is intended to influence the dice which, according to folk tradition, were an invention of Odin. Later, Kotruvers absorbed Christian elements. The spell cited by Bishop Árnason substitutes doctored church wine for the raven's heart. Because of this sort of magic, the church in Iceland was particularly harsh on magicians. The runes were prohibited in 1639, and anyone found using them was executed. Also, the laws of the *Jönsbok Code* (the Norse code of laws, named after the book *Jönsbok*) forbade Kotruvers, although this did not stop their use. Some paid the ultimate price for disobedience. In 1681, Árni Pétursson was burnt alive in the presence of the Icelandic Althing (Parliament) for using Kotruvers when playing back-gammon.

Some gambling talismans used crossroads as places of magic power. One works as follows:

Write a certain runic formula on new parchment, and wrap a silver coin in it. Before midnight on a Sunday, take it to a crossroads and bury the coin there. Then stamp three times on the ground with the left foot, calling the spell. Make the runic sign between each word, nine times in all. Then leave the crossroads without looking back. On the next day, go to the crossroads and recover the coin which you can then carry with you to the gaming table as a lucky charm. But you should always remember that gambling magic texts state that if you win, you should donate ten per cent of the winnings to the poor in thanksgiving. If you fail to do it, then you will never win again!

Hof- and Housemarks

Even when runes were no longer in everyday use, their descendants were everywhere. All over northern and central Europe, various runic-derived marks continued in use. They were the Hofmarks and Housemarks of trades- and craftspeople. Many are still in use today as trademarks. These ancient symbolic marks were used in all areas of trade and business. They were used to identify animals, being branded, clipped or painted on the animal with tiver. They were cut into the ears of domestic animals, and on the beaks and webbed feet of ducks, geese and swans. Housemarks were painted or printed on sacks (figure 17).

Figure 17 Contemporary engraving of a horseman dragging sacks on a sledge. The sacks bear the runic house mark of their owner.

They were branded on carts, wagons, sledges and boats. They were punched onto timber floated on rivers, so that individual owners' trees could be sorted out at the saw-pits. Magically, they were the first signs ploughed into fields at the beginning of the season. Lots used in 'run-rig' divinations sometimes carried individuals' marks. Housemarks were painted on the outside of houses, and carved into the woodwork of mills. They decorated stained-glass windows in churches and halls. Wrought iron wall anchors were also made in the shape of the owner's Housemark. The marks were woven into rugs and tapestries, and stamped on cutlery, plate and cups. Their owners wore rings and jewellery proudly displaying the sign. They are still prominent in central European burghers' coats-of-arms. Finally, they appeared on the coffins and tombstones of their owners.

The most mystical of these marks are those used by the operative freemasons of medieval and later times. Many of their signs are runic in origin. Their forms relate to the organisation of their craft, where each worker was a member of a 'lodge' which had its own sign, the individual's mark being in some way related to this lodge mark.

Traditional Hof- and Housemarks include the whole range of runic sigils. Some are long bind runes of names, some are elegant and simple, while others are intriguingly complex sigils. They can be analysed as bind runes, combinations of various runes that give the Housemark both its own identity and its magical power. Like several of the runes, some Housemarks are ideograms of tools and implements. The names of some Housemarks: key, windmill, ladder, flail, pot-hook, arrow, hanger and hourglass all have their runic equivalent.

In former times, each property-owning family had its own Housemark. Sometimes, as in heraldry, each individual in the family had a mark that varied in some special way from the basic form. By the addition of certain marks, the sign of the sons, grandsons and other relatives of the 'founder' of the family dynasty were made. In this way, individuals could be defined without breaking the basic unity of the original Housemark. Sometimes this was achieved by marks made next to the original bind rune. These are known as countermarks. Often they were stave-figures like double or treble crosses. Also used were points or dots, and small circles. If your trade or family has not already given you a personal mark, it is possible to create your own mark using runic letters. Unlike personal heraldry, which is controlled tightly by legal authorities, there is no restriction on personal marks. The methods are detailed in Chapter 5.

3

The Meaning of the Runes

On the horn's face were there
All the kin of letters
Cut aright and reddened.
How should I read them rightly?
The Ancient Lay of Gudrun

The Elder Futhark

Rune magic works on a system of correspondences. For example, there are certain elements which rule each rune. These come from the five-element system of the Northern Tradition: fire, air, water, earth and ice. Each rune has a polarity, either masculine or feminine. There are also divinities who are the major rulers of each rune. Each rune has a corresponding herb and tree which are linked symbolically and magically with the most important quality of the rune. We can use the corresponding wood or herb to empower the rune working. Finally, the rune has a corresponding sound, which is used in the calls and chants of rune magic.

Feoh
The Elder Futhark begins with Feoh. This is the primary rune of the first aett, representing all kinds of beginning. Literally, Feoh, means cattle, the same meaning as the first characters of the Hebrew, Greek and Gothic alphabets. The cow plays an important part in the Norse myth of creation: the legend tells of the primal cow, Audhumla, which licks

a crystalline block of salt, from which comes Buri, the father
of the human race. Symbolically, then, Feoh is the primal
origin of us all, while magically, it represents movable
wealth. To the herdspeople of ancient Europe, their wealth
was measured in cattle. In modern times, Feoh refers to
money. Fee, a payment, is the name-meaning of this rune.
More specifically, Feoh is the power to gain worldly success
and great wealth, and to keep it.

Magically, Feoh is used in workings for power and
control. It provides the power to begin a working, drawing
in all of the energy we need. But, as with all magical
workings, we must take account of the implications of what
we do. We must be responsible in our activities. This is
stressed in the reading for this rune in the *Norwegian Rune
Poem*: wealth can easily lead to greed and envy, which bring
the downfall of society:

> Wealth causes friction between relatives,
> While the wolf lurks in the woods.

Feoh's elements are fire and earth, and its polarity is female.
Fire's power of creativity and generation are present in
Feoh. Its ruling divinities are the twin brother and sister
Vanir deities, Frey and Freyja, the Lord and Lady of modern
Wicca. Frey is often shown with an erect phallus, one of the
meanings of the Gothic letter Fe. Feoh's herb is the Stinging
Nettle (*Urtica dioica*). Its tree is one of the most magically
powerful, the Elder (*Sambucus nigra*). The sound of Feoh is
'F'.

Ur

The second rune is called Ur. It represents the great
European wild ox known as the Aurochs (*Bos primigenus*).
This magnificent beast was once widespread in Northern
and Central Europe. Unfortunately, like so many
indigenous European species of animal, it is now extinct.
It was killed off in Britain in the 1200s, and the last Aurochs
of all was shot in Poland in 1627. Despite this tragic loss,
the magical power of Ur is still available. In addition to its
bulk and power, the Aurochs was noted for its long, sharp,
curving horns. The *Anglo-Saxon Rune Poem* describes it thus:

> The Aurochs is bold with horns rising high,
> a fierce horn-fighter who stomps across the moors,
> a striking animal!

Figure 18 Skull of an Aurochs, the extinct 'primal ox' whose power is reproduced by the Ur-rune. The last Aurochs was killed in 1627.

Because of their immense length and capacity, Aurochs horns were reserved for the use of aristocrats. The traditional Scottish ceremonial drinking cup, the Corn, was an Aurochs horn, lipped with chased silver. A set of nine Aurochs drinking horns were buried with a Celtic lord in his mound at Hochdorf near Stuttgart, Germany (6th century BCE). A fine example was used until recently at Dunvegan Castle in Scotland, 2,500 years later. People who drank from the Aurochs horn partook of some of the magical virtues of this noble beast.

Magically, Ur channels the untamed strength of the Primal Ox. It brings us into a direct connection with the boundless power of the universe. Above all others, Ur is the rune for power, stamina and perseverance. It is also a rune of healing. Overall, it is one of the most powerful runes, providing the basic empowerment for any magical working which requires a solid grounding of any kind. Here, it can be used for anchoring a working in a specific way or place. However, it should be noted that this basic empowerment can never be used selfishly. It cannot be owned or controlled by a single individual. Workings using Ur must be 'according to free will, for the good of all'. The influence of Ur can bring personal success, but it will not be at the expense of others.

In the Younger Futhark, Ur means drizzle or slag. The

magical herb of the Ur-rune is the lichen called Iceland
Moss (*Cetraria islandica*). Ur's magical tree is the Silver Birch
(*Betula pendula*). It is ruled by Asa-Thor and the eldest Norn,
Urd, 'that which was'. Its element is earth, with a male
polarity. Its sound is 'OO'.

Thorn

The third rune is Thorn, or Thurisaz, and is primarily
sacred to Thor. On the tree, the thorns protect the plant,
working passively, deterring attackers. Magically, this rune
invokes the powers of resistance present in thorn trees, and
the power of the earth giant known as Thurs or Moldthurs,
and can be used to channel defensive powers. These are
symbolised by the strength of Mjöllnir, the Hammer of
Thor. Like Mjöllnir, Thorn is that divine power which
resists everything that threatens us. Just like Thor's
lightning, the Thorn rune can produce a sudden change
without warning. Used effectively, it can significantly alter
the course of events. Depending on how it is used, Thorn
can be used for attack or defence. The shape of the Thorn-
rune is a magical protection, and it is still used in the
Icelandic alphabet.

The Thorn rune is especially powerful at places named
after Thor, for example, Thundersley, Thorley, Thorney,
Thornton, Thornbury, Torshavn, etc. Of course, this is only
the case for places which lie inside the historic rune area
of Europe and Greenland. This principle should not be
ignored: the geomantic awareness of people in the past still
remains in place names which describe these special local
qualities even today.

Thorn's corresponding trees are the Blackthorn (*Prunus
spinosa*), the May Tree or Hawthorn (*Crataegus monogyna*);
the Bramble (*Rubus fruticosa*) and the Oak (*Quercus robur*).
Thorn's corresponding herb is the Houseleek (*Sempervivum
tectorum*); when grown on the roof, this traditionally
protects the house against lightning, Thor's weapon.
Thorn's element is fire, and its polarity male. In this aspect,
Thorn represents the wilful direction of the generative
principle, the masculine creative energy in action. Its sound
is 'Th'.

As

As, the 'god rune' is the fourth stave in the Elder Futhark.
This rune is known also as Æsc, Asa, Ansuz and, in a

variant form, Os. As originated long before the runes. In the Hindu tradition, it is the Sanskrit primal sound, which created the present universe. This is the divine breath, önd, which powers existence, the divine source within the human being. As is a powerful controller of the consciousness and all intellectual activities. Magically, this rune invokes the divine force and is used in workings which aim to maintain and reinforce order.

This rune symbolises the Ash tree (*Fraxinus excelsior*), one of the most sacred trees of the Northern Tradition. The universal world tree, Yggdrasil, the cosmic axis linking the worlds, is an Ash. It is a symbol of stability. The *Anglo-Saxon Rune Poem* tells us that

> Humans love the Ash tree,
> towering high.
> Though many enemies come forth to fight it,
> it keeps its place well,
> in a firm position.

As well as the Ash, this rune is connected magically with the Linden tree (*Tilia platyphyllos*). The As rune's herb is the Fly Agaric mushroom, (*Agaricus muscaria*). This plant contains hallucinogenic substances, and those who eat it may experience sensations of flying. In the past, it may have been used in the rites of As magic, but it must be remembered that, in former times, magicians knew the correct way of taking this mushroom. It is not recommended that readers should use it, as fatal overdoses are quite possible. The god of this rune (and fungus) is Odin, in his role as master of Shamans. The black buds and horseshoe-shaped leaf scars of the Ash denote its dedication to the god Odin and also, in springtime, to the goddess of that season, Eostre (Ostara). The corresponding element of As is air, and its polarity is male. Its sound is 'AA'.

Rad

The fifth rune is Rad or Raed. This is a very important rune, representing ritual and process. The name 'Rad' means wheel and, by extension, the motion that the wheel allows. In magical terms, it represents the 'vehicle' used to achieve an objective, but, just as a wheeled vehicle cannot be used without a road on which to run, Rad also represents the road or process itself. It is both the way forward and the means to get there. Magically, Rad is the rune of 'command and control', for it allows energies to be transformed. It assists the transfer of spirit, matter or information from one place to another. We can use it to channel magical energies in an appropriate way, according to our will, to produce desired results. To take full advantage of Rad's power, we must be in the right place at the right time, doing the right thing. An important element of Rad is in personal transformation. It helps us to take conscious control of our destiny (Wyrd).

The Rad rune's associated element is air. Its ruling divinities are the fertile deities Ing and Nerthus. It has a male polarity. This rune's trees are the Oak (*Quercus robur*) and the Wayfaring Tree (*Viburnum lantana*), while its corresponding herb is the Mugwort (*Artemisia vulgaris*). Its sound is 'R'.

Ken

The sixth rune is called Ken. As with many other runes, we can find its meaning in language. The Scots dialect word *ken*, which means knowledge, is the general meaning of this rune. Thus it is a rune of teaching and learning. Ken can take a number of forms. Its most common forms are < and, alternatively, a branch arising from a straight stave. In this form, it signifies the active principle. It is the polar opposite of the eleventh rune, Is, the single stroke representing the static principle. This upright form is the shape of the ancient means of lighting, known in Germany as the *Kienspanhalter,* a floor-standing holder of the flaming of pine-wood.

Basically, then, the name Ken describes a fiery chip of resinous pine wood, burnt for lighting. The *Anglo-Saxon Rune Poem* says:

The torch is living fire,
bright and shining.
Most often, it burns
where noble people are at rest indoors.

Because Ken brings us light in the outer darkness, symbolically, it brings the inner light of knowledge. As the fire of the hearth, Ken represents the power of the forge in which material is transmuted by the smith's will and skill into something new. The disordered raw materials are put into order by human consciousness. In the Younger Futhark, Kaun can mean a sore or wound. This relates it to the Gothic letter Chosma, which means illness/ illumination in the shamanic sense. Wounds and illness are sometimes gateways to personal change. Ken is therefore a rune which connects the rune magician with the mystery of transformation.

Magically, then, the Ken rune can be used in workings concerned with personal illumination, or which produce mystical creation. This is achieved through the union and transmutation of two separate entities into a third, which did not exist before the operation. Ken can be used to channel protective energy and regenerative powers, and to empower all positive actions. It is under the overall rulership of the watcher-god, Heimdall. It has the corresponding trees of Pine (*Pinus sylvestris*) and Bilberry (*Vaccinium myrtillus*). Ken's herb is the Cowslip, (*Primula veris*). Its element is fire, and it has a female polarity. Its sound is 'K'.

Gyfu

The seventh rune is Gyfu, which means gift. It is the X-shaped sacred mark, the linking rune that symbolises connections between people or the gods. As the gift, Gyfu signifies unification through exchange. It denotes the unity between the donor and the person to whom the gift is given. The creation of balance is the key feature of this rune. It is personified by the goddess Gefn, whose title is The Bountiful Giver. Magically, Gyfu gives access to those powers which can link us with other people, or the human level with the divine. It is useful in magic which involves interchange between people, such as cooperation between two individuals. This can be to further a common cause or a business partnership. When used magically, this rune should not be written as a crossing of two lines, but as the combination of two strokes, > and <. When they are written horizontally, they represent a connection between two people on an equal basis. But when written one above the other, these strokes symbolise a connection between the human, on Middle Earth, and other powers, either above in Asgard or below in Utgard. This rune's element is air, and it has a bisexual polarity. The corresponding trees of the Gyfu rune are the Ash (*Fraxinus excelsior*) and the Wych Elm

(*Ulmus glabra*). Its herb is the Wild Pansy or Heartsease, (*Viola tricolor*). Its sound is 'G' as in 'gift'.

Wyn

The last rune of the first aett is called Wyn or Wunjo. Its shape represents a metal windvane, such as those used on Viking ships, temples and stave churches in Scandinavia. This rune signifies joy, the elusive state of harmony within

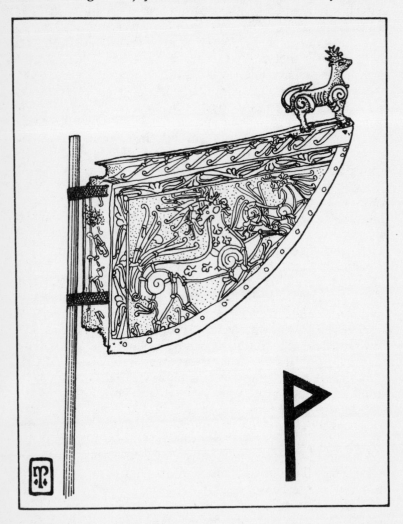

Figure 19 The joy rune, Wyn. Viking-age gilded bronze weathervane from Heggen Church, Norway.

a chaotic world. Magically, joy is obtained by being in balance with things, just like the windvane, which moves in harmony with the prevailing air currents. Wyn is the mid-point between opposites. It removes alienation and anxiety, whether they are caused by shortage or excess. It is a rune of fellowship, shared aims and general well-being. Magically, the Wyn rune helps us to realise our true will. Then we can use it to fulfil our wishes and desires. It does this by showing harmonious ways of doing things, transforming our life for the better. When used with Rad, it is very powerful. The Wyn rune is sacred to Frigg and Odin. Its element is air, and it has a male polarity. Its tree is the Ash (*Fraxinus excelsior*), and its corresponding herb is Flax (*Linum usitatissimum*), the plant from which linen is made. In legend, this was one of the gifts Frigg gave to human beings when she began the process of civilisation. Its sound is 'W'.

Hagal

The second aett, which is ruled over by Heimdall, the Watcher of the Gods, begins with Hagal, the ninth rune. The three runes at the beginning of this aett are icy and binding runes, expressing their place at the first part of winter in the year-circle. Hagal represents the most powerful sacred number of the Northern Tradition, 'by the power of three times three'. Because of this, it is sometimes called the *Mother Rune*. Literally, the name Hagal means *hailstone*. Hailstones are water transformed for a short while from its liquid into its solid phase, during which time it falls from the sky, sometimes so violently that it destroys crops or property. But when the damage is done, it melts, changing back into harmless, even beneficial, liquid water. More generally, Hagal represents all aspects of frozen water that falls from the sky – sleet and snow as well as hail. Everyone who has experienced a bad winter will know the sudden transformation that a snowstorm brings. Green fields and black roads are transformed rapidly into a sea of whiteness. Equally transformative is the thaw, when the colours of the landscape are restored.

The Hagal rune has a number of forms. The Elder Futhark form is like the letter H, whilst the Younger Futhark and more modern Germanic rune rows use a form like a six-branched 'star'. Symbolically, the Hagal rune is the crystalline primal seed, the basic geometry which determines the structure of the material universe. This is the basis of Guido von List's *Armanen* runic system of eighteen runes. Basically, Hagal represents the processes which have to take place for a project to be successful. Because of its icy nature, Hagal can be used in *Vardlokkur* – warding and binding magic. But Hagal is not the primary rune of magical binding – that is the role of the next rune, Nyd. Magically, though, Hagal can bring disruption, confusion and chaos, but it is more than that: it is one of the major runes of Wyrd. It expresses those patterns of events in our past life which make the present what it is today. The Hagal rune gives us access to those patterns of energy originating in the past which are active in and affect the present time. It represents the power of evolution within the framework of present existence, whose direction can be altered by the magical action of Hagal.

Personally, Hagal is the rune of the unconscious mind and of the formative processes of thought. On an impersonal level, it is the rune at the roots of things, both on a physical, material level, and in time. Thus it is used as a magical link between the upperworld and Middle Earth. Hagal is ruled by the deities who guard the passages linking the world of human consciousness with other planes. They include Heimdall, the watcher god who protects Bifröst, the Rainbow Bridge which links Middle Earth with the upperworld. The goddess Mordgud, who guards the icy bridge to the underworld, is also a ruler of Hagal. So are the Celtic guardians of the underworld entrance in Britain, Gwynn ap Nudd and Midir. This rune is also associated with Urd, the elder Norn, 'that which was'.

In folk magic, this rune is the protective sigil called the *lucky star*. This is drawn as a six-petalled flower formed of arcs within a circle. It can be seen on many old buildings, still protecting them magically against bad weather. Hagal's element is ice, the fifth element in the Northern Tradition, ruled by Rinda, goddess of the frozen earth. Its magic tree is the Yew, (*Taxus baccata*), the oldest-lived European species, and its herb is the Bryony (*Bryonia alba*). Both have been used magically for access to the underworld and upperworld through the arts of shamanry and, more permanently, death. Its sexual polarity is female. Its sound is 'H'.

Nyd

The tenth rune is called Nyd or Not. The form of the rune represents the two baulks of wood used for making the magical needfire in times of famine and pestilence. It has the literal meaning of need. This means both absence or scarcity of something, and 'necessity'. Need is constraint, and magically it refers to binding, the 'tight band across the chest' of the *Anglo-Saxon Rune Poem*. But the idea within the Nyd rune is that the power to release one from need is found within the need itself. Magically, the use of Nyd calls for caution, and the old adage 'know thyself' is particularly applicable to this rune. In using it, we must not attempt to strive against our Wyrd, but should use it in a constructive manner. Its main use in magic is for defensive binding spells, preventing magical attack and disempowering opponents. Nyd's element is fire, and its ruling divinities are the goddess Nott and Skuld, the Norn of the future. Its magic trees are the Rowan (*Sorbus acuparia*) and the Beech (*Fagus sylvatica*). In German tradition, the Beech is one of the most important trees for making rune slivers, whose name is said to be the origin of the word 'book'. The herb of the Nyd rune is the Snakeroot or Bistort (*Polygonium bistorta*). Its sound is 'N' and its polarity is female.

Is

The eleventh rune is Is. Its shape is an icicle, vertical and fixed. It represents static existence, the present time, and the element Ice. Is is the third 'binding rune' in the second aett. Magically, Is is primarily a rune of stopping activity. Ice is the result of a change in state from liquid to solid. It comes from energy loss. Static resistance replaces fluidity. The Is rune is the polar opposite of the rune Cen. It corresponds with the Gothic letter Iiz, destiny.

Magically, Is should not be underestimated. It does not only refer to motionlessness. As well as being static, ice can move. When it does, as in a glacier, it does so with irresistible force. Also, when it is in the form of an iceberg, the depth of floating ice is deceptive, for we can see only one ninth of the true mass above the surface. When the Is rune is used magically, although the results may seem small-scale, it will contain unsuspected depths. Magically, Is can be used to delay or halt the progress of something, or to terminate a relationship.

The magic tree of the Is rune is the Alder (*Alnus glutinosa*), whilst its herb is the highly-poisonous Henbane (*Hyoscyamus niger*), the Crann-gafainn of Scottish magical herbalism. Is's basic polarity is female, and, naturally, it corresponds with the Northern Tradition's 'fifth element', ice. This rune is ruled by Rinda, goddess of the frozen earth. It also relates to Verdandi, the Norn representing the present, 'that which is eternally becoming'. Its sound is 'EE'.

Jera

Jera, Jer or Jara is the twelfth rune. It means 'year' or 'season', referring to the cyclic nature of the seasons. Magically, Jera brings completion at the proper time. It can be used to bring forth a plentiful and rewarding harvest, but this can only happen after the right things have been done, to correct principles. Jera cannot act against the natural order of things but, if it is used under the correct conditions, results will be beneficial. When appropriate, it can speed up a process which is not proceeding quickly enough.

There are two basic forms for this rune. One is based on a standard upright stave, over which is written the diamond-shape of the Ing rune. Magically, this represents the stable state once it has been achieved. It symbolises the cosmic axis surrounded by the four seasons in their correct order. In this form, Jera is a pictographic representation of an actual object. It represents the harvest garland with its supporting pole (see figure 34, page 195). Its shape echoes its function, looking backwards to the old year, and forwards to the new, like the two-faced Celtic gods and the Roman Janus. In runic astrology, it is the rune of completion, marking the winter solstice, the end of the old year and the beginning of the new.

Jera's other form is made from two angled staves, like two Ken runes. These interpenetrate one another without touching. This is its dynamic form. It represents change towards completion. In turn, this can have two forms, the 'clockwise' and the 'anti-clockwise'. In rune magic, the deosil (clockwise) form of Jera accelerates a process, whilst its opposite, widdershins, form, brings a slowing-down.

Jera is related to the twin deities Freyja and Frey. Its shape reflects the mystic marriage between earth and the cosmos, or the transition through the seasons. Because it is a rune of balance, Jera's polarity is jointly masculine and feminine. It has the element earth as its ruler, and its tree is the Oak (*Quercus robur*). Jera's herb is the Rosemary (*Rosemarinus officinalis*). Its sound is 'J', as in 'jam'.

Eoh

The thirteenth rune of the Elder Futhark is called Eoh or Eihwaz. This is one of the most powerful runes. Eoh is the Yew rune. It represents a stave cut from a Yew tree (*Taxus baccata*). This is the magic double-ended stave of life and death. The Yew is the longest-lived of all European trees, and is green throughout the year, but its bark, leaves, roots, fruit and resin are all extremely poisonous. Because of this, numerologically, Eoh is 'unlucky thirteen'. But as it combines a remarkable longevity with toxicity, the Yew is also thought to be a tree of eternal life, possessing both the powers of death and regeneration. On occasion, older Yew trees which have partially died are regenerated by their own daughter trees which grow in their decaying interiors. Certain Yews have never-healing wounds. These are the 'bleeding Yews', from which red resin flows in an unceasing stream like blood.

In magic, the Yew has a number of related powers. Its wood is a magical protector and facilitator in its own right. In former times, the main use of Yew wood was for bow-making. As a killer of animals in hunting and of humans in combat, the bow was a death-bringer. In the times before firearms were invented, to carry a bow was a potent way of warding off any potential assailant. Because of this, Yew was physically as well as magically defensive. Northern Tradition magical alphabets such as Runic, Ogham and Gaelic recognise this in the qualities ascribed to the Yew-letters. In the Anglo-Saxon and Northumbrian rune rows, this bow-aspect has its own special stave, Yr. Gaelic, too, has two magical Yew-letters, and the Gothic letter Waer has the same meaning.

Bows made of Yew wood from a sacred grove, such as the Uetliberg near Zürich, were considered to have special virtues. Eoh is primarily the domain of the god Uller, dweller in Ydalir, the Valley of the Yews. But during the summer period, it is ruled by Odin. In its female aspect, it is ruled by Skadi, the destroyer-goddess of death and winter. Her skates, like Uller's skis and bow, are made of

Figure 20 The Eoh rune as a pothook, supporting the cauldron.

Yew wood. Skadi and Uller preside over the season of Yule, the 'yoke' between the old and new years. This affirms the power of Eoh as continuity and endurance.

Another use for Yew is in magic runic staves. Ancient Frisian runecraft has left us several. They use the Yew wood as the medium for banishing all harm, especially the powers of destruction and death. Yew staves, like the bow, can also be used for imposing one's will on other people, working both on the physical and on non-material planes. On a broader level, Yew protects the dead and provides the living with a means of access to the otherworld. Yew trees in churchyards and cemeteries are there to protect the dead. Access to the otherworld through Yew magic uses extremely risky life-or-death shamanic techniques. The ancient ecstatic-narcotic incense made from the resin or leaves of the Yew is very dangerous, perhaps lethal, so it is not recommended that the reader should make or use it.

Druidic tradition speaks of the Yew staff upon which are written the Powerful Oghams, which gives the magician the power to penetrate the kingdom of faerie without coming to any harm. With the Eoh rune, we need not fear death, for through the Yew we can gain passage from one state of being to another. In this aspect, Eoh corresponds with the Gothic letter Waer, meaning sacrifice and self-sacrifice. Mythologically, it relates to Odin on the Tree and Christ on the Cross.

The magical herb of Eoh is the Mandrake (*Mandragora officinarum*), a dread plant with a humanoid magic root. This rune is connected also with the Poplar tree (*Populus canescens*). It is considered a male rune, ruling all five of the elements (earth, water, ice, air and fire). Its sound is 'EO'.

Peorth

The fourteenth rune is Peorth, Pertho or Perthro. It has several meanings. The most popular interpretation is the 'dice cup', a mechanism used in former times for casting lots. Another meaning of this rune is a pawn or game piece. Both the dice and game piece represent the uncertainties of life. When Peorth is a piece in a board game, then it represents the interaction between the freedom of our conscious will-power and the constraints of our surrounding conditions. When a game is played, the pattern of the board and the rules of movement of the game pieces are already laid down but, beyond these limitations, the actual movements in any game are free. They reflect the conscious skill and will of individual players, and their interaction during the game. Similarly, in life, too, we are each in our own unique situation. But, as in the board game, we have free will within the constraints of our own Wyrd.

On another level, the Peorth rune represents the womb of the Great Goddess, Allmother. Here, magically, the Peorth rune brings things into existence. It exposes things which previously were concealed. The shape of Peorth is in the ends of the traditional Roman cartouche, in which texts are written. In this aspect, it is the bringer of knowledge. Thus, through all its interpretations, Peorth is the power of Wyrd in the world, bringing forth its potential into physical manifestation.

Peorth, then, is a rune of memory and recollection, problem-solving and esoteric knowledge. Magically, it gives access both to the inner secrets of the human world and to the inner workings of nature. It empowers us with the ability to distinguish things of value from those which are worthless. It is valuable in workings connected with initiation, where it can give meaningful insights into otherwise puzzling inner experiences. Peorth is sacred to the goddess, Frigg. Its tree-correspondences are the Beech, (*Fagus sylvatica*) and the Aspen (*Populus tremula*), whilst its herb is the lethal Monkshood, (*Aconitum napellus*), popularly called Aconite or Tyr's Helm. Its sound is 'P' and its polarity is male.

Elhaz

A powerful rune of magical protection comes fifteenth in the rune row. It is the stave known as Elhaz, Eiwaz or Eolh, whose shape symbolises the stupendous resistant power of the Elk. Magically, this is the most powerful defensive 'warding sign'. It has the power of repelling all evil. Above all others, it is the rune of personal protection. Visualisation of the rune around one's person provides a powerful protection against all kinds of physical and psychic attack (see pages 171–2). Equally, it is effective in protecting property, especially buildings and vehicles. The magic warding power of Elhaz promises protection against all of those forces or influences, known and unknown, which conflict with us. It is the power of the human striving towards divine qualities.

Elhaz is bisexual in polarity. Its herb is the Elongated Sedge (*Carex elongata*), which is shaped like the rune, and is very defensive. The Elhaz rune's element is air. It corresponds with the magically powerful wood of the Yew-tree (*Taxus baccata*), along with the rare Wild Service Tree

(*Sorbus torminalis*). Like the Yew, this is protective but, more specifically, against wild things and people. As primarily a defensive rune, Elhaz is ruled by Heimdall, the watcher-god. Its sound is 'ZZ'.

Sigel

The last rune of the second aett is known as Sigel, Sig or Sowilo. This is a rune of great force, which represents and channels the power of the sun. Magically, it brings the stupendous power of the sun and its light, helping us to achieve our objectives. Used properly, Sigel is the magical will acting beneficially. It can direct power in a devastatingly straightforward manner. Its shape is like a lightning-flash, and this describes its effects graphically. Using the solar power, Sigel resists the forces of death and disintegration, heralding the triumph of light over darkness. Because of this, it is the rune for gaining victory by magical means. In combination with Ur, it is also a powerful healer. Sigel is ruled over by the solar divinities of the North, the goddess Sól and the god Balder. Its sacred trees are the Juniper (*Juniperus communis*) and the Bay (*Laurus nobilis*). Its magic herb is the semi parasitic plant Mistletoe (*Viscum album*), one of the most sacred 'trees' of the Druids. This rune has a male polarity, with the element of air. Its sound is 'S'.

Tyr

Tyr is the first rune of the third aett, the Aett of Tyr. The spear-like shape of the rune represents the targeting of positive forces in the correct place for the greatest effect. Like As, Tyr is a god rune. Its name describes the power of the ancient sky god Teiwaz, known in England as Tīwaz, and in Scandinavia as Tyr. Symbolically, Tyr represents the courageous Asa-Tyr, who gave his right hand to allow the binding of the destructive Fenris Wolf which threatened the cosmic order. Tyr is the rune of positive regulation. Like Sigel, it represents victorious achievement of one's objectives. But when one uses Tyr magically, it should be remembered that achievement requires self-sacrifice. Any success that comes from the use of Tyr will be tempered by sacrifice.

A popular magical use of this rune is in legal actions, but here the success will come only if you are in the right to begin with. Travesties of justice, even when favourable to the magician, will not happen when Tyr is used. Tyr's polarity is male. Its tree is the Oak (*Quercus robur*), and its magically-effective herbs are Tyr's Helm (*Aconitum napellus*) and the purificatory Sage (*Salvia officinalis*). Air is its element, whilst its sound is 'T'.

Beorc

The eighteenth rune, representing the Birch tree (*Betula pendula*), is Beorc, Bar or Birkana. This rune's number is double the sacred nine of Hagal. In the Northern Tradition, eighteen is symbolic of completion, and new beginnings on a higher, organic, level. It marks the point at which the primal laws have been defined, and the stage is set for the play of life to begin in earnest. As the first tree which recolonised the barren land when the ice retreated at the end of the last Ice Age, the Birch is also symbolic of regeneration. Magically, Beorc is a rune of purification and new beginnings, sacred to the female side of magic. It can be used to 'set the stage' for a working, for the Birch symbolises purification, apparent in the rebirth of the sun's vigour in springtime.

Birch twigs are used for the 'brush' part of the witch's broomstick. Whole Birch trees are used traditionally for Maypoles. It is powerful in all women's magic, and in dealing with women's problems. Beorc's shape represents the breasts of the Earth Mother Goddess Nerthus or Berchta, making it a birth rune. The Beorc rune is identified with Beth, the first character of the Ogham tree alphabet. Beorc's polarity is therefore female. The element associated with Beorc is earth. Its corresponding herb is also sacred to the Mother Goddess, being Lady's Mantle (*Alchemilla xanthochlora*). Its sound is 'B'.

Ehwaz

Ehwaz or Eh, the horse rune, is the nineteenth stave. In former times, horses were the most sacred animals of Pagan Europe. In the Baltic countries, horses were used in divination, and horse magic is an integral part of the Nithstong rite (see pages 49–51). The *Anglo-Saxon Rune Poem* speaks of the horse as:

> the joy of peers,
> stepping out with pride
> when talked about by wealthy riders everywhere,
> and to the restless, always a comfort.

Magically, the horse rune is connected with combination, bringing things together into an unbreakable bond. But this requires absolute trust and loyalty. Loyalty, or faithfulness, is a necessity for those who use this rune. When you use Beorc, you must have serious intentions. Only work with Beorc if you intend to carry it through to completion.

Beorc helps us to create the movement which we need to undertake any task; more specifically, the task of life which our Wyrd has set us. It is valuable at the beginning of a psychic journey. On a more basic level, you can use it to assist any alteration in lifestyle, such as moving house.

The goddess of the horse rune is Freyja. Its element is earth, and it is bisexual in polarity. This runestave has two sacred trees, the Ash (*Fraxinus excelsior*), and the Oak (*Quercus robur*). The Ehwaz rune has the yellow-flowered Ragwort (*Senecio jacobaea*) as its magical herb. Its sound is 'EH'.

Man

Man or Mannaz is the twentieth runestave. It denotes the basic qualities of humanness that we all have, whether we are male or female. The Man rune is the shared experience of everybody's humanness. Its shape represents the archetypal human being in which all things are reflected, Man the Microcosm. Using bind-rune analysis, Man can be interpreted either as two overlapping and interconnecting Ken or Lagu runes. As a rune of magical connection, the Man rune is the symbolic embodiment of the social order, without which we cannot achieve our full human potential. Because language is the primary human quality, Man is one of the Hog runes, the runes of the mind. It is magically powerful in all things which use language, bringing advantage in disputes and academic examinations.

The Man rune has a bisexual polarity. Its major alignment is towards human beings, but it is also connected with the deities Heimdall, Odin and Frigg. The related Gothic letter is Manna, which means man and tree. This reflects the Northern Tradition legend that the first humans were made from trees. Askr, the first man, came from an Ash, and Embla, the first woman, an Elm. The Man rune connects magically with the Maple tree (*Acer campestre*), the Alder tree (*Alnus glutinosa*), and the Holly (*Ilex aquifolium*). The herb of the Man rune is the Madder (*Rubia tinctorum*),

whose red pigment, tiver, is used to colour runes. Its sound
is 'M'.

Lagu

The twenty-first rune, representing water in its many
phases and moods is called Lagu. The French word, *Lac*
(lake), and the English word lagoon reflect aspects of Lagu,
but, primarily, it is a rune of fluidity, signifying the flowing
powers of the tides, the force of waterfalls, and the vigorous
power of growth embodied in the Leek. Magically, Lagu
brings us into contact with the life force which is present
in physical matter, organic growth and waxing energies.

Organic growth proceeds in cycles, which can be seen in
the growth rings of seashells and tree rings. This is
manifested in Lagu as the ebb and flow of the tide,
reminding us that, to be successful, we should conduct all
magical workings when the times are right. Lagu is used
to clear blockages in progress and to accelerate any flow
already taking place. In my own work, I have found this
rune to be one of the most magically potent. The Lagu rune
can signify any of a number of polar opposites, and
appropriately, its corresponding deities are Nerthus and
Njord. There is also the lunar influence of Mani.

Lagu's element is water, with a female polarity. Lagu's
tree is the Osier (*Salix viminalis*), and its herb is the Leek
(*Allium porrum*). Its sound is 'L'.

Ing

Ing or Ingwaz is the twenty-second rune. It is a symbol of
light, representing a firebrand or beacon. The Ing rune has
two forms. The first is an inward-looking form, shaped like
the 'diamond' in playing cards. This concentrates the runic
energy of Ing, the inner fire. The second form is outgoing,
with spreading lines representing limitless expansion. This
carries the Ing energy outwards into the surroundings,
transmitting its light far and wide. Like Tyr, Ing represents
the god of its name. He is the male consort of the Earth
Mother of fertility and nurturing, Nerthus. Ing is god of the
hearth, the Inglenook, so this rune has a magically-
protective quality for households.

Magically, the Ing rune channels potential energy. It is a
'doorway to the astral'. Ing can bring together and integrate
various separate elements in a working. We also use it for

gaining access to the power of limitless extension. This is done using the outgoing form of the rune but, unlike that of the Sigel, Tyr or Ziu runes, the power of Ing is not available immediately. Ing requires a gradual build-up of energy for a period, before it is released as a single burst of power. Because of this, in sexual magic, it is connected with the force of the male orgasm.

The polarity of the Ing rune is both masculine and feminine. It is ruled by the elements of water and earth. Ing's herb is Selfheal (*Prunella vulgaris*), and its sacred tree is the Apple (*Malus spp.*). Its sound is 'NG'.

Odal

Odal, Odil, Ethil or Ethel is the twenty-third rune of the Elder Futhark. In the Frisian language, this rune is called *Eeyen-eerde*. This means 'own earth' or 'own land', a perfect definition of this rune's meaning. Odal has the form of an enclosure which is under the magician's control. Beneficial magical energies can be drawn into this rune, and kept there for later use. This is why Odal is used beneath the gable-end of houses. Odal's magic is most effective in the area of personal belongings, and ancestral heritage. It brings magical workings into being on the earthly level. It is the centre through which the magic can operate.

More generally, Odal strengthens our connections with other people in our group or family. Odal is powerful in maintaining the existing state of things. It resists arbitrary rules, and preserves individual and clan liberty within the framework of natural law. Its tree is the Hawthorn (*Crataegus monogyna*), used for hedging enclosures, and its herb is the White Clover (*Trifolium repens*), especially in its lucky four-leafed form. Its sound is 'OO' and its polarity is male.

Dag

Dag or Dagaz is the twenty-fourth, and final, rune of the Elder Futhark. Dag means 'day'. Its form represents balance between the polarities, especially light and darkness. Magically, Dag is a powerful blocking rune. But this does not mean that it is harmful. On the contrary, it is a very beneficial rune of light, health, prosperity and openings. Traditionally, it is painted or carved on doors, window shutters, doorposts and other uprights in the house. Its function is to prevent entry of harmful sprites, whilst admitting things which are desired.

Another magical use is to bring invisibility. Things, and people, 'sealed' with this rune are not noticed. On a more transcendent level, Dag gives us access to cosmic consciousness. The elements corresponding with Dag are fire and air. Dag is sacred to the watcher god Heimdall, and the goddess Syn, guardian of the door. Its trees are the Oak (*Quercus robur*), and the Norway Spruce (*Picea abies*). Its herb is the Clary Sage (*Salvia horminoides*). Dag's sound is 'D'.

Ac

The fourth aett (the aett of the gods – the Aesir) begins with the twenty-fifth rune, Ac, which represents the Oak, the holy tree of the god of sky and thunder. He has had many local names, among which the best known are Zeus, Ziu, Jupiter, Thunor and Thor. Ac is a rune of great potential power, symbolised by the acorn, from which the mighty oak tree grows. Although seemingly insignificant, this seed contains within itself the awesome potential of massive growth. Magically, Ac is the cosmic egg which channels the power of strong, continuous growth from small beginnings to a mighty climax. It should be used to reinforce magic which assists the creative and productive processes. The magical polarity of the rune Ac is masculine; its element is fire. Ac's corresponding herb is Hemp (*Cannabis sativa*), the now-banned plant which was used legally until the 1920s in rope-making, herbal tea and in smoking mixtures which provided access to altered states of consciousness. Ac's sound is a short 'A', as in 'cat'.

As

The second rune of the fourth aett is As, which is the fourth rune in the Elder Futhark. When extended rune rows are used, As is moved. It comes twenty-sixth, being replaced by Os. Naturally, there is a close connection between the meanings of As and Os. Os is the rune of Odin in his aspect as god of eloquence and linguistic communication. Os is literally the mouth from which comes the divine sound of creation. On a cosmic level, this signifies the primal vibration of existence. Magically, Os denotes the creative power of the word and hence wisdom itself. More generally, it refers to information, whose expression on a physical level underlies the very processes of life itself. Os reaches to the basic level of human culture, which is expressed in poetry, song, saga and literature. When it is used in magic, it is at its most powerful when connected with call spells (*galdr*). It serves to bring the divine breath, önd, into action. Like As, the rune Os is related to the Ash tree (*Fraxinus excelsior*), the Cosmic Axis tree Yggdrasil. As with Ac, the Herb of Os is a hallucinogenic plant, the Fly Agaric mushroom (*Agaricus muscaria*) used by ancient and modern shamans alike. Its polarity is male, and its element is air. Its sound is 'O', as in 'open'.

Yr

Yr is the twenty-seventh rune. It represents a Yew bow. Made from the Yew tree, the bow is both a weapon and an instrument of divination. When the rune Yr is used, it takes over this aspect of the Yew tree from Eoh in the 24-rune row. The form of the rune can represent the Arbalest or Crossbow, a more powerful form of bow, used in ancient times for hunting and military combat. In the Younger Futhark, this rune has the shape of the three roots of Yggdrasil, at the fateful entrance to the nether regions of existence. In this form, it is the 'death rune' of Teutonic magic. Because of this, it is sometimes used as a sigil denoting a person's death. The emblem of the Campaign for Nuclear Disarmament is also the Younger Futhark Yr.

In its Yr-aspect, the bow represents handicraft. This is the perfect combination of skills and knowledge applied to materials taken from Nature. As well as being a death-bringer, the bow was used for geomantic purposes. There were two different ways of using the bow to find a special place. One was to shoot an arrow, the place being selected where the arrow fell. This technique is mentioned several times in the legend of Robin Hood. The location of the graves of both Robin Hood and Little John were defined by the fall of arrows. So was the site on which Salisbury Cathedral is built. The other method was to use the tensioned bow as a divining rod.

Magically, Yr is used both defensively, as protection at the expense of others, and for finding the correct location – literally being on target. Yr magic is most valuable in finding lost objects, or the place in which to do something best.

The herbs of this rune are the Black-Berried Bryony (*Bryonia alba*) and the Mandrake (*Mandragora officinalis*). The magical poppets (small human-form 'dolls' or 'puppets' used for magical or sacred purposes) known as Alrauns are made from the roots of these herbs. When an Alraun is made, it is a magical link with the three roots of Yggdrasil, the powers of the Norns and the underworld. The Yr rune is also sacred to Odin, Frigg and Vidar, who symbolise all of the elements together, and hence is bisexually polar. Its sound is 'Y'.

Ior

Ior is the twenty-eighth rune. This represents the sea serpent, a beast once well known to mariners, but now endangered or extinct. In magical tradition, Ior is personified as the World Serpent, whose name is Iormungand. The form of this rune is very similar to that of the Younger Futhark character, Hagal, having a sixfold form. As Ior, this rune denotes the dual nature of matter, symbolised by the amphibious habits of many water beasts. According to tradition, Iormungand is an extremely formidable and dangerous beast, which sometimes threatens to destabilise the world. However, it is an essential part of the world's structure, which cannot be removed, and is recognised as such by Northern Tradition spirituality. Even if it became possible to eliminate the qualities that the World Serpent represents, then this would produce a catastrophe far worse than the consequences of its continued existence. Ior thus symbolises those unavoidable hardships and problems with which we must come to terms so that our lives can be tolerable.

Northern Tradition art often shows Iormungand, earth dragons and supernatural wolves as beasts of protection. In this role, they were made as roof or door guardians. They can be seen today on Norwegian stave-churches, and in Romanesque churches elsewhere (see Figure 15, page 59). Under the magical guardianship of Ior, these supernatural beasts represent certain forces in Nature which, rather than being killed, are quelled. Then, still living, they are integrated with the human-natural order. This can be seen

Figure 21 The effects of binding magic. Viking-age stone at Kirkby
Stephen, Cumbria, England, showing a supernatural being magically
bound.

in the two myths of Iormungand associated with Thor. The
first takes place in Utgard where, as a test of strength, Thor
is asked to lift a grey cat. Although the cat is small, Thor
can only lift one leg off the ground. Later, it transpires that

this cat was actually the World Serpent. Today, a Gaelic word for a cat, *iara*, reflects this Iormungand-nature. In another legend, Thor fishes for Iormungand using an Ox-head as bait. He succeeds in hooking it, but before he can drag it from the water, Hymir, the giant with whom Thor is fishing, cuts the rope, and Iormungand sinks back to the ocean bed. Similarly, in other Norse legends, both the Fenris Wolf and Loki are not killed, but are bound magically under the earth.

Iormungand, Fenris Wolf and Loki, are recognised as separate entities, but they are partly reintegrated with the powers of the Earth and the unconscious. This process is not yet complete, but whilst they remain dangerous, they are also essential parts of life. These legends are fine examples of the recognition of the law of the unity of opposites in the Northern Tradition, and their reintegration into their appropriate place in life. Unfortunately, the modern response to such dangerous forces as these is to seek to eliminate them completely, which is impossible.

Magically, Ior is a binding rune of great power. This is seen in one of the rune's corresponding trees, the Ivy (*Hedera helix*). The Ivy is a plant of binding and tying. Whilst it is said to strangle and kill other trees, it remains evergreen, making it a plant of life and death. Ior represents the serpentine, binding power of the water snake, the Ivy, or the seaweed. The deity of Ivy is the Morrigan, who can manifest herself as the dark water snake. According to myth, she is the binding and destroying hag who embodies all that is perverse and repulsive among supernatural powers. This dark water snake is the herb of Ior, the seaweed Kelp (*Laminaria digitata*), with which swimmers are sometimes entangled and drowned. The other important magic tree of Ior is the Linden (*Tilia platyphyllos*), which is the traditional central tree of villages in Holland and Germany, the Dorflinde. Sometimes this was the gallows-tree, too, upon which criminals were hanged with nooses woven from lime-twigs. Its element is water and its polarity feminine. Ior is ruled over by Njord. Its sound is 'IO'.

Ear

Ear is the twenty-ninth and final rune of the Anglo-Saxon Futhark. It represents the soil of the earth. Figuratively, this is 'the dust' to which our bodies return at death. Ear is symbolic of the grave, the termination of life. Without an end, there could never have been a beginning: without death, there cannot be life. Ear signifies the unavoidable end of all things, more specifically the inevitable return of individual, living human beings to the clay of which their bodies are made. Magically, Ear brings on the end of something. More specifically, it can accelerate the arrival of an inevitable end-point. It is therefore a useful rune for bringing about the swift conclusion of something that the user wishes to be terminated. Magically, along with Eoh and Yr, Ear is the third Yew-tree rune. Its herb is equally deathly, being the lethal Hemlock (*Conium maculatum*). Ear has the sound 'EA'. Its polarity is female, corresponding to the element of earth. Its deity is Hela, goddess of death and the lower world.

The Northumbrian Rune Row

Around the year 800, in England, north of the Humber, the Futhark acquired further characters, which are described below. This became the Northumbrian rune row, which has thirty-three characters. Conventionally, these are divided into four aettir of eight staves plus one additional, central rune. Some of these additional runes have a Celtic connection, being related to the indigenous Ogham alphabet of the British Druids. In many places, the Anglians of northern England and the indigenous Celts lived together in peace and cooperation. For example, the Mote of Mark, in Dalbeattie Forest, Kircudbright, Scotland, had a mixed Anglian-Celtic population. It was a centre of excellence of Hiberno-Saxon metalwork production, and a rune-inscribed bone, found there in 1973, proves that runes were used in that area.

Cweorth
The first of the Northumbrian runes is called Cweorth. This letter is related to the Ogham character Quert, the Apple Tree of the Celtic tree alphabet. It has the meaning of rebirth and eternal life, as does the related Gothic character, Quertra. Specifically, the Northumbrian rune Cweorth represents the climbing, swirling flames of the ritual fire.

It describes ritual cleansing by fire, and the sacred hearth.
It is the process of transformation through fire. In the case
of the funeral pyre, one of the aspects of Cweorth, fire
serves to liberate the spirit so that it can be reborn in a new
form. More commonly, Cweorth represents the festival
bonfire of celebration and joy. In this way, Cweorth is the
opposite to the binding need-fire Nyd.

Magically, Cweorth is used to bring about all kinds of
transformation. The Cweorth stave has a female polarity. Its
element is fire, and its deity is Loki in his aspect as the god
of Fire, Loge. The magic trees of Cweorth are the Bay
(*Laurus nobilis*), the Beech (*Fagus sylvatica*) and, through its
Celtic connection, the Apple (*Malus spp.*). The sacred herb
of Cweorth is the Rue or Herb of Grace (*Ruta graveolens*),
used in rites of purification. Its sound is 'QU', as in 'queen'.

Calc

The next rune in the Northumbrian Futhork is Calc. This
is the last-but-one letter of the fourth aett. It has the literal
meaning of a ritual container or an offering cup. The form
of this rune is identical to Elhaz inverted. If Calc is seen as
an inversion of Elhaz, it may be taken as symbolic of the
death of the individual. This is reinforced by the Younger
Futhark character, Yr, which also has the same form. In the
Armanen runic system, this is the shape of an inverted Man
rune. Often, this signifies death. However, Calc is not a
'death rune' in the sense of calling for or accelerating the
demise of someone or something. More generally, it stands
for the natural conclusion of a process. This can be seen in
its position as the final rune of the Scandinavian 16-rune
row.

Magically, Calc represents the successful conclusion of a
working, so it is appropriate to use it in a closing rite. Once
it is over, the transformation has been achieved, and no
more needs to be done. But also, what has passed was real.
It has become part of our personal history (örlog).

Calc may also be used magically in contacting absent
friends or the departed in an act of remembrance. It
connects us with areas of existence which appear to be
accessible, yet cannot be touched – the ungraspable,
unattainable unknown. Because of this, Calc is ruled over
by the three Norns, whilst medieval myth describes it as a
cup or stone, the Holy Grail.

The magical trees of the Calc rune are the Field Maple (*Acer campestris*), the Maplin Tree, from which sacred cups are made. The other sacred tree of Calc is the Quicken Tree or Rowan (*Sorbus acuparia*). Calc's sacred herb is the Milfoil or Yarrow (*Achillea millefolium*), generally an important herb in traditional Wicca and rune magic. This stave's working polarity is female, and it corresponds to the element of earth, having the sound 'K'.

Stan

Stan is the final rune of the fourth aett. It means 'stone', containing the magical power of stone in all its forms. At a basic level, Stan represents the Bones of the Earth, the ground beneath our feet. It can signify a blockage, such as a rock lying across a path, or a stone at the entrance to a cave. Additionally, Stan represents a megalith standing at a place of power in the landscape. On a more conceptual level, Stan may signify a stone or playing piece in a board game. The rune has the shape of the stone or bone playing pieces used in ancient Northern Tradition board games.

Magically, Stan is used to create a link between human beings, earthly and heavenly powers. In its appearance as a game piece or a geomantic stone, Stan can either provide protection or act as a block to our progress. An important magical use is in blocking and stopping, turning back opposition and driving away assailants. *The Lay of Hamdir* tells of a Stan spell by 'The High Gods' Kinsman' (Odin):

> Roared he as bears roar;
> 'Stones to the stout ones,
> That the spears bite not,
> Nor the edges of steel,
> These sons of Jonakr!'.

In this, Stan is linked to the Celtic Ogham letter Straif, which is the Blackthorn tree. This is the Ogham of magical turning and blocking, which can also be used in attack and punishment. Of course, the stone is the oldest offensive missile known to humans! The sacred trees of Stan are the Blackthorn (*Prunus spinosa*) and the Witch Hazel (*Hamamellis mollis*). Stan's magical herb is the stone-loving lichen known as Iceland Moss (*Cetraria islandica*). This stave is ruled over by the deities, especially the goddess Nerthus.

Naturally, Stan is allied to the element of earth. Its magical polarity is male. Its sound is 'ST'.

Gar

The thirty-third and final rune of the longest complete Futhork is Gar. It has the literal meaning of spear. More specifically, Gar refers to Gungnir, the spear of Odin. Asatrú lore tells us that this has a staff of ash wood, making it a portable version of the world tree Yggdrasil. Unlike the other 32 runes, which are assigned to their corresponding aett, in the Northumbrian system Gar stands outside. This is because of its magical meaning, the stable reference-point which is at once internal, external, everywhere and nowhere. When the four aetts are written, Gar should be the central point around which all of the other runes are laid out in a circle. But this is not the whole of Gar's function. It can also be used to represent the beginning of a new order of things, as a rune of fulfilment. In this way, it serves as the 'seal' in the completion of a magical formula or working. As a sigil, it represents the final statement, 'and so mote it be', or 'Ka!'. Magically, it can be used for any new beginnings. It is also valuable for wiping out any runic on-lays which are no longer needed.

When called, Gar has the phonetic value of 'G'. For magical workings, ruled by Woden as shamanic master of the Cosmic Axis, the sacred tree of the Gar stave is the Ash (*Fraxinus excelsior*) and the now-rare Spindle Tree (*Euonymus europaea*). The phallic Gar has a masculine polarity, which is related magically to all of the five elements. Its sound is 'G', as in 'gate'.

The Fifth Aett

Rune magic uses several other runes. Unlike the other 33, they have never been listed as part of any rune row. But along with Gar, they form the fifth aett of modern rune magic. Of course, when compared with the runes of the Elder Futhark, much less research has been done on them. However, their meanings are as well-defined as any other runes.

Wolfsangel

The first of these additional characters is the rune called Wolfsangel. It is in the form of the 'wolf hook', which was a device once used in central and northern Europe to trap and torture wolves. Wolfsangel's magical use is in capturing and binding. When called, Wolfsangel has the phonetic value of the diphthong 'AI', the wolf howl. In its shape, it resembles Eoh, with an additional crossbar and, like Eoh, it can be used negatively, causing sadness and distress. But its greatest use is in binding powerful forces of disorder and dissolution. In its use as a wolf-catching weapon, this runic form prevented the animal from doing any further harm to human beings. Also, as a wall anchor, it maintained order, prevented the spreading of walls, and the possible collapse of the building. As a magical protection of power, it was used in central European heraldry, and as a personal magical sigil. Wolfsangel is solely a metallic rune, the rune of Iron, the element earth and the god Tyr. Its sound is 'SZ' and its polarity is female.

Erda
The thirty-fifth rune is Erda. This is the rune of the Earth Mother Goddess, Erda. Symbolically, it signifies Mother Earth, our planet as the goddess. Magically, it is a rune of nurture, protection and enclosure. In its shape, the Erda rune resembles Odal. However, it has a distinctly different meaning and magical use. The two 'tails' that distinguish this rune from Odal represent the links between the protective enclosure of the Earth upon which we live and are nurtured, and the wider universe. Being composed of eight straight lines, all of the same length, Erda is thus a rune that engenders stability and the maintenance of wholeness. In this, it is related to the magic grid, known in Ogham lore as 'the eight ifins' or the hurdle of pine branches. Its tree is the Scots Pine (*Pinus sylvestris*), tree of illumination and marker of sacred places in the landscape. Magically, the application of the Erda rune is for all things which require a holistic approach, the bringing of reintegration of human actions with the wider world of which they are a part. When called, Erda has the sound 'OE'. Its polarity is female, and its element, earth.

Ul
Another rune of the fifth aett is Ul. This is the rune sacred to the ancient Frisian god Waldh. He is a divinity with some similarity to Ullr, the Norse god of wintertime and the arts

of skiing and archery. Magically, this is a rune of great of personal strength. Its use brings with it personal endurance and the inner power that one needs to overcome severe trials and to come out of them with success. Ul is the rune of personal empowerment and of healing, for another of Waldh's attributes was that of assisting recovery from illness or injury. The solsticial connection of Ul denotes its connection with 'turning points'. Ul is the runic element in Yule, the nodal point where the darkness of winter is turned back. It is the crisis point, the 'darkest hour before the dawn', corresponding with Thule, the mystic place 'where one is forced to turn back'. Thule was also the name of a shaman or runemaster.

Magically, Ul can be used to turn around a situation to the advantage of the user. It can give the runester the power to endure life's turning points unscathed. Such experiences, under the protection of Ul, become times of empowerment. When called, Ul represents the sound 'UE'. Its polarity is male, and its element, air.

Ziu

This is a very powerful rune named after the old Swabian sky god Ziu. He is a parallel of the southern European deity Zeus, known in Anglo-Saxon England as Tîwaz. At first glance, this rune might appear to be a bind rune of Sigel and Tyr. However, it is not a bind rune because the stem of Tyr is not carried to the bottom of the line. (Bind runes must include complete parts of all of the runes of which they are composed.) In its shape, it is the runic representation of the god's thunderbolt. Magically, Ziu channels devastating power, carrying the immediate power of a magical thunderbolt. It concentrates and channels magical energy, especially when maintaining the divine order. According to medieval symbolism, Ziu has the meaning of 'the past taking revenge upon the present'. This is usually interpreted as the process of justice and order asserting itself over disorder, no matter how long it might take. In this aspect, the magical effect of Ziu is described in the old adage, 'the truth will out'. In central Europe, the main place of power of Ziu is the German city of Augsburg, formerly called Ziusburg. In England, his major shrine was at Tysoe in Warwickshire, where his totemic beast, the Red Horse, was carved on the hillside. Modern German graffiti writers use this rune to denote that a building is occupied by squatters. Its sound is 'ZZ'. Its polarity is male, and its element air/fire.

Sol

Another rune named after a divinity is Sol, the rune of the sun goddess, Sól, at her elevation. Magically, this is connected with the rune Sigel, but it is more contained, more specific, and less transitive in its actions. The form of the rune Sol is the solar circle with a vertical stave below it, representing a straight sunbeam bringing light from the heavens above to the world below. Just as the sun provides warmth and light to the world, so the power of this rune brings illumination from outside. Magically, it is potent in healing and nurture. It is the embodiment of gentle growth and regeneration when the time is appropriate. When called, this rune represents the sound of 'SS'. Its polarity is female and its element is fire.

The Classes of Runes

The runemasters of old classified the runes into various types. These depended upon the runes' use, and they are still useful today. When any runes were used for magic, they were called Ram runes. These strong runes are given their power through ceremony. The word 'ram' means strength, as in the male sheep, whose horned head can batter its way through difficulties. A more general category of runes is the Wend runes. These are any runes which are written from right to left. When written this way, they have magical properties. Runes written upside-down can also be called Wend runes.

The runes have a number of specific uses. These are listed in the old Norse text called *Sigrdrífumál*. The most useful runes are those which can be used at any time. Because of this, the runes used most frequently are those of memory, speech and mental agility. Here, the power of the runes can be expressed and brought into action both through speech and writing. Of these, human speech is the most immediately effective. In *Sigrdrífumál*, spoken runes, called *Malrunes*, are described. The word Malrune comes from the Norse *mal* or *maal*, meaning speech. This word describes several old Norse texts, such as *Hávamál*, The Utterance of the High One. This text is literally the divine words of Odin, the spoken runes of the god of consciousness. The word Malrune also means any rune whose magic is to do with the spoken word.

Generally, the Malrunes are used in magic that brings advantage to the rune user by means of speech. Most basically, then, a Malrune is a runic formula that is spoken, called, or sung to achieve the desired magical result. Malrunes are effective in areas of life where words are important. They can be used to gain compensation against injuries, especially in legal actions. When they are used for this purpose, they should be written upon the walls, pillars and seats of the place where the case is being tried.

Malrunes are also used in the word magic of poetry and invocation. Closely related are the *Hugrunes* (or *Hog runes*). The word is related to the name of one of Odin's two attendant ravens, Huginn, 'thought'. These are the mind-power runes. Traditionally, they should be written upon the runemaster's chest and 'secret parts'. Their function is to bring mental excellence to the user. As in former times, Hugrunes are one of the most powerful and effective means of mind-concentration.

Other necessities are taken care of by other sorts of runes. The runes which are used to assist one in obtaining victory are known as *Sigrunes*. These are named after the solar power rune Sig or Sigel, and are used to gain advantage in all kinds of contest. They should be written on the runemaster's clothing, instruments, tools, or weapons. The function of Sigrunes is to bring success to any venture. When writing Sigrunes, the name of Thor should be invoked twice.

Not all of the rune magic of the past was just for selfish gain. The runes have always been used in benevolent ways, too. For healing others, people have used the *Limrunes*. To get the best results from Limrunes, they should be carved on the south-facing bark or leaves of the corresponding tree. The rune Ul is a Limrune of great power, invoking Waldh. *Biargrunes* are more specialised healing runes which invoke Berchta, the goddess of childbirth, to procure a safe birth. They also protect women and their babies at this hazardous time. Biargrunes are named after the Goddess Rune, Biarg or Beorc. This is the rune of the sacred white

Birch Tree, symbol of purity and new beginnings.

Magic that helps us to communicate with other realities has its own type of rune. *Troll runes* are runes that can be used for divination. This name comes from an old belief that prophecy comes from Trolls, who have knowledge of the future. Trolls are literally earth spirits, the elemental forces known to country magicians. Troll runes are also used for enchantment. Connected with these are the *Swart runes*, or 'the black runes'. They are necromantic characters used to communicate with departed spirits.

Another important aspect of rune magic is defensive. The runes can help us to 'ward off' harm coming from both the physical and the non-material realms. This aspect of rune magic is the realm of the Warlock, the cunning man skilled in the arts of *Vardlokkur*. This is the magic of warding and binding. There are many ways of using runes in binding magic. In ancient times, for example, men used the *Ale runes* to block the magical enchantments of strange women. Ale runes were written inside the cup from which the woman drank, and also on the back of the man's hand. The man would scratch the Nyd rune upon his fingernail as the final binding power.

Weather magic is a major part of all traditional magical systems, especially when connected with hunting, sailing and farming. This sort of magic tries to ward and bind the forces of the weather. The *Brun runes* are an example of this. Literally, they are the *Fountain runes*. Sometimes they are called, more accurately, *Surf runes*. But whatever their name, they are the runestaves that connect the runemaster harmoniously with the power of flowing and running water, including the sea. To protect a ship against harm, for example, Brun runes should be carved on the stern, oar or rudder. There are Brun runes carved on the late-eighth-century amulet found at Westeremden in Frisia. According to the runes carved on it, this yew stave gave power over the waves. The story of King Canute, who ordered the tide to retreat, may be an echo of the more successful use of the Brun runes in earlier times.

Runic Fire and Metal Magic

Some of the runes are in the shape of tools, weapons and utensils. By looking at the use and meaning of these objects, we can gain a greater understanding of the runes themselves. Magically, there are two sides to rune use. They have one meaning when used in wood-craft, and a slightly different one in iron-working. An example of wood-craft is the rune Ken. This is the stave of illumination which represents a chip of pine wood and its holder. Until the eighteenth century, chips of pine were burnt for lighting. They were held by an upright stand, which the rune represents. The rune Nyd is another classic example of woodcraft. It represents the two baulks of wood that were rubbed together to kindle the needfire. This was a magic fire lit only in times of dire need. During plague and famine, all of the fires in a village were put out. Then the needfire was kindled by friction. In Scotland, the ceremony of the *tein'éigin*, as the need-fire was known, survived until the 1820s. It is last known to have happened in North Uist in 1829. To start the needfire, 81 married men were called together. Taking turns, groups of nine men rubbed two planks of wood together. Finally, their efforts produced fire. Torches were lit from the burning planks, and from them, all of the fires of the district were lit again. Other wood magic involves the Yew tree, which is detailed elsewhere (page 158).

Iron magic was at its height in the Viking period, when the craft of the smith was highly sophisticated. Basically, smithcraft is a kind of alchemy. In pre-industrial times, the smith was responsible for every part of the process. This began with extracting metal from the ore, and continued with the creation of tools and weapons from that metal. The smith literally transmuted base minerals into shining metal. The symbol of alchemy, the tail-biting serpent Ouroboros, is a representation of the hand-crafted iron ring which was the hallmark of smithcraft. If you examine any smith-made iron ring, it will reveal its Ouroboros nature. The complex magic of metal rings is closely related to this eternal mystery. Also, the metal from which anything is made has its own örlog – it came from *somewhere*. Consequently, it has a magical link with the place from which it came. Metal taken from places of power still retains that link, no matter how far away it may be. Thus it was that iron extracted from the tiver-red mud of holy springs and lakes was magically linked with the powers of those waters. It was fitting to return objects there once they had been used. Hence the legend of Excalibur and other magic swords that were returned to the Lady of the Lake. Metal extracted from meteorites carries the extraterrestrial power of the worlds beyond the Earth. As in the Jewish tradition, anything which falls from the heavens is bound to be pure.

Swords were the high point of smithcraft, but of course smiths made many more mundane objects. If we look at these, we can find many runic connections that bring new insights into their standard meanings. An important example of this is the rune Eoh. This is the 'yew tree' rune, one of great magical power for protection and projection. Usually, it is depicted as a yew stave, with hooked ends. In this form, it represents a magical staff like the Westeremden stave. The hooked ends symbolise the rune's power of attachment and binding, but it also represents a cauldron hook, on which a cauldron was hung over a fire. In traditional society, this iron was used as a powerful magical tool in its own right. Its main use was in weather magic, to dispel clouds and act against bad weather in general. In this aspect, it is a rune of binding. In Scottish house magic, this iron rune form is called *drola*, a word which is connected with binding. The *Hahalruna* rune code is also related to this cauldron hook magic. Its name comes from the Old High German word for a pot-hanger rack, *hahal*. Because of this, Hahalruna are best used in binding magic.

In metalcraft, the rune Odal is another symbol of strong connections. It is the traditional form for the 'eyes' of the cauldron, which connect the handle to the body of the vessel. Here, twin Odal runes are the anchors for the hook, assuring the safe keeping of the cauldron's contents.

The Ing rune has its iron counterpart in a certain type of chain link. This is where the metal is twisted to make a link that cannot be reversed. Links like this were often used as connectors between iron chains and the leather parts of the harnesses of farm animals. Here, literally, Ing is a link.

The iron form of Ur is of another fixing device. It is the staple, hammered into the wall as a place to hang tools, harnesses, etc. The iron Ur is a strong anchor to which things may be attached. Traditional ironwork also uses staples on doorposts to hold the latch when the door is closed. As a multi-purpose object, the staple expresses the collective qualities of the rune.

The later rune Wolfsangel, the wolf-hook, is a stave which has no wooden equivalent. This weapon is described earlier in this chapter.

Another defensive and offensive rune is Tyr. In its iron aspect, this rune is in the form of a spear or harpoon. Carvings of the god Tyr on timber-framed buildings in Alsace show the one-handed god accompanied by his rune-shaped spear. Magically, Tyr in its iron aspect cuts through problems. In this it expresses the quality of the old Welsh word, *tyr*, which means 'to cut'.

As an iron object, the Is rune is a nail. In ancient Europe, nail-driving was performed as counter magic against psychic attack, such as the Evil Eye. Magically, it brings the static, binding power of Is into action to stop something happening. For example, Livy states that pestilence was stopped in ancient Rome when a dictator drove a sacred nail into a temple door or wooden post. In Roman times, nails were engraved with magic inscriptions and symbols to enhance their power. In the Northern Tradition, good luck is brought by nails hammered into doorposts, supporting posts and main beams of a building. In Norse temples, the High-seat Pillars (Öndvegissulur) were the most sacred part of the building, and had sacred nails hammered into them. Also, the symbol known as God's Nail is carved upon posts. This is an Ing rune containing an eight- or four-petalled flower, at the centre of which an iron nail should be driven. It represents the star called The Nail or Nowl, the Pole Star. This is a powerful magical symbol of stability, the power of Is.

Other runes represent iron weapons. In Viking times, the rune Is was also the sword. The Icelandic *Saga of Howard the Halt* has a poetic kenning that calls a sword blood-ice. Another weapon from the Northern Martial Arts is related to the defensive rune Elhaz. Some ancient drawings of Odin show him wielding two 'thunderbolts'. These are depicted as hand-held weapons with trident forks at each end. This is an ancient weapon used in the Northern Martial Arts. Basically a weapon of defence, it is similar to an oriental martial arts weapon, the Okinawan *Sai*. In medieval Europe, this trident-like weapon was called the Military Fork. Magically, the trident invokes the power of the defensive rune Elhaz. In the hands of a master of the martial arts, both the Military Fork and the Sai are formidable defences against swordsmen. The fork is used to deflect sword blows, and can even break the sword.

The final iron rune is the 'Joy' stave, Wyn. This is shaped like an iron weather-vane used on sailing ships in Viking times and later. The mast-top vane on the East Anglian sailing ships known as Norfolk Wherries is actually called a Wane. By complying with the changing wind, the vane symbolises the joy that one has in life when one can live in harmony with the conditions. Wyn is the rune of wind magic, a life-or-death matter for those who voyage in sailing ships or who operate windmills.

4

Principles of Rune Magic

Now this is my first counsel,
That thou with thy kin
Be guiltless, guileless ever,
Nor hasty of wrath
Despite of wrong done
Sigrdrifumal

One day, a Viking ship arrived at a small port. An official boarded it and asked one of the crew, 'Where is your leader?' The man replied, 'We have no leader, we are all equal, free men.'

This story, from the 'heroic age', epitomises the soul of the runic tradition. Unlike many systems, rune magic has no overall authority, no Popes, Imperial Wizards or Grand Masters. It is simply a matter of personal will, practised by free individuals. There is no dogma or fundamentalism in runework. But this does not mean that it has no order. Runework does have well-established principles which are worth keeping to. The guiding principle is free will. In performing magic, never subordinate your will slavishly to any 'master' or 'system'. A master's job is to shed light and to give guidance, not to control and use you. Also, as a rune magician, you must never cease to be conscious of what you are doing. Respect your own mind. Nobody else can tell you what you 'should' think or do. If you give up your critical faculties, then you will no longer be able to do rune magic effectively. This is because magic is worked through thought, will and consciousness. But, if words and conduct are not in harmony, then they will have no effect.

Form and Essence

Over the years, many magicians have tried to define the essential nature of magic. A master of the East Anglian tradition once described magic to me as 'the craft of willing things to happen (or not to happen)'. Similarly, the Thelemic magician Aleister Crowley described it as 'the art of causing change in accordance with will'. Later, Dion Fortune refined Crowley's definition by referring to it as consciousness: 'Magic is the art of producing changes of consciousness in accordance with the will'. No matter how magic is defined, the conscious, trained will is an essential factor. This is implicit in all interpretations of magic.

However we may believe it works, magic is not outside the universe. It is a natural phenomenon. It is an integral part of human consciousness like language. Magic gives us access to the process called *transvolution* – 'the way things happen' – giving us a way of altering them in accord with our will. The practice of magic is based upon understanding and then using the structure of transvolution in a creative way. In this way, magic is the craft of producing those synchronistic effects which the magician requires. This means that, theoretically, if there is only 1 chance in 100 of something happening, then the use of magic will tend to make that 1 in 100 chance occur in favour of the magician. Magic cannot produce extra chances, but it *can* channel those chances towards the magician. It does not violate the laws of statistics. The overall statistical audit will not be changed: there will still be only 1 result in 100, but the magician will have been in harmony with the outcome. Used properly, magic helps us to be in the right place at the right time, or to avoid being in the wrong place at the wrong time. By this means, meaningful coincidences happen, though no more than would be expected by chance in any one instance. This is the essence of magical practice, from the finding of lost objects and people, to the achievement of wonders. At the deepest level, rune magic is a work of self-transformation. It always tends to bring the magician into harmony with the conditions surrounding her or him.

Magic is a natural process. What could be more magical than existence itself? Magic works at a deep level, not on the surface. It always works with the inner essence of things, not the outward forms. When practised effectively, it will bring that essence into being. Do not confuse essence and form. Essence is the inner being of something; form is its outward expression. In magic, you should always work for the essence. Think about what you really need from a working. Examine your basic motives for wanting something to happen. When you work for something you should ask yourself: 'Why do I want this?' '*Do* I really want this at all?' If the answer is 'yes', then the question arises, 'Is this the best way of getting it?' 'Can I get it in any other way?' Always think about the *essence* of what you want. When you do this, banish precise forms from your mind. Working for form is too restricting: form is limiting, but essence is unlimited. There is often a better alternative which you have not yet thought of. Working through essence will bring the best possible results.

We are all looking for the perfect life that will fulfil all our needs. So why restrict the possibilities by asking for unimaginative trinkets? Many myths, fairy- and folktales tell of empty form-fulfilment. This occurs when someone asks for something magically, and receives it. But although the request is fulfilled literally, the essence of what was asked for is lost. The legend of Midas's golden touch is a classic example of empty form-fulfilment. When he could turn all to gold just by touching it, then he could no longer touch another human without killing them, and he was unable to eat.

Negative and Positive Magic

The rune teaching of 'The Way of the Eight Winds', described in this book, disapproves of all harmful or negative magic. The ancient charge known as The Wiccan Rede says: 'an it harm none, do what thou wilt' (so long as it harms no-one else, do as you will). If you follow this very responsible creed, then you can never work destructively. Unfortunately, destructive magic is often more spectacular than creative magic. Bad news always gets reported: healing may go unnoticed, but a car crash never will. It takes nine months to create a human being, but he or she can be blown away in a fraction of a second.

Destructive magic is essentially negative. It works by

diminishing the life force of a thing or person. It drains away its vitality. But the fatal flaw of destructive magic is that it disregards the fact that all things in the world are linked with one another. By diminishing the vitality of one thing, we deplete the vitality of all things. Because of this, destructive magic also has an effect on the sender, and is the most extreme example of empty form-fulfilment. It is well known that all evil magic will eventually come back upon the sender, threefold. 'He who lives by the sword will die by the sword.' There is no punishment sent from 'above', but what will come back are the natural consequences of doing things against right orderliness. You will suffer in the long term for these short-term mistakes.

In Viking times, when rune magic was at its height, revenge magic and cursing were part of the runemaster's repertoire. The Niding Pole was used frequently to curse people and bring them to destruction (see Chapter 1). The pole concentrated magical forces and projected them destructively towards the target. Hela, goddess of death, was invoked to smash the soul of the accursed person. Destructive methods were also used to interfere with the land on which the accursed lived. This magic caused places to become *álfreka* by driving away the earth spirits from a place. It was done to destroy the livelihood of the person who lived there, but it is a bad thing, the psychic equivalent of physical pollution, destroying the environment of all. Magic that invokes the forces of destruction is dangerous to the person who uses it as well as those close to its effects. For this reason, harmful magicians in all cultures have been punished. The forces of destruction may well visit themselves upon the person who calls them up.

Negative magic is nothing more than unskilled behaviour. It is not necessary to use magic to destroy someone. There are far more positive ways to use magic. Methods which harm none are better than those which aim to destroy. Positive magic is on the side of life. It builds up the life force within whatever is being protected so that it cannot be harmed. In this respect, defensive magic is quite different from negative, reactionary magic. It harms none. Instead, it may reflect ills upon those who send them. In that case, they are getting back only what they have sent, not anything new. Hopefully, in such an event, an attacker will learn from this that negative magic is counter-productive. Binding magic, too, should be done so that the binding works upon the harmful aspects of a person or organisation. It should not be done clumsily, so that their good aspects are also prevented from working.

In magical operations, you should always think about *all* of the possible effects of what you are doing. Sometimes, unexpected results arise from an action. Folklore and mythology are full of such tales. Clearly, magic which gets you something wonderful, but which destroys the environment, is not for the good of anyone, even the magician. Because of this, magical workings should contain some statement that you are giving away all negative effects of what you do. Wherever possible, the formulae should try to replace negative things with positive ones. To avoid unforeseen effects, we need to release the cause and effect of any negativity which might be in the working. We can do this by adding the words 'for the good of all' to the spell, or 'turn this to the good of all. Ka!' When you do a working for something, call upon it to come 'at the best time' rather than immediately. Ask for 'the perfect thing for me' rather than something specific. You should always work towards fulfilment according to your needs. Do not ignore your own needs, so long as 'it harm none'. Magic need never compromise our own interests or deprive us of something that is necessary. There is enough in the world to fulfil everyone's true needs. Greed only results from a lack of awareness of our true needs.

Önd – The Power of Life

The human being is a complex physical and spiritual system. To understand rune magic, we must first understand ourselves. In his excellent researches into ancient beliefs, Stephen Flowers has rediscovered the nine separate aspects of the human being taught by the Northern sages. These are the physical body (in Old Norse, the *lík*); the 'shape' or body image (*hamr*); the faculty of inspiration (*ódhr*); the vital breath (*önd*); a perceptive-cognitive power (*hugr*); the power of reflection, the mind (*minni*); an after-death image or 'shade' (*sál*); a permanent magic soul, the *fetch* (*fylgja*); and the power-material that gives protection and good fortune (*hamingja*). Traditional wisdom tells us that we are far more complex than we might think. The runes are a means to understanding this complexity.

Since the earliest times people have known that there is a power which underlies life itself. It is one of our nine components, the power which we contact when we do rune magic. Throughout history, this power has been known by many different names. To the ancient Greeks, it was *Pneuma*, the divine breath. In the Far East, Chinese geomants call it *Ch'i*, the *Ki* of the Japanese martial arts. Further south, it is the Polynesian magic power called *Mana*, whilst in India, this life force is *Prana*. It is the Celtic *Nwyvre*. Less traditionally, it has been called the *Universal Plastic Medium, Odyle, Vril, Orgone* and *Earth Energies*. In the Northern Tradition, it is called *önd*.

When we look at it in terms of 'material' energies, önd is difficult to categorise. It is not life and growth, but it is the power behind them. It is present everywhere, but it cannot be seen or caught. It has patterns that flow across the world like running water or the eight winds. It is dynamic; in some places it is strong, in others it is weak. This can vary according to the time of day or year, or because of other factors. Önd also has a component of physical energy, which can be detected by scientific instruments that pick up magnetism, electric charge and other physical radiations. In recent years, many valuable insights have been gained through the measurement of these radiations at places of power such as stone circles. But these physical radiations are only a part of the complex nature of önd. Ultimately, only its effects can be described in words. According to tradition, önd comes to us from three directions; from above the earth, on the earth, and within the earth. The *Heavenly önd* flows from the cosmos, above. *Terrestrial önd* flows along the surface of the earth, and just below the surface, *Chthonic önd* comes from deep within the planet. According to some rune magicians, places of great runic power are those where Heavenly and Chthonic önd coincide.

Although önd cannot be caught and preserved, certain things absorb and store it. They accumulate it gradually, and they can also release it under the right conditions. Among the best reservoirs of önd are crystals, stones and trees. A stone at a place of power fills up with önd; the quality or 'colour' of the önd depends on the type of stone. Different stones provide different sorts of power. This is the basis of crystal magic and the lore of gemstones. Önd is also present more dynamically in springs of fresh water, and in trees. Trees are dynamic, living systems. They seek out and channel water from beneath the earth, then they bring the water up through the trunk, and out into the air by way of the leaves. This energy-flow also channels önd. Each type of tree has its own special magical qualities. These are the special patterns and 'colours' of önd peculiar to that type of tree.

The önd present in an object can be visualised as an energy/information pattern. The overall pattern has been likened to a woven fabric, 'The Web of Wyrd', each individual coloured strand making up the pattern of the whole. The colour and patterns of önd affect things in the path of its flow. If önd is too strong at a place, or if a colour or pattern is incompatible with human well-being, then it is harmful to us. Places like this can be identified. We can use geomancy to discover whether the strength, colour or patterns of önd at a place are beneficial or harmful to humans and, if necessary, we can alter them. This is because human consciousness interacts with önd by a two-way process. Önd affects our consciousness, whilst we can use our willpower to cause alterations in intensity, colour and flow. We use this in the martial arts. There, external önd in the surrounding environment is drawn into the body. Then it is used to reinforce the body's own önd to achieve feats of strength and endurance. Objects charged by human willpower have an effect on the önd at any place. These can include painted patterns, consecrated talismans and sacred images. The flow of önd along spirit paths can be disrupted by geomantic mirrors. Land magic uses spirit posts and sprite traps to drain away önd which is harmful to humans.

Magic rituals can alter for a time the colour and patterns of önd at a place. This is what happens when a magic circle is cast. Magical consecration of an object or place colours or patterns the önd present there. The precise colours and patterns of the önd will depend on the object itself and the intention of the ritual. A ceremony can also charge up an object or place with a level of önd that it did not have before. When we perform a ritual, it produces a receptive frame of mind within us. This allows us to 'tap in' to a certain current of önd which corresponds with the ritual. When we put our full emotion into a magical act, we affect the corresponding current of önd as well as drawing from it. Through this, we can link into the consciousness of animals and birds as well as the patterns and colours of the önd in trees, crystals and rocks.

In rune magic, we use the runes to gain access to the flow of önd around us. The runes and the gods are images of certain complex patterns and colours of önd. The Armanen runes are very specific in this, for they are designed to link with the önd patterns of hexagonal crystals. Just like a stone or tree, the runes colour the önd. The colours depend upon the runes used, but also upon the time, place and consciousness of the person using them. Rune magic organises and colours önd according to the magician's will. From the other direction, divination uses the runes to tell us about the nature of the önd acting upon us at the present time. A runic reading is like a report on the intensity, pattern, colour and flow of önd present at this moment.

Önd and Sacred Images

In some periods of history, iconoclasm has caused religious leaders to order sacred images destroyed. They have done this because, they believed, people were worshipping the stone, wood or metal image rather than the deity which it represented. However, when looked at from the perspective of önd, this image of 'idolatry' is wrong. Like a stone, religious images store and channel önd. Gaining access to this power is a natural process, like getting water from a well. Worship at an image is not asking favours from a piece of stone or wood. It is the inner essence of önd that is being contacted, not the outer form which contains it. Because the image is charged with certain patterns of önd, related to the powers of the goddess or god represented, the worshipper can come into harmony with it. To be in harmony with the flow of önd is to be at one with the universe.

Rad Power: Turning and Winding and Setting Straight

In general, magic is used to 'turn' around circumstances in accordance with the will of the magician. Modern idioms

talk of things 'turning out for the best', or someone having
'a nasty turn'. This is an understanding of the possibility of
altering the course of events. Magicians do this consciously,
trying to transcend the Wheel of Fortune, on which all must
ride and take the good with the bad. This is the essence of
the rune Rad, the wheel-rotation-riding-ritual rune.
Northern European words for magicians and magic contain
this element of 'turning'. The Old German *drajen*, the
Danish *dreje*, and the Dutch, *draaien*, all mean 'to turn'. This
'turning' element is in the Irish name for a Druid, *draí*, and
a wizard, *draoi*. The Gaelic word for enchantment is
draoidheachct. The traditional Irish word for a whispered
magical chant, or hum, is *drann*. The Welsh name for a ritual
labyrinth is *Caerdroia*, 'the City of Turnings'. In Irish, the
thorny, winding and tangling Bramble and Blackthorn trees
are called *dreas* and *draion* respectively. In Scots Gaelic, a
thorn tree in general is *draigh*. Magically, they can 'turn
around' the unwanted attacks of sprites and magicians.

Whenever we visit the otherworld, then we must turn
back at some point. If we cannot re-turn to the everyday
world, we die. Then the insights and information we gain
can never be given to other people. In the Northern
Tradition, those who underwent magical seers' journeys –
sages and inspired orators – were called Thul or Thyle.
Thule is a Norse place name which means 'the place where
one is forced to turn back'. It is also the name of the mythical
land of the north, beyond which it is not possible to
venture. A Thule is a person who has journeyed to the
otherworld, and turned back again to this one. His or her
symbol is the Thorn rune.

Another magical connection with 'turning' can be found
in the Old English verb 'to wend'. Literally, this means 'to
turn'. In East Anglia, many crossroads, the sacred places of
Odin, are called Four Wentz Ways. This means 'four ways
to turn'. Winding magic, the creation of spirals and
labyrinthine patterns, part of the Warlock's craft of
vardlokkur, is an essential part of runecraft. The circle and
spiral dances of traditional sacred rituals are part of this
magic of winding and turning, as are the magic patterns
chalked on steps in traditional house and stable protection.

One of the attributes of the rune-bringer, Odin, is god of
roads, tracks and paths. Basically, this means that he rules
linear movement. Since ancient times, rulership of straight

lines has been connected intimately with authority. In European languages, the root *reg* has the meaning of setting straight, leading or guiding in a straight line. It means a true guide, a powerful one, a chief, king or queen. The old Celtic *rîg*, a king, the Irish *righ*, relates to the Latin word *rex*, 'king'. All Indo-European words related to this are connected with order. This can be seen in the word *rig*, which means to make something as one wants it. In East Anglian dialect, a 'rig' is a straight line furrow made by the plough. The Norse writings, *Rigsmal* and *Rigsthula* tell of how Rigr (Heimdall) organised society.

The runes themselves are part of this tradition. The straight lines with which they are written are the rite by which their power is disclosed. In the runes, this power is found in Rad, which is also called Rit or Raidho. The meaning of this rune is one of riding, linear movement and ritual action. Implicit in all of these meanings is the control of spatial order. Straight lines are connected with an ordered, conscious, ritual way of doing things. This can be seen in words such as upright, regular, right angle. Then there are the moral terms also connected with straightness: righteous, rectitude, correct. In all of these words, there is inherently the concept of order coming from ritual straightness. Conscious control achieves the desired result, resulting in the creation of order out of chaos. This is the magical power of the runes which can be seen in legend in the story of the Four Royal Roads of Britain which, according to Geoffrey of Monmouth, were laid out on the orders of King Belinus (390 BCE). They ran in straight lines between cities. The ancient tradition of straight royal roads continued in the *rides* laid out through aristocrats' forests in medieval, Renaissance and Baroque Europe. The wheel-shaped city of Karlsruhe in Baden, Germany, laid out in 1715, is the paramount example of this. There, 32 straight roads radiate from the Duke's palace into the surrounding city and countryside.

These elements of conscious control are present in the Rad rune, and its associated straight trackways. To travel along a sacred road is a sacred act in itself. In former times, sacred wagons were kept for this purpose. Among others, images of the god Ing and the goddess Nerthus were carried along ceremonial routes by cart. Ceremonial carts have been found in burials at Oseberg in Norway, and

Figure 22 Plan of the city of Karlsruhe, Germany, laid out in 1715 on the 'Rad' principle, radiating from the tower of the royal palace at the centre.

Hochdorf in Germany. Sacred carts running on straight ceremonial trackways combine the Rad-functions of the wheel and motion in a ritual journey. In some places, these trackways still survive. One is in the Swedish parish of Låssa, Uppland, where there is a sacred road of the dead. It lies close to a stone labyrinth and a series of Bronze Age cairns on a glacial hill called Rösaring. Constructed in the ninth century, this straight road was used for funeral rites in which corpses were drawn by cart along the trackway which linked a Pagan funeral chapel with the place of interment.

This ceremony was part of the worldwide tradition of straight spirit ways. The rural tradition of Ireland, Britain, France .. .d Germany preserves a knowledge of these magic tracks running across the country. In Ireland they are called Fairy Paths, and in the west of England, the Trod. Whatever their name, they are straight, linking ancient places of power. It is said that they can be identified easily because they grow with a different shade of green from the rest of the field. One such track, traversed by the Sybil on her chariot pulled by cats, can be seen at certain times of year near the Teck, a holy mountain in south Germany. It runs in a straight line towards a sacred cave where the Sybil once lived. In folk tradition such tracks are known to have magic properties and, in former times, people suffering from rheumatism would walk along them to gain relief. But they cannot be used continuously – at certain times of the year, when the inhabitants of the non-material world travel along them, they should be avoided. At these times, önd may be seen as balls of light or fiery dust shimmering over the trackways. In Wales, *Y Tylweth Teg* (the Fairy Folk) travel these trackways and are said to bring death to any mortal who meets them there. Corpse candles, lights whose appearance foretells a death, also travel along the straight trackways. These lights are manifestations of önd. In Brittany, these tracks are traversed by spirits of the departed. Like the Rösaring funeral road and the Welsh corpse candle tracks, they run towards graveyards.

Folk magicians have always used significant places on these trackways to contact the otherworld. A place where two straight tracks cross is most powerful. Each crossroads is a representation of the *Nowl*, the middle of the world. The central world tree, Yggdrasil, Odin's Steed, stands at the crossroads, linking the upper and lower worlds with Middle Earth. Because of this, magical acts performed there have a more powerful effect and such places are revered by country traditions all over Europe. Any crossroads with names such as 'carfax' or 'Four Wentz Ways' are especially magical. They are powerful places on which to conduct rune magic.

Legendary Magical Powers

The Norse sagas and later folk traditions tell of the many wonderful abilities of magicians and exponents of the Northern Martial Arts. These include teleportation, invisibility, distant viewing, shape shifting and feats of superhuman strength. In any generation, only a few people can ever acquire these special powers. That is why they are celebrated in sagas. In rune magic, these abilities are described by specific words from Old Icelandic. Magical learning, from which all other abilities come, is called *Fródleikr*.

People capable of seeing into the future were called *Framsynn* (far-sighted). Those with second sight, insight

Figure 23 Sixth century helmet panels from Torslunda, Öland, Sweden, with scenes from the northern martial arts, showing Berserkers, Úlfheðnar and Svínfylking warriors, also the binding of the Fenris Wolf by Asa-Tyr.

into the otherworld, were called *ófreskir*. In the Martial Arts shape shifting, the power to confuse and disorientate one's opponents, was important and was known as *Bregda Sér*. The related art of travelling in animal form is *Hamfarir*, whilst the power to do it so called *Hamrammr*. Possession of supernormal strength, *Rammaukinn*, is another necessity for the Martial Artist. As well as being descriptions of magical states, these words are also words of power. They can be used magically to invoke their corresponding powers.

Hamfarir

Hamfarir is an advanced magical technique. Literally, it means 'shape shifting', the shamanic transference of one's consciousness temporarily into an animal or bird. Some animal connections of the Northern Martial Arts have been mentioned already. The úlfhednar, Berserkers and Svínfylking warriors drew upon animal powers in their time of need. Bothvar Bjarki, Berserker champion of King Hrolf of Denmark, fought in the body of a bear, whilst his human body lay in a sleep-like trance. There were also Dog warriors like the Ulster hero, Cuchullain, and the Lion warriors of the later middle ages. Sometimes, for special purposes, more exotic animals were contacted. A whale was used by the personal wizard of the Norse king, Harald Gormsson: in trance, he mind-linked with a whale in the North Atlantic off Iceland. Then, in its consciousness, the wizard was able to reconnoitre the magical defences of the island. Merlin, King Arthur's wizard, sometimes appeared in the form of a Stag.

This is a remarkable example, but the most widespread connection of shamanry is with birds. In Norse scripture, we read of Freyja travelling in the form of a Peregrine Falcon, and Odin's consciousness carried in flying Ravens. He also flew in the form of an Eagle, as did Loki. Ondott Crow was a famous Norse warrior. In Arthurian literature, Sir Gawain is connected with a Hawk called Gwalchmai, and Merlin is identified with his Hawk, the Merlin. Early in the twentieth century, the wise woman Kate 'The Gull' Turner connected magically with seagulls, the prime birds of southern British sea magic. In another culture, the medieval Jewish magician, Abramelin the Mage, gives a procedure 'for flying in the air in the form of a crow'. Asiatic shamans often use a goose in their out-of-the-body journeys. The name for a male goose is a Gander, cognate with the Norse word *Gandr*, meaning 'projection of magic power'. Also, in southern English dialect, 'to have a gander' at something means to take a close look.

Viewing distant things is a form of Gandr. Transference of consciousness outside the body is one of the major techniques of advanced magic. It is the stage beyond visualisation, when one's personal magical power transcends the limits of the physical. In Hamfarir, the physical body lies in a trance whilst the consciousness is elsewhere, entered into the consciousness of an animal. To all intents and purposes, we become that animal for a time. As the *Ynglinga Saga* tells us:

Figure 24 Odin enthroned, flanked by Thor and Balder. Below is
Loki, bound, assisted by his faithful wife, Signy. Contemporary
engraving of a 19th-century German Pagan plaque.

Odin could change himself. Then, his body lay sleeping as if
dead, then he became a bird or wild animal, a fish or dragon,
and journeyed in an instant to far-off countries, on his own
missions, or those of other people.

Hamfarir is the power to send up a bird high into the air,
and literally see what that bird is seeing. It is to fly in the
air amid the eight winds, seeing all from a 'bird's eye view'.
But it is a dangerous procedure. If the animal should be
killed during the operation, then the consciousness will be
separated from the body. In the poem *Grímnismál* Odin tells
of this fateful possibility:

Hugin and Munin,
Thought and Memory,
Fly over the world every day.
I fear for Thought,
Lest he not return.
But I fear even more
For Memory.

This is why magicians like to use a bird of prey which is not likely to be killed by a predator. It is best to connect with a formidable bird like a Raven, Merlin, Peregrine Falcon, Buzzard or Eagle, whose chances of survival are good.

The composer Mozart had a remarkable rapport with a bird. Walking through a bird market, he heard a caged Starling sing the first seventeen notes of a piece he had just written, the *Concerto in G Major*. Recognising this psychic link, he bought the bird, which became his companion for three years. It is believed that in some of his compositions, he used certain other themes sung by the Starling. This is the principle of the 'familiar', an animal whose consciousness is linked with that of the magician. Mozart's case is unusual because it had artistic results. Mozart's Starling reminds us of the unlimited possibility of connecting with the consciousness of other species.

Irish folklore tells of the time when Jackdaws could speak human language. Captive birds taught by humans may have transmitted their ability to those in the wild, but this seems to have been lost when English took over from Irish as the everyday language. Other legends give examples of a rapport between humans and animals which is almost lost today. Now, it is a rather neglected part of magic. The relationship between horse and rider, or shepherd and sheepdog, are still recognised today, but their magical element is undeveloped. This is a step towards Hamfarir, but most people do not get beyond this stage.

The technique of Hamfarir is related to Astral Projection. There, the 'Astral Body', the Hamr of the Northern Tradition, separates from the physical body (*Lík*) and travels free from it into other realms of existence. But unlike the experiences of Astral Projection, Hamfarir does not involve travelling outside the body in the same form as the physical body. The Hamr passes into an animal or bird, in which it travels on its mission. To achieve Hamfarir is a long and difficult process. It involves developing some unusual abilities, which cannot be told in print. The other version of shape shifting is appearing for a short while as an animal. This is done by altering the perception of others, who actually see you as that beast. This ability is useful for scaring off intruders. As with other magic powers, you should not use it negatively, to attack other people.

The Goddesses and Gods of Runecraft

Rune magic works most effectively when it is performed in its own cultural context. This is the Northern Tradition, the world view that contains the Teutonic deities, worshipped by the runemasters of ancient times. Traditionally, each deity rules over a specific aspect of life, so it is useful to invoke their powers when appropriate. These powers are best recorded in the Norse scriptures, where many teachings describe the special qualities of each deity, including their magic weapons and tools. In this tradition, there are three main groups or dynasties of gods and goddesses. The older deities are the gods and goddesses of the elemental powers. These appear to be the most ancient of all, coming from prehistoric times. They include the ice, fire and earth giants, and non-humanoid, elemental beings. They are so archaic that they have no recorded collective name. Next come the more human deities of the nomadic pursuits of hunting and fishing. They are called the Vanir. Both groups of divinities were superseded and absorbed by gods of a more settled life based on agriculture. These are the Aesir, the gods headed by Odin and Thor, and the Asyniur, the goddesses headed by Frigg. Having come from Odin, the runes are mainly associated with the Aesir and Asyniur.

Perhaps the most basic deity of all is Tvisto, the ancestor-god of the people who come originally from Europe north of the Alps. Without him, this book would not be here now. His name should be used in magic concerning ancestral matters of all kinds. Tvisto's runes are Odal and Erda.

The elemental deities are equally primal. They connect us with the basic forces of material existence. They are Loge, god of wild fire, Kari, the air deity, and Hler, the water god. The symbol of these three primal deities is the rainbow, made of fire, water and air. The fourth and fifth elements are represented by Erda, the fruitful earth goddess, and Rinda, goddess of the frozen earth. Together, the pentagram symbolises these five primal elemental deities. In rune magic, they are represented by the Ur rune. Also included are the elemental giants, such as Surt, the fire giant and Ymir, the primal giant, from whom the physical earth was formed.

The Vanir

The chief deities of the Vanir are Frey and Freyja. Their names mean 'the Lord' and 'The Lady'. Frey's by-name (an official 'nick name') is Fro, Freyja's is Vanadis. They are the deities of modern Wicca. Frey is the god of growth, male sexuality and the fruitful rain. He has two companions: Byggvir, the grain god, equivalent to the English folk-song character, John Barleycorn; and Beyla, the bee divinity. Frey's animal is the golden-bristled wild boar, Gullinbursti. Freyja has two consorts: her twin brother, Frey, and the god Odur. Freyja's two daughters by Odur are named Hnossi and Gersemi, and they govern all beautiful, wonderful things in the natural world. Their rune is Wyn.

Freyja rules over the plants of the earth, the trees and animals of the forest, natural love, female sexuality and magic. Her chariot is drawn by two snow-white wildcats. She also flies in the form of a Peregrine Falcon, and rides a Siberian Tiger! Her magical power-object is the necklace, Brisingamen. Freyja is the patron goddess of shamanry (seiðr), one of the arts of the pre-Aesir era. These were the older times ruled by the five ancient deities of the elements, and the Vanir. It was Freyja who taught the craft to Odin. Among the Aesir, only Odin and Loki practised it, and through this primal technique the runes were revealed to Odin. Together, Frey and Freyja should be invoked for success in love, prosperity and increase. Together, their rune is Feoh, and they govern the first aett of the Elder Futhark. Collectively, the Vanir are represented by the rune Wyn.

The Aesir and the Asyniur

The Aesir and Asyniur include many deities. They are represented by the 'god rune' As. Some are aspects of others, and there are many by-names. The chief god of the Aesir is Odin, called Allfather. He is the god of inspiration, shamanry and battle who brought the runes into human use. His major runes are Odal and Os. Odin is one of three brothers – Odin, Vili and Vé. Together, the trinity represents the spirit (Odin), the will (Vili) and holiness (Vé). Frigg, Odin's consort, is Queen of Heaven, 'most magnificent'. She rules over food, clothing and married sexuality. Her magic 'tools' are the distaff and spindle, upon which thread is spun. Her cloak is the night sky, spangled with stars. Her attendant goddess is Sága, the goddess of events in time: invoking her assists memory recall. Her rune is Peorth, allowing the recall of hidden things. Gná is Frigg's messenger. Her name is powerful in women's mysteries.

Other members of the Asyniur provide us with our vital human needs. Hlín is the goddess of infinite compassion, whilst Gefn is goddess of giving. Hlín has the power to rescue us when the situation appears hopeless. Gefn is the ruler of the rune Gyfu. Sjöfn, goddess of love, and Hlín, both share the Gyfu rune with Gefn. Gefjon is goddess of unmarried women, whose shrine was the holiest place in Denmark, Lejre – seat of the Danish kings. Lofn brings together men and women in love in conditions where marriage is forbidden or impossible. The goddess of healing and medicine is Eír. She is equivalent to the Irish goddess, Airmed, gatherer of the holy herbs. Her runes are Beorc, Lagu, Ul and Sól. Gentle wisdom is the realm of Snotra. Two sister goddesses go together naturally. Vor is a witness of oaths, and Var the punisher of those who do not keep their word. Vor can see through deception, whilst Var is the goddess of awareness, seeing clearly and without prejudice. Both should be invoked in magic to do with seeing things as they are. Finally, the goddess Syn guards the door. She admits desirable people and things, whilst keeping out the undesirable. Her rune is Dag.

The Aesir rule the more violent and muscular areas of human existence. Tyr, (Tîwaz), is the sky god of battle and victory. His magical weapon is the sword. Naturally, his rune is Tyr. Thor is the god of thunder and lightning, defence and strength. He is the god of the working man, labouring in the fields and forges. His sacred 'tools' are a belt of power, iron gauntlets, a magic oath ring and, most powerful of all, his hammer, Mjöllnir. These power items embody the power of his rune, Thorn. He is powerful in defence, but can also be invoked in all matters connected with handwork. Thor is the god of the old Scottish Guild of Hammermen, whose badge was the crowned hammer. All those who worked with the hammer – from goldsmiths to stonemasons – were members of this guild. The wife of Thor is the golden-haired goddess, Sif. She is a swan goddess, ruling over the bright, fertile days of summer. She is a bringer of peace and happiness, which can be invoked with the runes Beorc and Ing. Sif's sons by Thor, Magni and Modi, 'might' and 'wrath', survive Ragnarök, the Day of Change.

Ing is the god of male sexuality, enclosed protection and regeneration. His power object is the ceremonial wagon in which his image was paraded along the holy roads of ancient Denmark. Ing is patron god of England, having been brought here magically by the ancient Heardings. His runes are Ing and Rad. Baldr 'the beautiful', is the deity of solar power who is slain, to be reborn again after Ragnarök. He is believed to be the same as Phol, a god of fertility. His rune is Sigel, the solar power. The goddess Sól is his female counterpart. Forseti, the axe god, son of Baldr, is champion of justice. He is the god of the sacred island of Heligoland. His runes are Sigel and Tyr, usually as a bind rune. Bragi, the Bardic god of poetry and eloquence, is consort of Iduna, goddess of the golden apples of eternal life. Bragi's magic 'tools' are the lyre and the *Bragaful*, a cup in the shape of a ship. His are the runes of consciousness and eloquence, As, Ken and Os. Fjölnir is another deity of wisdom whose rune is Ken.

The White God, Heimdall, is guardian watcher of the gods and keeper of the Rainbow Bridge. As Rig, Heimdall organised the classes of traditional society – bondsman, yeoman and lord. His magic is that of 'rigging' things, ordering matters according to the magician's will. His rune is Hagal in its structural aspect. Hermod, one of Odin's sons, is the messenger of the gods. He can be invoked in communication magic. His runes are Rad, Ehwaz and Lagu. Vidar, also Odin's son, is the future destroyer of the demonic Fenris Wolf. His runes are Stan and Wolfsangel. Vali, another son of Odin, is the archer god, assimilated with St Valentine as god of lovers. His runes are Gyfu and Yr.

In Norse tradition, there are five water divinities representing different aspects of the element. Most ancient is Hler, one of the five primal elemental deities. Chief of the Aesir water deities are Aegir, god of the stormy sea, and his consort, Ran, destroyer of ships. Ran is goddess of death for all who perish at sea. She is the goddess of gold, 'the flame of the sea'. Her magic 'tool' is the net. Aegir has a grappling-hook. As well as Aegir and Ran, there are Mimir,

god of the waters beneath the earth, and Njord, deity of
coastal waters. Mimir's magic connects us with the primal
depths of being, the önd of holy wells and mineral waters.
Njord is an ancient god, father of the Vanir deities Freyja
and Frey. His function is to still the storms whipped up by
Aegir. Magically, Njord brings calm to stormy situations.
His sacred objects are an axe and a crown of sea-shells. His
runes are Feoh and Lagu.

For a time, Njord was consort of the goddess Skadi,
sometime lover of Odin, finally the wife of Ullr. Her name
means 'shadow'. In her powers, she parallels the Celtic
Sgathach, dark warrior goddess of Dunscaith on the Isle of
Skye. She is a scathing goddess of wintertime who travels
the icy wastes on her skates. Skadi is a destroyer, the
northern equivalent of the Hindu goddess Kali. Her magic
is dark and destructive. Her runes are Eoh, Hagal and Is.
Ullr is the Yew tree god of midwinter, skiing, sledges and
archery. His sacred 'tools' are the bow and skis. Ullr's magic
deals with travel in difficult conditions, reaching his
objective successfully – and rapidly. His runes are Eoh and
Yr. His holy mountain is the Uetliberg, which overlooks
Zürich.

Another dark goddess is Hela, ruler of death and keeper
of the underworld. Her runes are Eoh, Hagal, Nyd and Is.
Loki the trickster god, and the Fenris Wolf are both bound
in the nether world. Their powers remain unresolved in
Northern Tradition magic. They have not yet been fully
reintegrated. Although bound, they are still present as
dangerous powers which it is unwise to contact.

Other Deities

There are a number of other goddesses and gods not
included in the Vanir, Aesir or Asyniur. Some of them are
local, clan or tribal and include some Celtic deities. But
their fame and power have spread beyond their original
location and time. They have come down to us as powerful
ancestral forces with which we can make contact today.

Walburga, a lunar goddess, and Eostre (Ostara), deity of
the dawn and springtime, are still remembered each year
at the festivals which bear their names: Walpurgisnacht
(May Eve) and Easter. Walburga's rune is Lagu and Eostre's,
Beorc. Waldh, the forest god of Frisia, is patron of the

powerful rune of healing, Ul. Nehallennia is the Frisian goddess of the sea and vegetation. Her sacred images show her accompanied by a dog and a basket of apples. Like Skadi, she is a holy island goddess. Her main shrine was on the Frisian island of Walcharen. Nehallennia's runes are Hagal and Lagu.

The Celtic Deities

There are a number of Celtic deities whose powers can be invoked in rune magic. In the main, they represent specific qualities or powers. Some are alternative names for the same deity. For example, Lugh and Gwydion are parallels of Odin, whilst Ambisagrus and Sucellos resemble Thor. Cernunnos, the Lord of the Forest, also known as Herne the Hunter, may be equated with Frey. The Irish goddess Flidhair, deity of forest animals, parallels Freyja. Like the Asyniur, the Celtic goddesses personify many important human qualities. Rosmerta, consort of Lugh, is goddess of material wealth (Feoh). Brigantia (Brigit) is goddess of learning, poetry and handicrafts (As, Ken, Os). The northern martial arts have their patronesses in Artio, the bear goddess, and Arduinna, the boar goddess. Bird magic is ruled by Abandinus, whilst Belutacadros, the Gallic warrior god, is powerful in conflict magic.

The Three Norns

Finally, the Three Norns must not be overlooked. These Norns, or Weird Sisters, are not strictly goddesses. They are the guardians of fate, personified as the three stages of existence – beginning, middle and end. They are called Urd, 'that which was', Verdandi, 'that which is becoming', and Skuld, 'that which is to come'. They represent the grandmother (Urd), the mother (Verdandi), and the daughter (Skuld). Magically, they are represented by three cords. Urd has a white cord, Verdandi a red one, and Skuld, the maiden-destroyer, a black one. Urd's rune is Hagal, Verdandi's is Is, and Skuld's is Nyd. Nornic magic is very powerful. It should be conducted only with great care and foresight.

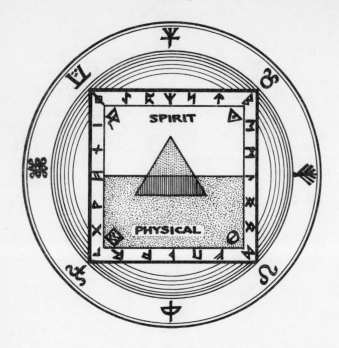

Figure 25 The west British Elven magical system, showing
corresponding directions, elements and runes.

The Elven System

The Elven System is the underlying principle of a
hereditary tradition practised in Wales and the West of
England. It was revealed publicly by Dr David B. Shirt in
1988. It has powerful possibilities in rune magic.

The Elven System is described by a diagram which
depicts the seven aspects of being, each ruled by an Elven
power. This power is called a 'Lord', but it has both female
and male aspects. The diagram is an equilateral triangle
within a square. A line cuts both square and triangle in two.
The four corners of the square represent the four rulers of
the elements. These elements are the Light, the Rocks, the
Waters and the Airs. They are ruled by the Sun, the Earth,
the Moon and the Stars respectively. Fire and Ice are not
elements in the Elven System. They are considered to be
the destructive aspects of Earth and Water respectively. The
outer square of the elements is orientated with its corners

towards the cardinal directions. Light is located in the East, the Rocks in the South, Waters in the West and Airs in the North. The triangle represents the three Lords of Life. At the apex, towards the North-East, is Oberon. He is the High Lord of Elves and Humans who appears in William Shakespeare's *A Midsummer Night's Dream*. The other two angles of the triangle are dedicated to the Lords of animals and plants, respectively, although no names are given in what remains to us of the Elven system. Unlike the female/male aspects of the other six 'Lords', Oberon is 'complete'. The full complement of Elven powers is thus 13. The line which cuts both square and triangle is the 'horizon'. It runs from North-West to South-East. Above the horizon, to the North-East of the line, is the light and airy spiritual world. Below the horizon, to the South-West of the line, is the damp and earthy physical world.

Runic Time and Tide

Time is important in rune magic. In everyday life, it is always better to do something at the right time rather than the wrong one. This is even more vital in magical terms. In any magical work, we must look at time in all its aspects. Every *sele* (specific time) has its own special qualities, which make it good for some things, and bad for others. The *sele* of the day and year when we work magically matters greatly. For doing magic effectively, we should select a *sele* when the ever-changing qualities of önd are most favourable for the working we want to do. Firstly, the season is important. Certain types of magic work better in the dark half, and others in the light half of the year. Other ceremonies are bound to certain festival days. It is not appropriate to do them on any other day. Clearly, celebrating a spring rite in autumn is not appropriate. Yule should not be celebrated in summertime. Each season has its own special qualities. So do the calendar months and runic half-months. Certain times of year and day correspond with certain runes. These runes are more powerful magically at their corresponding *seles*, so it is sensible to carry out their magic at the best possible time. The phase of the moon is important, too. Magic connected with growth or increase should be done during the waxing

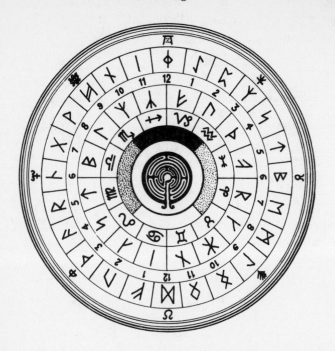

Figure 26 Runic time circle. Ring 1 (reading from outside to inside), the eight year festivals, midwinter at top; 2, the Elder Futhark circle; 3, the hours of the day (midnight at top); 4, Younger Futhark correspondences; 5, equivalent zodiac signs; 6, the four quarters; 7, the central mystery of Mother Earth.

moon. Sunrise, Noon, Sunset and Midnight are good times for wood-taking and divination.

Each day of the week also has its own qualities and powers. Since antiquity, these weekdays have been observed in unbroken continuity. Folklore attributes various good or bad qualities to them. In the English-speaking world, the days of the week are named after the gods of the Northern Pantheon. Their qualities relate to the powers of the corresponding goddesses and gods. Magically, they also have correspondences with an astrological planet, a tree, number, element, power and rune. These are:

In rune magic, specific runes are related to certain directions. These runic directions are based on the wheel of time. In the Northern Tradition, the horizon is divided into eight sectors called airts (*aettir*). Although they have

Day	'Planet'	Deity	Tree	Herb	Number	Magic Square	Element	Rune	Quality
Sunday	Sun	Sól	Birch	Polygonium	1	36	fire	Sigel	healing growth
Monday	Moon	Mani	Willow	Chickweed	5	81	water	Lagu	psychic powers
Tuesday	Mars	Tyr	Holly	Plantain	2	25	fire	Tyr	strength
Wednesday	Mercury	Odin	Ash	Cinquefoil	6	64	air	Odal	knowledge, wisdom
Thursday	Jupiter	Thor	Oak	Henbane	3	16	fire	Thorn	material wealth
Friday	Venus	Frigg	Apple	Vervain	7	49	earth	Peorth	sexuality
Saturday	Saturn	Loki	Alder	Daffodil	4	9	earth	Dag	destiny

different names in different languages, they are the same throughout northern and central Europe. These are the eight directions, which correspond with the eight winds of Roman geomancy. Each airt has its major direction at its centre, the *aetting*. Thus the northern airt, Septentrio, has true north at its middle, the south-western, Africus, has south-west at its centre, and so on.

Time is defined by the position of the sun in relation to the directions. It takes three hours to travel through each airt and, therefore, exactly 24 hours to travel through the whole circle. When the sun stands due south, in the middle of the southern airt, it is midday, High Noon. Correspondingly, when it is due north, at the middle of the northern airt, the time is midnight, Bull's Noon. At any time of day or night, then, the sun is in a corresponding airt. During daylight hours, at any given time, we can see the sun in its airt. At night we cannot see the sun, but it is still in its corresponding airt. Each Tide of the Day is the time-period corresponding with an airt. Each airt/Tide contains three runes. They are shown opposite.

Each quarter also has its own correspondences. These can be used to augment work done with the airts. The Eastern quarter corresponds with the Spring season of the year; the South, Summer; West, Autumn; and North, winter. These quarters are defined by the four Fire Festivals. Spring begins at Imbolc (February 1), Summer on May Day (May 1), Autumn at Lammas (August 1), and Winter at Samhain (November 1). They are ruled by the runes of the corresponding equinox or solstice. The quarters also have their own corresponding colour, element and deity.

Quarter	Season	Weather	Colour	Element	Deity	Ruling Rune
East	Spring	Windy	Red	Air	Kari	Beorc
South	Summer	Sunny	White	Fire	Loge	Dag
West	Autumn	Rainy	Tawny	Water	Hler	Ken
North	Winter	Snowy	Black	Ice	Rinda	Jera
Centre	All/No time	Still	Blue	Earth	Erda	Gar

Finally, at any given time of day or night, the sun is in a corresponding hour-direction relative to us. The önd from the sun is flowing towards us from that direction. Even

Wind	Airt	Clock times	English name	Welsh name	Runes
Solanus	East	04.30–07.30	Morntide	Bore	Tyr, Beorc, Ehwaz
Eurus	South-east	07.30–10.30	Daytide	Anterth	Man, Lagu, Ing
Auster	South	10.30–13.30	Noontide	Nawn	Odal, Dag, Feoh
Africus	South-west	13.30–16.30	Undorne	Echwydd	Ur, Thorn, As
Favonius	West	16.30–19.30	Eventide	Gwechwydd	Rad, Ken, Gyfu
Cautus	North-west	19.30–22.30	Nighttide	Ucher	Wyn, Hagal, Nyd
Septentrio	North	22.30–01.30	Midnight	Dewaint	Is, Jera, Eoh
Aquilo	North-east	01.30–04.30	Uht	Pylgeint	Peorth, Elhaz, Sigel

during the hours of darkness, the sun is still in its hour-direction, even though it is below the horizon. Each of the 24 hours in the day corresponds with a rune, the time when that rune is most active. These hours run from the half-hour to the next half-hour, e.g. the hour of Beorc runs from 5.30 until 6.30. During each runic hour, the sun's önd is coloured according to the rune ruling that hour. The most active point of the hour is when the sun is at the middle-point of any rune. Of course, rune magic will work at any time, but it is especially effective at the correct time, when the colour of the önd is in narmony with the working. These are the runic hours. The cycle of the year is divided in the same way as the day, into 24 half-months. Each is ruled by a rune, whose quality refers to the season over which it rules. In the year cycle, Midwinter corresponds to Midnight of the day cycle, Midsummer parallels Noon, and so on. The correspondences appear in table form in Appendix 3, page 220.

Using this table, you can determine the two runes that rule any day and any time in that day. For example, 6.15 p.m. on April 17 is under the hour rune of Ken and the half-month rune of Lagu. The interaction between these runes and the specific weekday will affect any magic carried out then. When the rune of the day coincides with the rune of the half-month, it is an especially powerful time for workings connected with that rune. Birth runes and runic astrology are also based on these cycles. For details of this, see my *Runic Astrology* (Aquarian, 1990).

5

Runic Numerology and Colours

In Valhalla I think there are more than six hundred and forty doors; out of a single door at a time, will march nine hundred and sixty men, warriors advancing on the monster.

The Lay of Grimnir

The Numerological Tradition

As well as representing sounds, the letters of ancient alphabets also denote numbers. In ancient Israel and Greece, for example, there were no separate characters to represent numbers. Instead, letters of the alphabet were used in calculations. Each letter of the Hebrew and Greek alphabets corresponded with a certain number. This meant that each word and name also represented a number. From this came the art of numerology. The number of a word or name is calculated by adding together the numbers of the letters. In turn, numbers themselves have symbolic meanings. So the word or name becomes symbolic of the number it represents. Also, objects with similar or identical numbers are connected magically.

This is an important aspect of Jewish and Greek mysticism, where certain names are substituted for other names which have the same number, or a number different by one. In Greek, both of the names of Zeus (God), 'Dios' and Theos' (ΔΙΟΣ and ΘΕΟΣ) add up to 284. Sometimes, sacred symbols also have the same number as the divine principles they represent. The great mother goddess Cybele (ΚΞβΕΛΕ), 455, was called 'Mother' (ΜΗΤΗΡ), 456.

Poseidon (ΠΟΣΕΙΔΟΝ), the sea god, has the number 1219. His sacred fish, 'ichthus' (IXVYS), is also 1219. The Christian counterparts of Pagan divinities have the same numerology, too. The number of 'Christos' (XPISTQS) is 1480, equivalent to the 1379 of Odysseus (OΔYSSEYS), and so on.

The Basic Runic System

Modern numerology using the Roman alphabet usually adds the numbers together repeatedly until a single digit remains, (e.g. 754; 7 + 5 + 4 = 16; 1 + 6 = 7). This sort of numerology has only nine possible interpretations, making it very limited. As with Hebrew and Greek, Runic numerology does not reduce numbers by addition. Runic numerology has several alternative systems. The most popular has each letter of the Elder Futhark representing its number in the rune row. This means that Feoh is 1, Ur is 2, Thorn is 3, As is 4, etc. Each rune then represents a number from 1 to 24. In this system, the symbolic meanings of each number are present. The Scandinavian runic calendars use runes in this way to represent the numbers 1–19. The first 16 numbers were the 16 runes of the Younger Futhark, whilst 17–19 were represented by three special numerical runes.

The Elder Futhark has the following numerical meaning:

Number	Sound	Rune name	Numerical meaning
1	F	Feoh	unity
2	U	Ur	two horns, spiritual substance
3	Th	Thorn	triangle, enclosed energy
4	A	As	universal creation, the soul of the universe
5	R	Rad	universal life
6	K	Ken	divine intelligence
7	G	Gyfu	lucky seven, a gift
8	W/V	Wyn	balance
9	H	Hagal	the nine worlds, substance of existence
10	N	Nyd	potential force

Number	Sound	Rune name	Numerical meaning
11	I/Y	Is	static force
12	J	Jara	the twelve months of the year, harvest
13	Z/Eo	Eoh	unlucky 13, destruction/creation
14	P	Peorth	involution, entry of spirit into matter
15	X	Elhaz	destiny
16	S	Sigel	divine power
17	T	Tyr	wisdom, immortality
18	B	Beorc	twice nine, new beginnings, a higher plane
19	E	Eh	the solar/lunar number, transmission, correspondence
20	M	Man	actualised force
21	L	Lagu	flow, facilitation of the will
22	Ng	Ing	connection, expansion
23	O	Odal	the 'weird' number, things outside conscious experience
24	D	Dag	day, 24 hours

Any magical alphabet is a magical formula in its own right. The whole-rune row is known on ancient stones and other articles. By using the entire rune row, one can draw upon the power of the runes in general. The total of the whole rune row, the numbers 1 to 24, is 300. The fifth-century Kylver Stone has a rune row which adds up to 310. This is the number of years in the Aun Cycle. (For details of this, see my book *Runic Astrology*, Aquarian 1990).

Of course, some numbers are more important than others. Nine is of prime importance. It is the number of Hagal, which represents the basic crystalline form of matter. It symbolises the substance of all existence, the astral light of classical occultism. It is the operative number of önd in the world. Geomantically, nine represents the central point of the eight winds. To gain the runes, Odin hung on the windswept tree for nine days and nights. Nine also symbolises the grid of nine, the first square in which another square appears. The power of three times three is invoked in folk magic. Multiples of nine occur in the numerology of some important runic names. For example, the powerful runic formula ALU adds up to 27 (3 x 9: As = 4, Lagu = 21, Ur = 2). Details of the numerology of sacred names and words are given below.

Sometimes, individual runes are multiplied for numerological reasons. Multiples of nine and eleven are favoured. The number 66 is often found on ancient amulets.

Ancient runic inscriptions sometimes contain apparently meaningless 'words'. Many of these are encoded symbolic numbers. In runic inscriptions, staves marked in some way (e.g. larger or smaller, inverted, wend runes) can be used to single out special runes. Runes can be made larger or smaller. Their staves can be made longer, as in ancient times, to mark them out in relation to the others. These runes should be chosen so that they add up to a number which brings a further, related quality to the rune magic.

In rune magic, it is useful to use words which carry the appropriate number. These should relate in some way to the purpose of the magic. When you make a runic word, try to get the numbers of the runes to add up to a significant number. The 'names of power' below give a guide to this, but you may also find it valuable to develop your own personal 'kit' of words and numbers.

Names of Power

When we meditate on runic numbers, we can gain fresh insights into the subtle connections between the powers of gods, supernatural beings and other sacred things. Then, we can use these numbers in our own magical spells. When we use the Elder Futhark in runic numerology, the letter V is represented by Wyn, and Y by Is. Also, as in Hebrew, Greek and Gaelic numerology, a difference of one is allowed when comparing numbers. (See Chapter 7 for further information on runic Names of Power.)

Numerology helps us to understand the mystic by-names of Odin. Many of them have numerical connections with the names of other beings. Odin's wolf, Freki, and Baldr's wife, Nanna, have the number 38. Grim, ('the masked one'), a by-name of Odin, and the moon-hunting wolf Hati, both 41, are related numerically to the destroyer giant Thiazi, Iorth ('the Earth'), and Odin's other wolf, Geri, all

42. This is an important number in Odinic tradition. The magic word, Salu, invoking health, is 42. There are 42 members of the Wild Hunt which Odin leads, and only 42 days in the year when it does not ride. Furthermore, Woden and Gangleri, both Odin's by-names, share the number 84, twice 42. Other by-names of Odin have significant correspondences, too. Ómi has the number of God, 54, and of Hlutr, a portable sacred image. The primal god of water, Hler, and the goddess of the icy ground, Rind, are also 54. Two more by-names, óski (fulfiller of desires), and Alfothr (Allfather) add up to 56. Odin's actual number is 68. This is one less than that of the by-names Harbard ('grey-beard') and Vératyr ('god of men'). Sixty-nine is the number of the future Norn, Skuld, and of the goddess of springtime and renewal, Ostara. It is also the number of Erilaz, 'runemaster'. Alraun, a carved magic root in human form, has the same number as Burin, a carving tool, 46.

The power animals of the Northern Martial Arts all have significant numbers. Ulf, the wolf is 24, the number of runes in the Elder Futhark, and hours in the day. Bar (the bear) is 27 (3 x 3 x 3 or 3 x 9). Vé, the name of a sacred enclosure, and also one of Odin's brothers, has this number. It is also that of the powerful word 'Alu', used to start the flow of magical energies. Svín (Swin, the wild boar) adds up to 45 (5 x 9), the number of the Moon god, Mani, whose crescent form resembles the boar's tusks. The magic word Wihaz, 'sanctified', is also 45, as is Bragi, god of magic words.

Multiples of nine are significant in other areas, too. The fertility god, Frey and the goddess of all knowledge, Vor, are both 36 (4 x 9). So is Hela's underworld guard dog, Garm, the magic word álag (on-lay), and the Celtic sprite, Bucca. The personal beneficial force, Mattr, has the number 63 (7 x 9). Baldr, the solar god, and Sjofn, the love goddess, are 72 (8 x 9), whilst Tvisto, the ancestral deity of northern European people, is 90 (10 x 9). This is also the number of Voland (Wayland), the patron of metal-working.

Eleven is another important number. It is the number of the rune Is, interpreted as static force, the power of stability. It is also the bind rune of As (4) and Gyfu (7), *Gibu Auja*, a powerful lucky charm. When the letter-numbers are added together, Auja is 22, equivalent to the rune Ing. This is part of a series of magic words based on the number 11.

Gothi, a priest is 44; Ehwe, transmission of magic power, 55; and Framsynn, 'far sight', 77. Multiples of eleven are also important in runic god-names. Written as the rune itself, the god-name Ing is 22. When it is written as I-ng, it equals 33. Tyr written in full is also 33. The gods Ull and Vali are 44. Ull's alternative name, Ulli, adds up to 55, as does the earth goddess, Nerthus. It is the same as Christ (Krist) and Sigyn, Loki's wife. Numerically, this also corresponds with Odin's by-names, óski and Alfothr, 56. Borvo, Celtic deity of prophetic bubbling springs, has the number of far-sightedness, 77. Herigast, the ancient Germanic war god, has the number 88. So does Midgard, Middle Earth upon which we live.

Numbers ending in '1' occur in holy names. Of these, the number 31 is one of the most significant. It refers to the god Thor, the goddess Frigg, the oldest Norn, Urd, and the first man, Askr. The Celtic lord of the underworld, Arawn, is also 31. Grim has the same number as Hati, the wolf that tries to eat the moon, 41. Hlín, the goddess of compassion, and Iduna, goddess of eternal life, both have the number 51. The trickster god Loki and the destroyer goddess, Skadi, both have the number 61. The historic weapons, *Thorih* and *Gaois* have the numbers 51 and 61 respectively. The magic words Ungandiz, meaning 'unaffected by magical attack', and Mell, a by-name of the sacred hammer, are both 81. As well as being a number ending in '1', this is the powerful square of nine (9 x 9). The Rainbow bridge, Bifrost, which links Middle Earth with the realm of the gods, is 91.

Some numbers relate to certain periods of time. Gungnir, Odin's spear, is 52, the number of Erda, and the weeks in a year. The giant Thjalfi is also 52. Asgard, the home of the gods, has the number 60, the number of minutes in an hour. So does the sun goddess, Sól, and the Celtic goddess of bears, Artio.

Other numbers make important connections between deities and qualities. The rune of Tyr, god of justice, is 17, the same as the name of the goddess, Vár, who punishes liars. Vak ('the alert one'), Odin's by-name, has the number 18. Ymir, the primal being from whose body the world was made, is 47. This is the same as Bor, Odin's father. Gandr, the magic wand and its power, and Laukaz, the power of irresistible growth, have the number 50. Valhalla, Odin's hall, has the number 92, as does Forseti, god of order. Ninety-four is the number of Aurgelmir, the primal being of Norse tradition. It is also the number of Othroerir, the cauldron of inspiration, Gwydion, the Celtic god of inspiration, and the Frisian moon goddess Wilbet, whose emblem is a cauldron. The sacred enclosure known as a *Vébond*, and the cursing pole, *Nithstong*, are both 102.

Many numbers over 100 are connected with motion, especially up and down the cosmic axis, Yggdrasil. This axial quality is reflected in the posts of the *Vébond* and *Nithstong*. Hermod, who rides to the underworld to free Baldr, is 100. Verdandi, the Norn representing the present, whose name means 'that which is becoming', has the number 105. This is the number of Mordgud, guardian of the entrance to the underworld, and also Odin's by-name Hroptatyr. Odin's horse, Sleipnir, has the number 107. Numerologically, it is the same as the World Tree, Yggdrasil, 106. Literally, the name Yggdrasil means 'the horse of Odin'.

As in Greek numerology, opposites sometimes have the same numbers. The heavenly upperworld, Asgard, 60, corresponds with the gloomy underworld, Utgard, 59. Sól, goddess of light is the same as Nudd, celtic goddess of night, also 60. *Álfreka*, desecration, is also 60. The sky god Tiwaz has the number of the underworld goddess Hela, 53. This is also the number of one of Odin's ravens, Munin ('memory'). Wihyan, 'to make sacred', and Vitki 'rune magician' are both 53. Audhumla, the creative primal cow, is 86, whilst the sun-destroying wolf, Skoll, is 87. This is also the number of Wodiz, 'divine frenzy'.

Runic numerology also works outside the area of the Northern Tradition. For example, the number of Odin's spear, Gungnir, 52, is that of Zeus. Nerthus, 55, corresponds with Venus and Christ, also 55. The Anglo-Saxon hunting god, Herne and the Roman goddess of good luck, Fortuna, are both 62, twice the 'god number', 31, of Thor, Frigg, Askr and Arawn. Hermes, 88, corresponds with Herigast and Midgard. Krishna has the god number 61, and Buddha 81.

Advanced Runic Systems

As far as is known, this simple number-letter corre-spondence was not used by other ancient civilisations.

When it is used magically, this system is clumsy and limited because it does not allow large numbers to be expressed easily. The number system of Hebrew and Greek was different from the modern one. Firstly, the alphabet was divided into three groups. Each of them represented a sequence of numbers. The first stood for the digits, the second for the tens, and the third for the hundreds. Like Hebrew and Greek, the Elder Futhark is also divided into three parts, the three aettir. This makes it easily possible that the runes, too, have a similar numerical system. Unfortunately, there is no direct correspondence with the Greek alphabet, because the runes have their own special order. But the runes can be arranged in a similar way. The ancient Greek alphabet, like the runes, had 24 characters. This brought problems with numbers, and extra letters were used. With the runes, no comparable system has been worked out.

The Elder Futhark can have numbers allocated in another way, using a base of nine. This means that the staves of the first aett represent the numbers 1 to 8. The second aett's letters represent 9–72. Those of the third aett stand for 81–651.

Number	Rune	Number	Rune
1	Feoh	45	Eoh
2	Ur	54	Peorth
3	Thorn	63	Elhaz
4	Os	72	Sigel
5	Rad	81	Tyr
6	Ken	162	Beorc
7	Gyfu	243	Eh
8	Wyn	324	Man
9	Hagal	408	Lagu
18	Nyd	489	Ing
27	Is	570	Odal
36	Jera	651	Dag

So far, this system has not been closely studied. It is an area where further work may reveal many new startling insights. If this is a workable system, as with Hebrew and Greek, we should expect similar principles to have similar numbers. This is indeed the case. For example, the fire god Loge, number 1228, is close to the solar god Baldr, 1230. In this system, Frigg is 47, Odin is 1266, Thor is 578, and Loki 1011.

Finally, German students of the Armanen system have developed complex numerical schemes based upon Norse cosmology. I do not intend to deal with this here.

Runic Colours

In former times, the names of colours were different from those we use today. It is possible that people's perception of colour was different in the past. Some 'colours' now thought different were included within others. In the Viking age, the rainbow had three colours. It was seen as red, green and blue. Then, colours called 'red' included some we now think of as separate. Orange, orange-yellow and yellow of the rainbow were included in red. There were different types of red: ruby-red, rose-red, blood-red, etc. Also, brown was seen as a type of red. Even today, we talk of 'red' hair, a 'red' fox or a 'red' cow. In rune magic, we use traditional names, but in the context of the modern perception of colour.

Each colour has a meaning. The colours are useful in visualisation and runic meditation. Also, certain runes are allocated to each colour. This is a modern system, as it is not known what was done in ancient times. The runes' literal meanings may appear to indicate a different colour, but the colours here are magically the most important.

Colour	meaning	runes
Red	Magic power, strength, vitality	Feoh, Thorn, Rad, Ken, Tyr, Man, Wolfsangel, Ziu
Tawny (orange)	Material power, transforming	Cweorth, Ul
Gold (yellow)	Divine power, sunlight	Wyn, Elhaz, Ing, Odal, Yr, Sól
Green	Plant power, life, fertile growth	Ur, Beorc, Lagu, Ac
Blue	Sky power, ever-present	As, Gyfu, Hagal, Jera, Eoh, Dag, Os, Gar
Silver (white)	Moon power, light in darkness,	Sigel, Eh, Calc

	purification	
Brown	Earth power, nurture	Ear, Erda
Stone (grey)	Stone power, immovability	Stan
Black	Potential power, gestation, hidden things	Nyd, Is, Peorth, Ior

6

Trees and Wood Magic

There is nothing sought after but what is precious.
There is nothing precious but what is beneficial.
The Lesson of Tydain

Wood is used in rune magic for slivers, amulets, talismans, bracteates, wands, shields, cudgels, runestaffs and mete wands. Each of them has special uses. The wood from every tree has its own magical qualities. These qualities should be taken into account when you decide what wood to use in your rune magic. The following section gives the physical, symbolic and magical functions of all of the common trees of northern Europe. There is not only one tree per rune. Different aspects of the rune relate to different aspects of the trees.

Alder (*Almus glutinosa*)

Alder grows near water. Its cut wood is also resistant to water. Because of this, it was used for support beneath buildings and bridges in the days before steel piles. This gave Alder the symbolism of foundation. It was also the favourite wood for making clogs, whistles and flutes with magical powers. Alder charcoal made the best gunpowder. Its static, basic, qualities make its corresponding rune Is, and its goddess Rinda. Alder is the tree of Saturday.

Figure 27 The 38 runes commonly used in modern rune magic.

Apple (*Malus* species)

The Apple is symbolic of eternal life. It is the tree of Iduna, goddess of eternal youth. Sacred islands are islands of the apple, where fertile soil and a good climate bring health and long life. The Isle of Avalon in England (around Glastonbury), and Insel Reichenau in Germany (near Konstanz), are examples of this. Their form reflects the Apple's rune, Ing, representing fertility and limitless expansion. Peorth and Cweorth are also runes of the Apple. The Apple is the tree of Friday.

Ash (*Fraxinus excelsior*)

Ash has its own rune, As. According to Nordic tradition, the world tree, Yggdrasil, is an Ash. The first man, Askr, was made from an Ash tree. (His wife, Embla, was an Elm.) Ash-tree wood is good for making fence posts and the handles of tools and weapons. In Ireland and Wales, the slats of coracles are made of Ash. The staves of traditional broomsticks are made of Ash wood, as are the wands of Druids, wizards, wise women and cunning men. Because Ash attracts lightning ('courts the flash'), it is also a good conductor of önd (magical force). Wood cut at the Summer Solstice is best, making it a strong protection against ill-wishers. In former times, the sacred *High Seat Pillars* of halls and temples were made of Ash.

Ash-tree leaves are also lucky, especially those with an even number of divisions on each side. These are very rare and are called Even Ashes. When you find one, you should pick it for good luck, saying:

Even Ash, I do thee pluck,
Hoping thus to meet good luck.
If no good luck I get from thee,
I shall wish thee on the tree.

Then you can wear the Even Ash in your hat, as a buttonhole, or carry it in your pocket. Finally, the smoke of burning Ash-wood is a benevolent incense, driving away all evil and bad luck. In addition to As, the Ash corresponds with the runes Gyfu, Wyn, Hagal, Ehwaz, Os and Gar. Ash is the tree of Wednesday.

Aspen (*Populus tremula*)

Like the Ash, Aspen is magically protective. It was used for making magic shields and mete wands (measuring rods). Known also as the Shiver Tree, the Aspen is said to have

the power to heal fevers or 'the ague'. This is done by
pinning a lock of the patient's hair to the tree trunk, saying:

Aspen tree, Aspen tree, I pray thee
To shake and shiver instead of me.

Then return home in complete silence.

Another way is to put parings from the sufferer's finger-
nails into a small hole bored in the trunk, then fill in the
hole. If the bark grows over the hole, the patient is cured
permanently. The Aspen's rune is Peorth.

Bay (*Laurus nobilis*)

The Bay tree is protective, too. Bay trees are never struck
by lightning. Planted by the door, they ward off illness. In
cities, Bay trees planted in tubs give magical protection to
restaurants and shops. Often, they are garlanded with
ribbons, offerings to the tree spirit. A Bay leaf under the
pillow at night will bring pleasant, useful dreams. Bay
corresponds with Peorth as well as the solar runes Sigel and
Sol.

Beech (*Fagus sylvatica*)

In former times, Beech wood was used for writing tablets
and magical talismans. It is the tree of letters, which stores
and protects knowledge. Its runic correspondence is Nyd.

Birch (*Betula pendula*)

Like the Ash, the Birch has its own rune, Beorc. It is the
white tree of spring growth and purification, sacred to the
Mother Goddess. When the ice sheets retreated at the end
of the Ice Ages, it was the first tree to recolonise the land.
In Scandinavia, the first leaves of the Birch showed farmers
that it was time to sow their corn. Maypoles should be
made of Birch wood. Birch branches set up inside or outside
houses brings good fortune, driving away harmful
influences. At Yuletide, the Birch is stripped of its white
bark and burnt as the Yule Log. Traditionally, the hard but
resilient Birch wood was used to make babies' cradles. The
magical qualities of the wood are especially appropriate for
this. Birch trees sometimes bear Witches' Brooms,

outgrowths of magical power. As well as Beorc, Birch corresponds with Ur and Erda. Birch is the tree of Sunday.

Blackthorn (*Prunus spinosa*)

Magically, the Blackthorn is a very powerful plant. Its fruit is the Sloe, used to make the medicinal and magical drink, Sloe Gin. The Blackthorn grows freely, eventually making impenetrable thickets. These are physical barriers which also work on the psychic level. When cut, Blackthorn is good for making magic staves, sticks and slivers which have the power to protect us against all forms of psychic harm. Blackthorn staves are used for projecting protective energy – *blasting*. For centuries, the 'black rod', a Blackthorn staff, has been the sign of the cunning man and wise woman. One of the thorn trees, Blackthorn corresponds with the outgoing aspect of the Thorn rune, and the blocking aspect of Stan.

Bramble (*Rubus fruticosa*)

The Bramble or Blackberry is another thorn tree. Magically, it has medicinal properties. Bramble leaves are a remedy for scalds, burns, and inflammations of the skin. Nine leaves are floated in water from a holy well. Then, in turn, each leaf is drawn over the burn. This spell is said three times for each leaf:

> Three angels came from out the east,
> One brought fire and two brought frost.
> Out fire, and in frost,
> Out fire, and in frost.

Branches cut from the Bramble are used for making Sprite flails. To make one, take nine Bramble branches about an Ell in length (16.4 inches, 67 cm). These must have plenty of thorns on them. Then tie them together near one end, using willow bark collected in spring. Sprite flails are useful in clearing pathways and land from harmful on-lays. To use it, hold it in your left hand, and flail the ground with a nine-fold sweeping action. Magically, the Bramble corresponds with the Thorn rune.

Buckthorn (*Hippophaë rhamnoides*)

This coastal plant is sacred to the Frisian god, Waldh, deity of healing. Like Blackthorn, Bramble and Hawthorn, it is magically protective. Its main use is in thorny garlands to ward off illness. It corresponds with the healing rune of Waldh, Ul.

Cedar (*Cedrus libani*)

The Cedar is not native to northern Europe, but it has been grown here for centuries. Its wood has the runic correspondence of Hagal. Cedars sometimes bear Witches' Brooms, and its cones and resin burn well, making a good incense of illumination.

Cherry (*Prunus padus*)

The Bird Cherry is a small tree related to the Blackthorn. It does not bear thorns, and its leaves turn blood-red in autumn. Magically, it has some of the powers of Blackthorn, but without the harshness which Blackthorn can bring. Cherry trees sometimes bear Witches' Brooms. A fine runestaff can be made from Cherry-wood. It corresponds with the runes Jera and Man.

Cypress (*Cupressus* species)

The Cypress is an evergreen tree of the dead. In Roman times, it was sacred to Pluto, lord of the underworld. Correspondingly, in the Northern Tradition, it is the tree of Mordgud, guardian goddess of the gates of the Underworld. Its wood is useful in magic concerning binding and on-lays, corresponding with the rune Ear.

Elder (*Sambucus nigra*)

The Elder is also called the Bourtree or Lady Elder. It is the major fairy tree. Its German name, *Holunder*, links it with Hela, the goddess of death. Elder trees planted in front of a house entrance ward off evil sprites, bringing vigour to those who live there. Elder branches can be hung in front of stables or garages to protect them against lightning and other harm. But to bring Elder wood indoors is unlucky. The wood brings us into contact with the supernatural realms. Elder twigs woven into a garland and worn around the head on May Eve help the wearer to see otherworldly beings. Whistles made from Elder wood are magical, summoning spirits. Do not use one unless you are prepared for the results! Never burn Elder wood. Some say that it will prove fatal to do so. Magically, it is harmful, anyway. The Elder-tree fruit, the Elderberry, can be used for jam and jelly. It can also be fermented to make Elderberry wine, a potent sacramental drink. Elder's runic correspondences are the protective aspect of Feoh, and Erda.

Elm (*Ulmus* species)

The Elm is the tree of femininity. In the Norse creation myth, the first woman, Embla, was formed from an Elm tree. There are several types of Elm: the smooth-leaved Elm (*Ulmus minor*), the English Elm (*Ulmus procera*); and the Wych Elm (*Ulmus glabra*). The first two types are uncommon now, owing to the scourge of Dutch Elm Disease. Elm wood was used once for coffin-making, expressing the death aspect of the Earth Mother goddess. Elms, especially diseased ones, bear Witches' Brooms. The rune Gyfu corresponds magically with the Elm.

Fairy Trees (Ash/Oak/Thorn ingrowth)

Natural amalgams of trees are called Fairy Trees. Usually, they are hedgerow standards, where an Ash, an Oak and a Hawthorn have grown into one another to make a single composite tree. Fairy Trees only grow at places of concentrated önd, where the special qualities of the trees, the location and the spirit of the place come together to create a magical atmosphere. They combine the qualities and powers of the three trees in a very special way, corresponding with the powerful bind-rune of As, Ac and Thorn. But this power is not for human use. You should never take wood from a Fairy Tree.

Fir (*Abies alba*)

The European Silver Fir, the Tannenbaum, is the tallest tree native to Europe, growing to 225 feet (70 metres). Its height makes it a tree of the gods, and its resin makes it a tree of light. In this aspect, the Fir corresponds with the runes As and Ken. It is also one of the trees of power of Tyr, symbolising orientation and keeping on course. Like the Cedar and Pine, its cones can be burnt as a magical incense. Fir trees sometimes bear Witches' Brooms.

Hawthorn (*Crataegus* species)

Hawthorn is another protective thorn tree. With its strong thorn-bearing branches, a Hawthorn hedge makes both an excellent physical barrier and a psychic shield, protecting sacred enclosures. As an enclosure, it corresponds with the rune Odal, being guarded by Oberon, Lord of Elves and Humans. But it is the main aspect of the rune Thorn. It stands for active protection when upright and passive protection when reversed. It is very bad luck to cut down a Hawthorn bush or tree.

There are three distinct types of Hawthorn. Each has its own magical character. The Common Hawthorn (*Crataegus monogyna*, the Whitethorn or May Tree) produces the brilliant white or pink May Blossom that covers the whole plant. This blossom is sacred to the Mother Goddess, its fragrance imitating her most intimate perfume. Its appearance marks the beginning of the summer half of the year, with the saying:

Ne'er cast a clout,
'Til May be out.

This means: do not change from your winter clothes until the blossom of the Hawthorn has come out. ('Clout', in this context, means clothing, or a piece of clothing.)

Another type is the Midland Hawthorn (*Crataegus laevigata*). This flowers a week before the May Tree, and is mainly a hedgerow plant. Its wood is stronger in binding magic than the Common Hawthorn. The third kind is the Glastonbury Thorn (*Crataegus monogyna 'Praecox'*) which flowers at the Winter Solstice. It is powerful when used in Yuletide and New Year magic.

According to folk-tradition, if you sit under a Hawthorn bush on May Day, Midsummer's Day or Samhain, then you risk being enchanted or fetched away into the faerie kingdom.

Hazel (*Corylus avellana*)

In the Northern Tradition, the Hazel is the tree of wisdom. It gives the best wood for making ceremonial and magical shields. Hazel is the tree of inspiration of the Celtic poets. Hazel wands were carried by the Druids as a sign of office. The wand was said to guarantee the carrier a fair hearing in times of trouble. In Viking times, open-air courts were sanctified by the *Vébond*. This was a fence made of Hazel posts linked by ropes. It formed a magical as well as a physical barrier. The runes of the Hazel are Ken, and Ziu in its aspect as a flash of insight. Hazel nuts are symbols of fertility and wisdom. Hazel's rune is Os, in its inspirational aspect.

Holly (*Ilex aquifolium*)

Holly is sacred to the gods of lightning, especially Thor. Magically, it suppresses lightning. Fixed to the door frame or handle, Holly blossom prevents harmful people or forces from entering a house. For all-year protection, door handles and sills can be made of Holly-wood. Holly staves and cudgels are magically protective. Holly has the protective warding power of all thorn trees, added to the magical qualities of the evergreen Ivy and Yew. Its runes are Thorn, Man, Stan and Wolfsangel. Holly is the tree of Tuesday.

Ivy (*Hedera helix*)

Ivy is a broadleafed evergreen, which retains its leaves in winter when other plants have lost them. It is also thought to strangle trees. Thus it is an eternally living plant which brings death. These qualities give the Ivy a dual significance of death and life. Like the Holly, the Ivy is especially connected with Yuletide, the time of death and birth. When a house has Ivy growing on its walls, its inhabitants are protected from psychic attack. Ivy corresponds with the rune Ing in its outgoing aspect, and Ior, for the biggest ancient Ivy vines resemble the serpent which snakes around the world tree Yggdrasil. In this aspect, it is valuable in binding magic, where it also corresponds with Nyd.

Juniper (*Juniperus communis*)

Juniper protects against harm. Its twigs are used in Scotland to ward off the Evil Eye. Savin Charcoal, made from the Juniper, burns surely and rapidly. Added to its magical qualities, this made Savin Charcoal the favourite for gunpowder among the shooting magicians of former times. Also, Juniper smoke is a powerful anti-demonic incense. It is especially powerful in fire magic. In this aspect, Juniper corresponds with the runes Sigel, Ziu and Sol.

Linden (*Tilia* species)

The Linden or Lime Tree has three forms: the small-leaved Lime, (*Tilia cordata*), the broad-leaved Lime (*Tilia platyphyllos*) and a hybrid form of the two. The Linden is an emblem of feminine power, sacred to Freyja. It was the lovers' tree, under which they would come together to get the blessing of Freyja. Because Linden wood is fine-grained, it is a wonderful medium for fine-detailed wood carving. It is ideal for making sacred images.

The broad-leaved Linden is the *Law Tree* of the Northern Tradition, the tree of justice. In Holland, Germany and Switzerland, Linden trees mark geomantically important points such as crossroads and marketplaces. Traditionally, these are places of public assembly and celebration. In former times, these Lindens were pruned and trained to make representations of the Cosmic Axis or World Tree. Linden's runic correspondences are related to this theme: As, Os and Ior. Linden wood is especially useful for shamanic world-travelling magic.

Maple (*Acer campestre*)

Maple trees give the wood from which traditional ceremonial bowls are made on the lathe. These Mazer and Wassailing Bowls were used for drinking ceremonial toasts at the old festivals. Maple is the tree of spiritual longevity. To gain a long life, a young child should be passed through the branches of a Maple tree. Maplin wood is especially useful for magic connected with perpetuity. The runic correspondences of the Maple are Man and Calc.

Mistletoe (*Viscum album*)

Mistletoe has always been revered because it does not have roots in the ground, and grows instead on the branches of other trees. It is most powerful when it grows on Apple or Oak. In Nordic mythology, the white god, Baldr, was slain by a Mistletoe dart. Also, to the Druids, it was of prime importance. At the festival of Samhain, the Archdruid cut a branch of Mistletoe with a golden sickle. As it fell, it was caught in a white cloth held by virgins. Then the Mistletoe was consecrated and distributed to the congregation. People put it over their house doors for good luck. The runes of Mistletoe are Sigel and Sol.

Oak (*Quercus robur*)

The Oak has its own rune, Ac. The Oak is the major sacred tree of Europe. It was venerated as the holy tree of the chief sky god. Its acorns, leaves and wood have always been used as a protection against lightning, though the tree itself is rather prone to lightning strikes. Oak wood is very strong. Before it became scarce, it was favoured for the main load-bearing members in timber-framed buildings. It was also used in ship-building – the 'heart of Oak'. Because Oak wood is protective, doors, especially, were made of it. It corresponds with the letter 'D', which means 'door' in several alphabets.

The Oak's fruit, the acorn, symbolises potential: mighty Oaks from little acorns grow. Kept in the house, acorns bring good luck and keep away lightning. The Oak is said to live for 900 years, the magic number nine, one hundred fold:

> An Oak is three hundred years growing,
> Three hundred years blowing,
> And three hundred years decaying.

As an important tree, it is connected with several runes: Rad, Jera, Tyr, Ehwaz, Dag, Ac and Ziu. The Oak is the tree of Thursday.

Pine (*Pinus sylvestris*)

Pine, also known magically as Deal, is a tree of illumination. This is the meaning of the rune Ken, the Pine torch of knowledge. Pine resin is a pungent incense, suitable for magic worked to gain information. The tree is sacred to the fire god, Loge.

Poplar (*Populus canescens*)

In former times, Poplar wood was used for arrow shafts. In this aspect, its rune is Yr. It is a wood of divination, with special affinity to the rune Eoh.

Rowan (*Sorbus aucuparia*)

Rowan or Mountain Ash is a tree with great binding power which is used in protecting the house. When planted by the garden gate or near the door, it wards off unwelcome psychic visitations. In Norse mythology, Rowan was the tree which saved Thor from being swept away in an underworld river. Amulets of Rowan wood are used to protect the wearer against drowning.

Generally, Rowan is used to deflect all malevolence. Rowan twigs should be removed from the tree without the use of a knife. Then they are tied with red thread into an equal-armed cross. Use these to protect stables, byres, sheds and garages. On quarter days, Rowan wands are put over the lintels of house doors to bring good luck in the following quarter. A necklace of the berries is considered a strong protection against magical harm. Magically, it imitates *Brisingamen*, Freyja's necklace of amber. In traditional building, Rowan wood was used magically for the crossbeams of chimney breasts and other key parts of the cottage. Rowan's runic correspondences are with all of the binding magic runes, especially Nyd, and also Calc.

Service Tree (*Sorbus torminalis*)

The Service Tree is related to the Apple, Hawthorn and Rowan. Magically, it protects against all sorts of wild things, natural and supernatural. Service wood should be used for wands and talismans. Its runic correspondence is Elhaz.

Spindle Tree (*Euonymus europaea*)

The Spindle tree was once used in hedging, and its wood was used in making spindles for spinning wool. It is thus the tree of Frigg, the Heavenly Queen. Unfortunately, it is uncommon today. Spindle trees were destroyed wantonly when scientists proved that Broadbean blackflies spend the winter on them. Its runic correspondence is Gar.

Spruce (*Picea abies*)

The Spruce is the Yule tree. This represents the eternal cosmic axis and all permanent things. Sometimes, Spruce trees bear Witches' Brooms. Its runic correspondence is Dag.

Wayfaring Tree (*Viburnum lantana*)

This tree is related to the Elder. Like the Spindle Tree, it is rare, being restricted to southern England, but magically its wood makes powerful travellers' talismans. Its corresponding rune is Rad.

Whitebeam (*Sorbus leyana*)

Ley's Whitebeam is only native to Britain. Of all trees, it is the most endangered species. There are now fewer than a dozen examples known to be still growing in nature. It is one of the magic trees of the Earth Mother Goddess, and its corresponding rune is Erda. Of course, nobody should even think of cutting wood from such a rare tree. Plant one yourself, and cut the wood in nine years' time!

Whortleberry (*Vaccinium myrtillus*)

This is a protective plant whose twigs are used in the seasonal ceremonies of Little Yule (December 13), a festival of lights which precedes Yule itself. It is connected magically with the star known as the Torch Bearer (Procyon). This is the precursor of Loki's Brand (Sirius), the marker of midwinter. Magically, Whortleberry is a light-bringer and shower-of-the-way. Its runes are Ken and Ziu.

Willow (*Salix* species)

There are several species of willow, each of which has its own special characteristics and uses. Some Willows like wet ground. These are the White Willow (*Salix alba*) and the Crack Willow (*Salix fragilis*). They are pollarded, to grow straight poles used in hurdle-making. Cricket bats are made from the Willow *Salix alba var. calva*. Another type of Willow is called Osier. The Common Osier (*Salix viminalis*) and the Purple Osier (*Salix purpurea*) are used to grow the rods used in basket-making.

In springtime, the Great Sallow (*Salix caprea*) and the Common Willow (*Salix cinerea*) bear the catkin. This is the Pussy Willow, sacred to the goddess Freyja.

Magically, these trees produce wood that can be used for corresponding purposes. In general, Willows are symbolic of purification and rebirth. Willow staves can put forth roots and leaves and grow into new trees. Because the wood is good for basket-making, fencing and cricket bats, the Willow is also magically powerful in enclosing and turning back psychic attack. All Willows correspond with Lagu, the power of growth, and the primal water god, Hler. The Willow is the tree of Monday.

Witches' Brooms

These are dense bundles of twigs which can be seen hanging in the branches of trees. Most common in the Birch, they are also found occasionally in Elm, Cedar, Cherry, Larch, Silver Fir and Pine trees. They are caused by the fungus *Taphrina turgidus*. Magically, they concentrate the corresponding power of the tree in which they are found. Witches' brooms from the Birch have the most potent power of Beorc.

Witch Hazel (*Hamamelis virginiana*)

Although it was originally native to eastern North America, Witch Hazel has grown in Europe since the 1600s, and is part of the magical tradition. Magically, the products of Witch Hazel are related to blood-staunching magic. Its runic correspondence is Stan.

Yew (*Taxus baccata*)

The Yew is associated with the paradox of life and death. It is the tree of eternal life, because it lives longer than any other European native tree. The Yew is a very poisonous tree – small quantities of all parts of it can kill. In hot weather, it exhales a resinous vapour which shamans have inhaled to gain visions. Magically protective of the dead, it grows in holy places where the dead are buried and is common in British churchyards. In Norse tradition, plantations of Yew trees are sacred to Ullr, god of archery and winter. His home was Ydalir, a sacred Yew grove. In former times, Yew was a death-bringer because bows were made from its wood. In medieval times the Uetliberg, the holy mountain near Zürich, was a major Yew grove which exported wood for bow-making all over Europe. Eoh, Elhaz, Yr, Ear and Wolfsangel are all Yew tree runes.

Essential Oils

Scientific aromatherapy was unknown in the days of the original runemasters. Pure essences were few. But today, with pure essences available, the power of different aromas for mood creation and healing is well established. In 1988, in collaboration with the essential oils expert Charla Devereux, I determined the following correspondences. The powers of the oils most closely correspond with the qualities of the runes. The corresponding essential oil can be used in any ritual which relates to its rune.

Rune name	Essential Oil	Rune name	Essential Oil
Feoh	Spearmint	Beorc	Dill
Ur	Oak Moss absolute	Ehwaz	Juniper
Thorn	Frankincense	Man	Ylang Ylang
Os	Clove	Lagu	Fennel Sweet
Rad	Basil	Ing	Cedarwood
Ken	Pine	Odal	Marjoram
Gyfu	Hyssop	Dag	Clary Sage
Wyn	Marigold	Ac	Aniseed
Hagal	Rose absolute	Os	Cypress
Nyd	Eucalyptus	Yr	Myrrh
Is	Lavender	Ior	Lovage root
Jera	Rosemary	Ear	Laurel leaf
Eoh	Benzoin	Cweorth	Sandalwood
Peorth	Verbena	Calc	Thyme
Elhaz	Peppermint	Stan	Nutmeg
Sigel	Bay	Gar	Garlic
Tyr	Lemongrass		

7

Practical Rune Magic

Let there be fog,
And let there be phantoms.
Weird marvels
To puzzle your hunters.
Njal's Saga

Starting Rune Magic

The techniques described here are those I use in the teachings of *The Way of the Eight Winds*. They are the basic principles which, when mastered, are a solid basis for exploring further the limitless possibilities of rune magic.

Visualisation

To begin to do rune magic properly, you must know the runes well. It is important to be able to call up any rune in your mind at once without difficulty. The simplest way to get to know the runes in this way is to make up a set of rune cards. It is best to make your own cards, as they will contain your own essence. Printed cards, while useful in divination, are not so good when beginning rune magic. Carefully draw each rune upon a card, thinking about the meaning of the rune as you do it. You should draw the rune in red ink upon a white card about nine inches (23 centimetres) square. Call the name of the rune as you draw it, humming its sound. It is best to start with the 24 runes

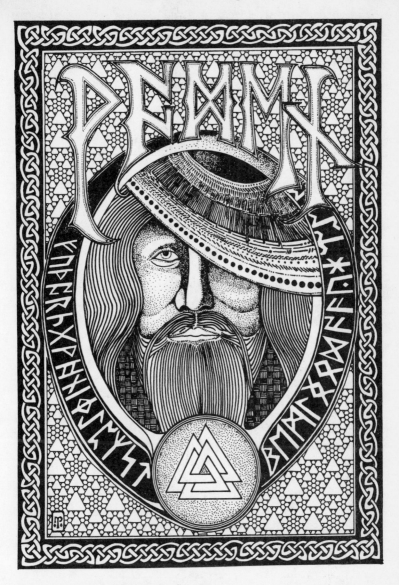

Figure 28 Woden (Odin), the deity of rune magic.

of the Elder Futhark. When you have mastered these, you can go on to the remaining runes.

To start using your rune cards, you should sit comfortably in good, but not dazzling, light. Go through the cards in order, beginning with Feoh and ending with Dag. Put a rune card in front of you in a place where you can see it without holding it. Look at the rune, concentrating on its form. Contemplate the meaning of the rune as you view it. When you shut your eyes you should continue to see the rune for a short time. This will help you to develop the ability to see the rune without the help of the rune card.

Runic Meditation

Progress in rune magic is only possible through inner discipline. The runes are the means by which we can draw knowledge from within, to illuminate the outer world. Traditional spiritual techniques bring us into communion with other levels of reality. Of course, to master this is not simple. Before starting, you must have worthy intentions. You should commit yourself to using the powers you gain only for needs which do not subvert the free will of other people. Also, so that you do not raise the wrong sort of energies, you should do runic spiritual exercises only in a state of 'purification' – after you have performed rituals of cleansing and protection. This includes bodily cleanliness, and wearing clean clothes. It is a good idea to have some special clothes used only in meditation.

There are several stages in runic meditation:

1. Each time you meditate, you should sit or stand in a definite posture. You should feel relaxed, yet alert. There are two ways of sitting. One is with your legs crossed, whilst the other has your legs under the body, as if kneeling. There are also some standing postures. You can stand in the posture of the shape of the rune being meditated upon. Another, rather difficult, posture is The Crane Stance of Clarity. To do this, you must stand on one leg with one eye closed. In this way, you emulate the one-eyed god, Odin, to achieve an altered state of consciousness.

2. You should control your breathing. Quiet, deep, regular breathing brings the correct physical conditions. When you control your breath, you become calm.

3. You should banish all unwanted thoughts. This is one of the most difficult parts of magic, at least for the

beginner. Firstly, you must withdraw your attention from external objects and other distractions. Then you should close your eyes. Suppress the mental images you see. Once you have done this, your bodily sensations will fade and eventually you will lose consciousness of them.

Once you have mastered the first three stages, then you are ready to go on further.

4. Concentrate on the rune. You may find it easier to banish your unwanted thoughts and mental images through concentration. You can do this by visualising the rune. You should meditate upon it until it becomes part of your consciousness.

5. Making the call. Speech and song release the psychic energy present in sound. Runic calls are the name of a deity, or a sacred formula, broken down into its sounds. You should repeat these during meditation whilst you visualise the appropriate rune.

When you have finished the runic exercise, you must complete it formally. This is the 'reawakening', where you re-enter the world of normal consciousness. You can do this by using the methods in reverse order. Consciously order each part of your body, in turn, to begin functioning normally again. Your body, as well as your mind, should feel revitalised after the exercise.

The Five Elements Meditation

Each rune is related to one of the elements. The Northern Tradition has five elements: Earth, Water, Ice, Air and Fire. They are ruled by the five primal deities who represent the five ways that things can behave in the material world. The Five Elements Meditation helps you to gain some insight into the characteristics of each element, and how it relates to each rune.

Each time you work with an element, use the same technique. It is best to proceed from the most dense, Earth, to the lightest, Fire, systematically: Earth, Water, Ice, Air, Fire. The elements relate to directions: Earth lies at the centre, Water in the West, Ice in the North, Air in the East,

and Fire in the South. The sequence of meditation is thus
Centre, West, North, East, South. It is a sunwise spiral of
expanding consciousness.

1. Earth Meditation

Put some earth in a bowl and place the bowl in a convenient
location. Use this as the focus for your meditation on the
element of Earth. Explore in your mind the many
possibilities of Earth symbolised in this small sample.
When you have done this, let your consciousness enter into
the Earth. Experience its many forms, relationships and
possibilities. Finally, concentrate upon the runes that relate
to the Earth element: Feoh, Ur, Wyn, Jera, Beorc, Ehwaz,
Ing, Odal, Ear, Calc, Stan, Wolfsangel and Erda.

2. Water Meditation

Pour some water into a bowl. This should be natural water,
from a spring, well or stream, not from the mains supply,
which is chemically treated. Place the bowl in a convenient
location. Focus your meditation upon the water. Explore the
many forms and qualities of water. When you feel you have
done enough, let your consciousness enter into the water.
Experience its many moods, forms and possibilities.
Concentrate upon the runes related to the element of Water:
Peorth, Lagu, Ing and Ior.

3. Ice Meditation

If it is wintertime, fetch some ice from Nature. Put this in
the meditation bowl. It is always best to use natural ice. But
when this is not possible, freeze some natural water. Do not
use mains water. Focus your meditation upon the ice in the
bowl. Explore the coldness, the crystalline forms, and the
many ways that ice occurs in Nature. Then let your
consciousness enter into the element of Ice, experiencing
its forms and possibilities. Finally, concentrate upon the
runes that relate to the Ice element: Hagal and Is.

4. Air Meditation

Light some incense. It is best to use an incense you have
collected yourself, such as Pine resin. Burn it in a fire-proof
dish. Watch the spiralling smoke rise, and explore the forms
and qualities that the air can take. When you have done
this, let your consciousness enter into the element of air,

experiencing its many moods, forms and possibilities. Concentrate upon the runes which relate to the element of Air: As, Rad, Gyfu, Elhaz, Sigel, Tyr, Man, Dag, Os, Ziu and Ul.

5. Fire Meditation
For this, use a candle. It is best to light one which is the colour of fire. Watch the brilliant flame and focus your meditation upon the forms and qualities of fire and flame. Then let your consciousness enter into the element of fire, experiencing its many forms and possibilities. Finally, concentrate upon the runes that relate to the element of Fire: Feoh, Thorn, Ken, Nyd, Dag, Ac, Cweorth, Ziu, Sol.

6. The Subtle Power Meditation
Finally, you can meditate on önd. This is the subtle power that underlies all things, including your own consciousness. It is the flowing energy-matrix of the universe upon which all things are patterned. You can visualise this as flowing patterns of colours, forming ever-changing geometrical shapes. Traditionally, this power is shown as a dragon with wings and front legs. Its rear part is a prehensile serpent tail. This is the Nwyvre that contains the runes of all the elements, most specially Eoh, Yr and Gar.

When you have finished each meditation, direct your consciousness away from the object. Return to a full awareness of the things around you. It is best to work several times with each element, until you feel ready to move on to the next one. Once the whole programme is completed, you will find your understanding of the runes has been greatly enhanced.

A Runic Self-Initiation

Once you feel comfortable with runic meditation, you may feel ready to do the basic runic initiation. This takes 24 days. Each day is dedicated to a rune from the Elder Futhark. The first day is dedicated to Feoh, the second to Ur, and so on, ending with Dag on the 24th day. The day before the first rune day, make 24 ferridges (ceremonial biscuits). Using a sharp point, prick a different rune upon each biscuit in the proper rune order. Then bake them. Eat one biscuit for breakfast on the day corresponding with that rune (Feoh on the first day, Ur on the second, and so on). As you eat it, remember that this is the day of that rune.

On the first day, make a promise to yourself that you will carry through to the end what you have started. Breaking off in the middle for any reason means that you must start again at the beginning. So make sure that you can carry it through for 24 consecutive days. Every day during this 24-day period, you should do a meditation on the day-rune. This will bring you into deeper contact with the inward essence of that rune. Analyse each thing that you do in terms of the rune of that day. You may be surprised at how even everyday events relate in unexpected ways to the rune of the day.

Sitting Out, Taghairm and Seers' Journeys

Sitting Out or útiseta is where a person 'sits out' at night under the stars to be integrated with the önd there, hearing inner voices and communing with the universe. The best locations for Sitting Out are high places. If possible, they should be away from populated areas. Unfortunately, sites near cities almost guarantee interference, no matter what the time of day or night. Ideal places are solitary, wild locations, especially those known to be ancient places of power. Ancient earthworks, holy hills or burial mounds are best. Explore a wild area until you find a good place.

Another technique, once popular in Scotland, is the Taghairm. This means 'the gathering summons', or 'the cloak of knowledge'. One is wrapped in a cow's hide or blanket, with only the head free, and left lying all night by a waterfall. During the night, visions come.

The Seer's Journey can be a journey inward, without any physical motion, or it can be a physical pilgrimage to a place of power. You can make the inward journey as a pathworking. To do this, you should visualise a journey through a symbolic, mythological landscape which contains specific 'stations' or stages. Runic meditation does this through the images of myths from the *Edda* or the *Sagas*.

In former times, the Seer's Journey was a pilgrimage. The pilgrim had to travel along a special route to a holy site, performing ceremonies at wayside sacred places. As the physical journey progresses, it is paralleled by an internal spiritual journey. Ideally, the outer pilgrimage reflects the inner one. Physical progress and spiritual progress go hand in hand.

Seers' Journeys, Sitting Out and Taghairm are all very powerful ways to access other levels of consciousness. But, as with any powerful magical technique, they should be approached carefully and gradually.

A Runic Exercise

Go out into Nature and put yourself in a receptive frame of mind. Then look for runes wherever they appear. You may see them in the branches of trees, cracks in the earth, the flight patterns of flocks of birds, shadows and shafts of sunlight. The runes are everywhere. But we see them only when our minds are receptive. When you are tuned into this way of seeing, you can do an awareness meditation. This means seeing all of the runes in order, beginning with Feoh, and ending with Dag, Gar or Sol. Walk through your surroundings, looking for runes. It is best to do this in the countryside, but it is not impossible in an urban environment. Once one rune has made itself known to you, go on to the next one. It is not easy to 'find' all of the runes in their correct order. Sometimes, the next rune will not appear for a long time. This can be very frustrating. But do not cheat if you cannot connect with the next rune in the sequence. Not seeing a rune is as important as seeing one. This 'failure' will tell you something about yourself. The rune that you cannot find represents something repressed or blocked inside you. This exercise is an effective way of finding out what this block is. Once you have realised what it is telling you, then the rune will appear, almost miraculously.

Making Magical Space

In rune magic, a consecrated place is called a Vé. This is a place, either indoors or outside, which has been set aside from the normal uncontrolled world. Before we perform any ceremony there, we must cleanse and consecrate it by making a circle. We neutralise any harmful patterns and colours of önd present there. Then, with an invocation, we fill the space with new patterns and colours of önd. To neutralise harmful forces, we use holy water, incense and the runestaff. These techniques and the reasons for them are basically the same as in many other, different religious systems.

To make holy water, take about a pint of water (say, half a litre), from your local holy well. Water from the domestic mains supply is useless. It does not have the önd qualities of holy well water. Put it in a suitable container, then stir it sunwise with your right forefinger. Visualise a vibrant stream of blue-white light streaming through your finger into the water. Say:

> In the name of Hler,
> Into this water, I direct the might of önd,
> That it will be pure and clean,
> In the service of the Goddesses and Gods.
> Ka!

When you feel the water is charged, take enough sea salt crystals to cover a circle one thumb (1.1 inches, 2.8 cm) in diameter. Drop this into the water, then stir it sunwise nine times with the forefinger, saying:

> Audhumla!
> Here is salt,
> Salt is life,
> To clean this place,
> Free from strife.
> Ka!

Try to use salt from one of the world's less polluted seas. When the salt has dissolved, sprinkle the water, with your fingers, sunwise around your circle. Start at the north, acknowledging the four cardinal directions as you go. At each direction, say, 'With water and salt, I purify this holy Vé'. When you have used all of the water, light some incense at the middle of the Vé. Any magical incense of protection can be used. Then take the burning incense around the circle. Again, acknowledge the four directions with the words, 'With fire and air, I purify this holy Vé'. Finally, carry

the wand or runestaff around the circle. At the north, say,
'I call upon Rinda, and the power of completion, Jera'. Walk
to the east, and say, 'I call upon Kari, and the power of
birth, Beorc'. Then, at the south, say, 'I call upon Loge, and
the power of daylight, Dag'. To the west, say, 'I call upon
Hler, and the power of enlightenment, Ken'. Finally, take
the staff to the centre, and say, 'I call upon the centre, Erda,
the power of Earth, and Gar, the tree of measure, Ash spear
of Odin'. As you do this, visualise a dome of protective light
forming over the Vé. On this dome, visualise a circle of 24
runes blazing with red fire. The rune Dag will be in the
south, with Jera to the north. Raise your runestaff towards
the pole star and call upon the Gods to be present:

O Erda and Hler,
Rinda, Loge and Kari,
Vanir and Aesir,
May your power be present in this holy Vé.
Ka!

Now, the Vé is ready for any magical operation.

The Harrow

A Harrow is a consecrated table upon which magical
workings are conducted. Outdoors, a natural stone, or an
ancient recumbent megalith can be used as a Harrow. It is
best to find a stone at an ancient place of power. Indoors,
a wooden table or platform is ideal. If at all possible, it
should stand at the centre of the Vé. When it rests against
a wall, it is known as a Stall. Wherever it is, a Harrow
should be raised from ground level, even if only by a few
inches. It should be covered by a cloth. This should be as
beautiful as possible, embroidered, printed or painted by
the person who intends to use it. Ready-made printed or
embroidered cloths are not recommended. Unless it has a
design from central or northern European folk tradition, it
is possible that it will have other sigils which may hinder
the work of rune magic. The Harrow or Stall carries the
magical objects used in workings. Depending on the
working, these include bowls, braziers, candles, power
objects and tools.

Techniques of Protection

Proper preparation is essential for success in anything. The Cosmic Axis Rite below is the basic technique of self-preparation for any work of rune magic. It brings sufficient önd of the right patterns, colours and intensity so that the working will be a success.

The Cosmic Axis Rite

Stand facing north, holding your runic wand in your right hand. Then visualise a ring around yourself at waist level. This should be a blue belt of smoky light. It will bear the 24 runes of the Elder Futhark in fiery red. Begin visualising the ring almost behind your head, slightly to the left of centre. This is the position of the rune Feoh. Jera should be towards the north, and the final rune, Dag, precisely behind you, to the south. The other runes are in their normal sequence. Once this is done, extend your arms outwards east and west to make a cross. Visualise the four cardinal directions as lines of blue light. These run from your front and back to the north and south, and from your right and left hands, to the east and west. Then visualise your body as part of the cosmic axis, running below your feet into the underworld, and above your head into the upperworld. You are standing at the centre of a sphere of magic blue light. Open yourself to the önd which is beginning to flow into you from the six directions. In this state of consciousness you become the Nowl at the centre of the world, through which all power is flowing.

When you feel that the flow of önd into yourself is sufficient, bring your hands above your solar plexus. Touch the wand to your navel area, visualising önd flowing into it as you do so. Then use the charged wand to draw your chosen power sign in the six directions. As you do so, face the direction and acknowledge it. Here, I will use the Ing rune as an example of how the rite is constructed.

You are already facing north. Make the sign of Ing with the wand, visualising it on the sphere of blue light which surrounds you. Call: 'In the north, the realm of Rinda, Ing keep watch over this holy place'. Then, turn deosil (sunwise) one quarter, make the Ing sign, saying, 'In the

east, the realm of Kari, Ing keep watch over this holy place'.
Turn again one quarter, to face south. Make the sign and
say, 'In the south, the realm of Loge, Ing keep watch over
this holy place'. Make a third turn, to the west. Make the
sign, and say, 'In the west, the realm of Hler, Ing keep watch
over this holy place'. Turn again. Facing north, look
upwards, Make the sign of Ing, and call: 'To up-north, the
realm of Odin, Ing keep watch over this holy place'. Still
facing north, look downwards, making the sign and saying,
'In the centre, middle earth, the realm of Erda, Ing keep
watch over this holy place'.

When this is complete, draw the wand back towards
yourself. Rest your hands on the solar plexus area. Centre
the önd in your own body. Visualise the sphere of blue light
collapsing inwards, protecting and empowering you. Now
you are ready for anything!

The Armour of Elhaz

A related runic visualisation is the Armour of Elhaz or
Shield Spell. This is a potent means of protecting yourself
against all physical and psychic attack. It can be done
anywhere, so the actual directions are not important. To
invoke the Armour of Elhaz, visualise six shields. They
stand in front and behind, to the right and left, above and
below your body. Their exact shape is not important. It is
best to think of the form which most represents a shield to
you. These shields are gleaming silver in colour. Upon each
of them, visualise an Elhaz rune in flaming red. Feel the
irresistible power of its önd, like a giant Elk standing
between you and everything harmful. As you erect the
armour, intone the spell:

> By the power of Erda and Kari,
> Rinda, Hler and Loge,
> Elhaz before me,
> Elhaz behind me,
> Elhaz to my right,
> Elhaz to my left,
> Elhaz above me,
> Elhaz below me.
> Elhaz protect me.
> Ka!

You do not need to turn to the corresponding directions when you perform this rite. Remain conscious of the runes flaming around you as long as you need them. They will fade away once they have done their job. Instead of the Elhaz rune, you can visualise the Hammer of Thor, the Aegishjalmur, the Double Axe of the Goddess, a pentagram, or any other power symbol which has a personal meaning for you.

Making Talismans

To make a runic talisman, you will need:
Consecrated water
Fire (or a candle)
Incense
Talisman material
Your magical knife, Ristir (rune carver) and colouring tool
Tiver (red colouring)
A piece of black cloth large enough to wrap up the talisman
A leather thong or thread long enough to wind nine times around the object

Making a talisman is a straightforward operation. Talismans of a constructive and protective nature are made during the waxing Moon. If possible, it should be at the runic hour corresponding most closely to the talisman's quality. First, consecrate the place where the working is to be made. All you need is to set up the Vé, using salt, water, fire and incense. When this is done, you should begin work on the materials of the talisman. Of course, these should be prepared beforehand, and the inscriptions or design already worked out. Wood for talismans must be cut from the tree using the wood-taking ceremony. The type of wood should relate to the magical purpose of the sliver. Similarly, the qualities of stone or metal should correspond with the magical purpose of the talisman. If the talisman is to be made of wood, stone or metal, then the runes and sigils will be engraved with your Ristir.

You should carve each rune carefully and precisely, calling the rune's name as you do it. Concentrate upon each rune, visualising it on the wood before you carve it. Visualise its power entering the work from the corresponding part of the runic circle which surrounds you. Feel the önd of each rune flowing through your body into the Ristir and then into the runes. When you have finished, you can cut lines above and below the runes, joining them together. This helps to unify them magically. Finally, make the sign of Thor's Hammer over the talisman. Give a runic call that corresponds with the power of the talisman.

Once the runes are carved they should be coloured. We give runes their magical power by 'making the runes red'. This empowers them with önd, bringing magical vitality. In former times, some magicians used blood for this. Today, we use the natural red colouring called tiver. This is a colouring paste which is drawn into the carved runes with a special tool. Take some tiver on the colouring tool and carefully draw the colour into the carvings. Call the runic sounds as you apply the tiver, making sure that you colour the cuts in the same order that they were carved.

Tiver can be made by grinding natural red ochre or the rust-red iron particles from a holy 'red' well. It can also be made from the root of the Madder plant (*Rubia tinctura*). You can make the tiver paste by grinding the colour with linseed oil. As you do this, call the runes which will be coloured with the mixture:

Lagu, Lagu, Lagu!
Bless this Tiver
With the power of [name of runes]:
Give strength to my runes.
Ka!

Tiver should be made in advance of the ceremony. It can be kept in a suitable container until needed. Tiver made in this way should only be used for colouring runic inscriptions.

When the colouring is finished, allow the tiver to dry. Once this has happened, enclose the talisman for a period in 'the womb of darkness'. This is its period of preparation before it is born into the world. In darkness, it is increasing in power. Wrap it completely in the black cloth, excluding all light. Then tie up the package with nine turns of the cord. As you wrap and tie it, say:

> Go into the womb of darkness.
> There to grow in power.

Once the talisman has been enclosed in darkness, rotate the package nine times in a deosil (sunwise) direction. As you do this, say:

> In the name of the goddesses and gods,
> And by the might of earth, wind, water, ice and fire,
> I Ward off all harmful evil sprites,
> The ill-natured demons,
> The fiends who injure our bodies,
> Who sap our strength,
> Who blight our lives,
> Who try to destroy us.
> Ward off the ill fortune of bad spirits,
> The awesome Giants,
> The fearful Trolls,
> The mischievous Yarthkins,
> Envious Humans,
> Bad omens, injurious portents,
> Unwanted on-lays and laid air,
> And the ministrations of malignant entities.
> May we be freed from all kinds of injury,
> And instead be favoured with those real gifts
> Which we seek.
> In accordance with eternal Law,
> According to Free Will,
> Ka.

The talisman remains in darkness for a symbolic nine-fold period. This can be nine minutes, nine hours, nine days, nine weeks, nine runic half-months, nine months, nine moons, nine quarters, nine seasons or nine years. The length of time is your decision. The longer the period of gestation, the greater the power of the talisman will be. If you intend to leave it for a long time, you should close down the place of working magically, and reopen it later for the next stage of the work. The talisman should be kept in a protected place for the time period.

The next part of the operation brings the talisman back into the light of day. This is its symbolic birth, when it is hailed as a newborn being. The talisman is then given a name. As an example, I will use the name Joybringer here. The naming ceremony has a number of stages. First, the package is unwrapped. Walk or dance around the package nine times sunwise before unwrapping it. Pass the newborn talisman over a candle or other flame three times. As you do so, call on the powers of light and life to bring its qualities to their full strength. Then name it, scattering consecrated water over the talisman, saying:

> I sprinkle water over thee
> And name thee Joybringer
> By the might of water, wind, earth, fire and ice.
> And so must it be.
> Ka!

The final part of the magical operation identifies the precise powers the talisman needs to perform its task. For this, you should create a call especially for each talisman you make. This call should state the special function of the talisman, for example:

> Joybringer, bearer of my will,
> I charge you to do as commanded,
> For the purpose of *bringing joy*
> [at this point, state what it is intended to do and where it will do it]
> May the talisman do my will
> Until its work is done,
> In accordance with eternal law
> And so must it be.
> Ka!

Finally, you should visualise the sign of the Triple Circle (three interlinked circles) on and around the talisman. When the operation is over, the enclosure should be psychically closed down, and the ceremony ended with the concluding words:

> Now the work is ended,
> In which Joybringer
> Was brought out of the unformed world
> Into the world of being.
> In the name of the goddesses and gods,
> According to Free Will
> And so must it be.
> Ka!

Now the talisman is ready for use, fully empowered.

You may now put the talisman to work. If it is to be worn, then it can be hung around the neck on a leather thong, or carried in a pouch. A metal talisman is best worn around the neck on a chain of the same material. If you intend to put the talisman in a building, three circles can be chalked on it, or carved where they are not visible. This is an ancient magical sigil that can be found, concealed, on roof beams and brickwork in many old buildings.

Sometimes, a talisman will be needed for a specific, limited, purpose. Then, after it has done its work, it should be disempowered and destroyed. This is done by cutting the rune Gar across the runic inscription. Then the runes must be scraped off. Say the formula:

Now your work is done
I thank you.
Return to formlessness
Ka!

As you do this, visualise the önd in the talisman flowing back to its source. It is best to burn wooden objects ceremonially, along with their scrapings. Stone or metal talismans should be thrown into natural waters, preferably a lake or river of ancient sanctity. Acknowledge the water sprites as you throw in the disempowered talisman.

Equipment For Rune Magic

It is possible to do perfectly valid rune magic with very little equipment. The amount of equipment you use is your own choice. But of course, fully-fledged rune magic uses its own special paraphernalia. The garments and tools are derived from existing historic objects and ancient descriptions. For example, the full equipment of a wise woman (Völva) in Viking times is described in the *Sagas*. She wore a dark blue cloak with hood, a kerchief, traditionally red with white spots, and gloves made from wildcat skin, with the fur on the inside. Around her neck was a skin medicine bag containing objects of power. In her hands she bore a mete wand (ceremonial measuring stick) and a runestaff. For the ceremony of Sitting Out, she carried an animal skin large enough to sit upon or be wrapped in. She also had a small rug woven with magical designs. During Sitting Out, these were placed on a wooden platform.

Clothing

It is often necessary to do rune magic in everyday clothes. But as a rune magician, you may find it useful to own the following: a hooded robe or cloak; a groundsheet to sit out upon; a bag for magical power objects; various knives, and a wand or staff. Ceremonial robes are made simply, from a piece of material related to the size of the wearer's body. The fabric should be as wide as the wearer's personal *Fathom*, the measure from hand to hand with outstretched arms. It should be twice as long as the wearer's body measured from the nape of the neck to the heels. The material is folded over, and four triangles cut from it to form a pair of sleeves and the flared sides of the robe. A slit is cut for the head and the sides are sewn up. All of the openings should be protected with a magical pattern. Traditionally, this should be a *tangled thread* pattern, such as a Celtic interlace or the 'running eight' design. A cowl-shaped hood can be made with a quadrant-shaped piece of similar material. In ancient times, the law ordered that only certain classes could wear certain colours. Today, thankfully, we are free to wear any colours we like. In rune magic, the earthly colours, such as greens, browns and yellows are desirable.

Belts and girdles are bringers of magical power. Wearing a belt around the body helps to contain and channel önd. Rune magicians often use a magic knotted cord around the body. In ancient times, shape-shifting magicians wore belts of animals skin or hair. To connect with wolves, for example, they wore wolf-skin or wolf-hair belts. Whatever it is made of, your magical belt should measure three fingers in width (two thumbs). It should also have seven tags or tongues. Belts with pockets are useful for carrying magical power objects.

A runic headband is a useful magic object to have, for it brings magical protection during ceremonies. It is made from a strip of white cloth, onto which all of the 24 Elder Futhark runes are embroidered in red. You should make it yourself, singing each rune as it is sewn in. It is best to do this over a 24-hour period during the waxing moon. Then, you can embroider each rune at the correct Runic Hour, facing the correct runic direction. In this way, you face the sun as each rune is made. When it is finished, a complete circle of time and space has been woven into it. Finally, as with all magic objects, it should be dedicated a place of power. If possible, it should be an ancient place of sanctity, such as a holy well, stone or hill.

Magical Tools

You will need a knife for working rune magic; unlike ceremonial clothing, it is essential. The knife is used to cut slivers of wood, to gather herbs and for protective magic. It can also be used to carve runes. The knife blade should be made of iron or steel. This is a magical material. It is better to make your own knife than to buy one in a shop or market. You should never use someone else's magical knife. A second-hand knife may carry bad on-lays. You should, if possible, make a new, dedicated, magical knife from a piece of metal shaped and ground to sharpness yourself so that you know everything about the knife. The knife should be a Natural Foot (nine thumbs) in length. The handle is four thumbs long, and the blade five. The handle should be made from wood, bone, tusk or horn, not plastic, but do not use tusk or horn from an endangered species of animal. The best wood is Rowan, Hazel, Blackthorn or Ash. It is desirable to cut and season the wood yourself. When cutting it, you should use the ceremony for taking wood, described below. You may engrave runes of divine power upon the handle. This helps to consecrate it to its special use, enhancing its power.

It is really only strictly necessary to have one knife, which can be used in all magical workings. The more a knife is used magically with conscious will, then the more beneficial power known as *megin* will accumulate within it. But as well as the ceremonial knife, it is useful to have a carver (known as a *Burin* or *Ristir*), for making runic inscriptions. Mine has a boar's tooth handle. To colour carved runes, some people like to use a *Reddener*. This is a triangular tool, made of metal, horn or wood, used to put the tiver (red colouring) into the carved runes. Some people use yet another magic knife, the *Boleen*, for gathering herbs. This is a small sickle.

Wood Magic

Objects made of wood have always been important in rune magic. The magical qualities of specific trees are described in Chapter 6. There is a ritual for taking the wood, which will empower it. You should remember that whenever wood is needed ceremonially, it should be cut from a living tree or shrub. Wood from a dead tree is useless. The önd has departed from a dead tree. Also to be avoided is wood which has been cut already by someone else. This is because the person who cut it will have put their own on-lay into the wood, knowingly or unknowingly. This could easily distort or thwart the magical operation. There is no sure way of knowing. When you cut wood ceremonially, you put your own magical power into it. You create an on-lay that interacts with the önd of the wood. To find the right tree, you should explore local woodland and hedgerows. Of course, you should first get permission from the landowner before taking wood. The best time to cut wood is at sunrise, high noon or sunset. When you have found the tree, you must approach it reverently. It is best to use wood which faces the correct runic direction for the operation. The branch to be cut should face towards the Airt that corresponds with the required use.

Before cutting the wood, you should perform a short ceremony of personal protection. Then, taking the knife, you speak to the tree's soul, saying:

Hail to thee, O [tree's name]!
Old Lady, give me of this wood,
And I will give thee some of mine,
When I grow into a tree.
Into this branch send thy might,
That thy power will work through it
For the good of all.
Ka!

Then you must cut the branch with a single stroke, starting the cut underneath and cutting upwards. You must not let the branch fall to the ground. If it touches the ground before it is worked on, then its power is lost. If you have to climb the tree to get the branch, then it should be passed to an assistant. Once you have cut the branch, you should thank the tree for its gift. You should speak to the tree again, saying:

Old Lady [tree's name]!
Accept my thanks
For thy might in this branch.
That its power there will remain,
Working for the good of all.
Ka!

Then you should make a small offering to the tree in thanks for the wood. You can leave a coin, a piece of red ribbon, pour a libation of ale, or light a candle in front of the tree. If you burn a candle, then you must stay with it until it is finished, as there is always the danger of fire in woodland. When you have finished the ceremony, then you should take the wood to the place where it will be used. There, you should consecrate it.

Runestaves, Croomsticks and Wands

There are many different sorts of magical object that can be made of wood. They range from the smallest talismanic runic slivers to long staves and building materials. A magic runestaff can be made from a whole sapling, using the root end as the knob on top. When you take a sapling, though, do be sure to plant a new one in its place (the tradition in East Anglia is to plant one's own tree, tend its growth, and then take it), or to take it from an area where culling is necessary. Staves such as this are carried upside down relative to the way that the tree grows, but only the largest staves are held with the lower (root) end of the tree uppermost: all other staves are held in the direction of growth, with the smaller end uppermost. Croomsticks and other hooked magical staves can be made by deliberately pinning a growing sapling in a certain way. It is harvested anything up to five years later. Croomsticks and staves created in this way are especially powerful. As an alternative, you can look for a distorted sapling or bush which has grown that way naturally. Natural forces sometimes make saplings grow in ways perfect for magical uses. A Croomstick is a magic stave with a curved top rather like a shepherd's crook. It measures about four feet (122 centimetres) long. You can use a croomstick to lay out a magic circle, hook down Mistletoe and Witches' Brooms, and in protective magic. When you hold a croomstick at arm's length, it should let you see exactly one sixteenth or one twenty-fourth part of the horizon through the space made by the curved part. The sixteen-fold croomstick is used for viewing the eight Airts and their mid-points, whilst the twenty-four-fold stick is for the runic directions. Excepting wands and Pilebogar, staves can be ornamented and empowered with ceremonially-plaited threads. The colours of the threads should always relate symbolically to the use of the stave.

Rune magic uses the wand for directing magical energy. In the Northern Tradition, the wand is called a *Gandr*. The best wood for a wand is Hazel or Blackthorn. Wands should be between a Shafthand (3.3 inches, 8.38 cm) and an Ell in length. An Ell (26 2/3 inches, 66.96 cm) is the best length. At the thicker (lower) end, it should not be more than a thumb (1.1 inches, 2.79 cm) in diameter. Most wands are rounded at the wide end, tapering to a point at the other one. This shape is most effective in directing önd, but there are other sorts, too. For example, wands sacred to Frey have either a pinecone or a phallus carved at the end. Whatever shape it is, your wand should be carved with runes. A useful formula is the whole rune row. Depending on your preference, it can be the 16 Scandinavian runes, the 24 runes of the Elder Futhark, or the 33 Northumbrian runes. Experienced rune users can create a formula which affirms their personal power.

You may find a mete wand useful in rune magic. This is a measuring rod or stick, an Ell in length, graduated in the subdivisions of Natural Measure – Shafthands, Thumbs and Barleycorns (there are three thumbs in a Shafthand, and three Barleycorns in a Thumb). You can use a mete wand for making sure that magical objects are the correct ritual size in Natural Measure. Unlike a *Gandr* (wand), a mete wand is not a magically-charged talismanic stave. (For full details of Natural Measure, see my book, *Practical Magic in the Northern Tradition*, Aquarian 1989.) Another sort of protective stick is the Albion Knot. These are about a Shafthand long with a knob-like projection at one end. Finally, Pilebogar can be useful. They are wooden staves which have a small fork at the top. Into this you can wedge a crystal or a blown egg painted red. It is used as a psychic protector, rather like the sprite trap described below.

Hammer and Nail Magic

Thor's hammer, Mjöllnir, is a symbol of runic power. The sign of the hammer was used in Viking times for consecration and personal protection. Priests made the sign over couples in the marriage ceremony, wives made it over the meal, and ploughmen made it over the fields. It is still as powerful today. Many followers of the Elder Faith today wear the hammer as witness to their beliefs. The hammer is used in traditional nail-magic. When you nail up a horseshoe over a door for magical protection, you should recite this rhyme:

> Thrice I smite with holy crock,
> With this mell I thrice do knock,
> One for God,
> One for Wod,
> And one for Lok.

In this charm, 'God' means Thor, the god of the hammer. He is invoked along with Wod(en) and Lok(i). The nails which fix the horseshoe are the magical protection, invoking the stable power of the Is rune. In Viking times, the sacred nails of temples were used in divination. At certain times, wise men and women would interpret the runic patterns made by the sunlight reflected from them.

All over Europe, people have continued to drive nails into holy trees, posts and doorframes. In Britain, we can still see ancient nails in the doorposts of many old inns. The binding power of the Is rune is activated whenever we hammer a nail into wood.

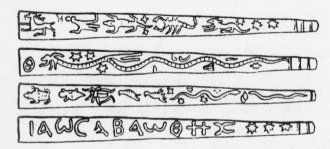

Figure 29 Gnostic magic nails, late Roman Empire. The tradition of nail-driving against evil is known throughout Europe.

Glory Twigs

To protect yourself against the hostile sprites of the night (unfavourably coloured and patterned önd), you should use red thread for binding. During the waxing moon, cut a twig each of Ash, Oak and Thorn using the wood-taking ceremony. Bind them together at each end, using red thread to make a faggot. Place the faggot over the door or window through which you feel the harmful forces are coming. It is effective for only one cycle of the moon, after which you must remove the faggot and make a new one. Bury the old faggot somewhere safe, where it is not likely to be dug up again. You can also carry the glory twigs as personal protection. Ash, Oak and Thorn represent the powers of As, Ac and Thorn. The glory twigs combine the protective power of Thorn with the divine force of As and the growth potential of Ac.

Sprite Traps

'Rowan tree and red thread gar the witches tyne their speed' is an old Scots rhyme, meaning, 'Rowan tree and red thread make the witches lose their speed'. This tells of the traditional use of red cord in binding magic. Its red colour has the same meaning as the tiver used in rune colouring, i.e. it is magically active. Red thread is important in the Northern Tradition spirit traps which are used to stop psychic interference at any place. To make one, you should first cut a Dag rune from a metal sheet. Silver is best, although aluminium or tinplate are also effective. The Dag rune also brings invisibility to the trap. Dag is the rune of doorways. It allows good things to pass by, whilst stopping bad things. Call the runic sound when making the Dag and consecrate it at noontide. For the support, you should cut a Blackthorn stave. Attach a loop made of copper wire to the stave, and suspend the Dag rune by wire or thread inside the loop. Twine red cotton thread around this, making a radial web, saying:

> Thread, tie up this sprite,
> Free us from its spite,
> Tangle up the bane,

Let not a jiece* remain.
Ka!
[* A small piece.]

With the final 'Ka!', you must put your full concentration
into the meaning of the words and act. This will give it its
maximum magical force. You should put the sprite trap
together at sunrise on the day when it is to be set up. To
set it up, you should concentrate on what you want it to do.
Call on the powers of the trap to entangle, ensnare and
entrap the harmful sprites which are causing the trouble.
Then you must put it in a place where it can be effective.
This should be between the place of trouble and any
possible source of psychic interference – this could be
between a cemetery and a house, or at the entrance to a
desecrated place.

Every few days, examine the sprite trap and repair any
damage. If the psychic trouble has lessened, give it a few
more days. When it stops, the trap has caught the offending
spirit (drained away the harmful önd). Now is the time to
take the trap away. Use your knife to cut away the thread
from the copper loop and carefully put each length of
thread into a consecrated bottle. When all of the pieces of
thread are inside, seal the bottle with a cork and red wax.
Finally, bury the bottle in a place where it will not be found.
It must be buried in a place known only to you. As you bury
it, say,

You will go
Down Below!

Then fill in the hole, saying:

In this place
I put this power,
Do no more mischief
From this hour.
Ka!

The Knotted Cord

Magical clothing includes a girdle which is made of knotted
cord. Like the glory twigs, this is also part of thread and

binding magic. It uses the encircling power of the rune Ior, holding in the magician's power and keeping out harmful influences. The Northern Tradition cord has nine knots. Each one stands for one of the nine worlds of the runic cosmos. To make the girdle, you need a piece of red cord one Ell in length. Protect it with the shield spell (see below). Then tie nine knots at equal distances along the cord. As you tie the knots, say:

> By knot of one, it is begun,
> by knot of two, the power comes through,
> by knot of three, so must it be,
> by knot of four, the power will store,
> by knot of five, the power's alive,
> by knot of six, the power to fix,
> by knot of seven, the power to leaven,
> by knot of eight, ties up the fate,
> by knot of nine, what's done is mine.
> Ka!

You should wear the knotted cord whenever you perform rune magic.

Protective Pouches

Pouches filled with herbs and other magical things are powerful protection. They can be made for protection, health, gaining wealth or love. Although you can buy ready-made magical pouches, it is better to make your own. Only then do you know the exact ingredients.

As a beginning, you can easily make a pouch for magical protection. Collect together nine magically powerful ingredients – Ash, Basil, Clover, Elderberries, Mandrake (or Bryony root), Rosemary, Rue, Tarragon and a clove of garlic. Put equal parts of each ingredient in the mixture.

Ceremonially create a Vé for your working. Consecrate the materials. Draw the nine-square pattern on a piece of parchment (paper will do if you cannot get parchment). Write bind runes inside the nine squares. You can use the bind runes in the diagram, or make your own. As you write them, call their runic sounds. Next, make the pouch from a square of blue or white cloth. This should be nine thumbs square (9.9 inches, 25 cm). Put a piece of each active ingredient on the square of cloth. As you do so, say the formula:

> Ash, Basil, Clover, Rue,
> Elder, Tarragon, Rosemary too!
> Mandrake and Garlic,
> Herbs old and new,
> For preservation,
> I summon you!
> Ka!

Finally, put the runic parchment on the herbs and tie up the pouch with red thread. You should use 13 knots, one for each moon of the lunar cycle, to tie up the pouch. As you tie each knot, say:

> I bind thee to preserve [name]. May the virtues in this pouch preserve and guard the cause which I intend and for all who surround it. Ka!

If you are making a pouch for yourself, then this formula is used:

> By the power of three times three,
> This pouch is bound to preserve me.
> Ka!

Practical Rune Work

Insigils

Magical signs or letters can be arranged to make the powerful amulets called insigils or runic wheels. Four, six, seven or eight lines are drawn from a centre, making a 'star'. Magic letters are then written on these lines, and a circle is drawn around the whole sign. In the Irish tradition, Ogham letters arranged like this are the *Feisefín*, Fionn's Shield. They are named after the hero, Fionn MacCumhaill (Finn McCool), who is said to have used them as a protection against magical attack. In ancient Ireland, protective signs like this were painted on warriors' shields. Some, known as *liuthrindi* dazzled opponents who looked at them. When an insigil is worn around the neck as a pendant, it is called a Bracteate.

The best insigils are based upon the Heavenly Star. This is an eight-branched figure which represents the eight-fold nature of space and time. It is a symbol of balance and right orderliness. The Heavenly Star can be used by itself as an insigil. When making an insigil, you should use runes of power and protection. Insigils have almost unlimited possibilities. You can use precisely the runes you need for a magical working. One shown here has the runes of the eight directions in their corresponding positions (figure 30). This reinforces the basic meaning of the Heavenly Star. Your own name, or a title such as Erilaz (runemaster), written in runes on the star, makes a good insigil.

You can also put a number of bind runes together to make the runic wheel. Doing this creates an insigil of great power. The most powerful insigil of all is the Aegishjalmur. It is the 'helm of awe', a symbol of irresistibility which disempowers opponents on both the human and non-material level, and is one of the magic objects gained by Sigurd in his victory over the dragon Fafnir. It is made of eight Elhaz runes combined with crosspieces that represent the 24 runes, drawing upon the combined power of all the runes and projecting them outwards from the centre. The centre of its power is between the eyes, the Third Eye, where önd enters the head. In ancient Iceland, Aegishjalmur amulets were made of lead, the metal of Thor. Before combat, they were pressed between the eyes, with the affirmation 'I bear the helm of awe between my brows'. In medieval England, it was the heraldic crest of the knight, Sir John de Warenne (c.1320).

Other possibilities for insigils include using cryptic runes, such as Branch or Tent runes. These make powerful, striking designs. Another form of insigil is a wheel with eight 'spokes'. Runic words are written around the rim of the wheel, and another circle is drawn around them.

When you make an insigil, you should consecrate the object in the usual way. Then carve the main stems of the 'star'. These should be done sunwise, starting from the centre. Even where lines are opposite one another, they should still be carved from the centre outwards, not across the centre in one stroke. Once you have made the star, carve the runes upon it. Again, this should be done sunwise,

Figure 30 Insigils. Clockwise from top: 1, seasonal year sigils; 2, year runes; 3, Mjollnir; 4, Ungandiz; 5, runic wheel; 6, Iarnsaxa; 7, bind rune wheel; 8, heavenly star; 9 (centre), Aegishjalmur, sigil of irresistibility.

starting at the highest point on the right. As you carve the runes, concentrate upon their meanings and call their names. For bind runes, cut each part of each rune, even when this means going over the same line two or more times. When you have finished the 'star' and its runes, make a circle around it. Then you can colour the runes in the same ceremonial way by going over each rune in turn, even when it means going over the same line twice. Finally, colour the circle, bringing out the combined power of the runes written there.

Runic House Protection

Historically, the runes have played a major part in house protection. When used properly, the power of the runes

Figure 31 Liuthrindi pattern on a figure-mounting from a bucket
found in the Viking-age ship burial at Oseberg in Norway.

affects the quality of önd entering the building to the benefit
of those living there. Today, they can be used just as
effectively as in the past. When you make any of these
protectors, you should do it ceremonially, for you are
creating a talisman. It is not possible to enclose a painted
rune in darkness, but as you paint or cut the rune, you
should make the corresponding runic ritual. In this way,
the divine powers, the colours and patterns of önd, will be
present in the rune.

We can see the possibilities of runic protection from their
historic uses. Runes were used on walls, roofs, over doors,

Figure 32 Relationship between the 'Man' symbol in German *fachwerk*
timber-frame building construction, the body of 'Man' and 'Man'
runes.

in windows, on shutters, and on beams. They occur in the patterns of beams in timber-framed buildings, where they combine sometimes to make complex bind runes. The X-shaped Gyfu rune in timber framing is a physical link between uprights. Other forms may be less necessary structurally, but more potent magically.

On the roof of a house, Wyn, in the form of a weather vane, brings joy to the household. The Younger Futhark form of Hagal, drawn with compasses as a six-petalled 'flower', is the Lucky Star. It protects entrances. It can be cut from window shutters, carved or painted on either side of an arch. This pattern is known in North America as the Pennsylvania Dutch 'hex' sign. Is is a powerful rune of binding. Nails, the iron versions of Is, are hammered into main beams or supporting posts for good luck and protection from fire and intrusion. They hold up horseshoes, which contain the primal power of the Ur rune. Traditional blacksmiths made wall anchors in Is form, straight with pointed ends. Sometimes, Dag runes were struck into each end with the cold chisel. The Eoh rune is also used in wall anchors. It can be found in its angular form, but it is more common as an S-shape, when it may have a serpent's head. Eoh's magical function is to ward off lightning. On a physical level, it earths charged particles.

Like Gyfu, Elhaz in timber framing has a structural function. It ensures physical stability and magical protection against harmful effects. As the Man pattern, it is well known in German timber-frame work. It represents the protection of conscious collective strength, 'together we stand'. This is the form of Younger Futhark rune, equivalent to the Elder Futhark's Elhaz. A more complex version of this, the 'Wild Man', is found in certain parts of Germany. This is a powerful figure, both structurally and magically. The Elder Futhark form of Man was also used by the timber frame builders and has the same magical meaning.

Ing is the most common runic building protector. It can take either form, the enclosed or the outgoing. Traditionally, either is used, according to aesthetics. In either form, the Ing rune has the power to protect the walls of the building from harm. Carved on a door frame, the enclosed Ing rune is God's Nail. There, the Ing shape contains a four- or eight-petalled flower, with a nail at the centre. This invokes the power of the sun standing due

Figure 33 Symbolic magical protection of a timber-frame hall (Little Moreton Hall, western English style), containing Ing, Jera and Elhaz runes and sunwheels (Celtic Crosses).

north at midsummer midnight north of the Arctic Circle. It is the power of the Pole Star and the Sun in alignment. Ing runes can be found in old timber-framed buildings, where they protect the space beneath the gable, or inside larger timber panelling. It is one of the traditional patterns used in the East Anglian plasterwork called Pargetting, and in tile patterns on roofs. Most commonly, though, Ing runes are used in brickwork. They are made from bricks of a colour that contrasts with the background wall colour. In its outgoing form, Ing is often extended and repeated to

make 'diaper work' (a diagonal grid). This was very popular
in the Tudor period. Magically, it extends to protect the
whole wall. Ing became very popular in the nineteenth
century, when vari-coloured bricks became available
everywhere. The recent revival in the use of ornamental
brick in building has led to a renewed use of Ing runes. All
over Britain there are new houses, shops and office
buildings with brickwork containing the protective Ing
rune. It is a vital, living, tradition.

Ing is also used to protect openings. In France and
Germany, many doors are panelled in the Ing pattern. Ing-
shaped cutouts can be made in window shutters, and as
small windows in doors. The diamond-shaped 'leaded
lights' in windows are also Ing runes. The Ing Grid is a
development of this rune, which is constructed by drawing
two squares over a horizontal Ing rune. These squares are
subdivided into chequerboards of 25 squares each. It is a
magic sigil invoking the power of dynamic balance between
two interchangeable states, and resists attack by both direct
and hidden means.

Odal is an invocation of the power of ownership – our
'own earth'. Usually, the Odal rune is used in brickwork like
the Ing rune. It can also be used on gable ends. According
to Westphalian tradition, it is put there to draw in beneficial
powers from the air. Dag, the rune of oak doors, is a
protector of openings. It has the magical effect of preventing
bad things from entering, whilst allowing good things to
come in. It should be carved on the door frame, or painted
in blue and white. The Dag rune was carved on internal
posts of timber-framed houses as 'witch posts', to ward off
psychic attack. In former times, blacksmiths would
hammer the Dag rune into the metalwork of gates, latches,
locks and hinges. Gar is used in timber work, and as
wrought iron railings and balconies. It has a blocking,
terminating effect. Wolfsangel is another wall anchor form.
Like Eoh, it wards off lightning. Magically, it is powerful in
binding harmful forces. Finally, Erda above the door
invokes the blessing of Mother Earth on all who enter.
Although it is not traditional, any of the runes above can
be combined to make a decorative – and magical – insigil
which can adorn and protect any flat or house.

Other magical sigils are used in rune magic. Even when
they do not contain actual runes, they all have some special

runic connection. Like the runes, they can be painted or carved. Also, certain sigils are effective as lead talismans. The Aegishjalmur has been mentioned already. The Sun Wheel, a circle containing a cross of four 'spokes', represents the power of the rune Rad. This invokes the careful, ritual application of the sun's power, bringing sanctification. Carved on top of a stone pillar, this simple insigil is the Celtic Cross, echoing the rune Sol. The pentagram – the equal five-pointed 'star' – is one of the most powerful magical sigils known. In the Northern Tradition, it was used rarely in ancient times. There are, however, some ancient rock scribings with pentagrams. But in modern magic, the pentagram is used widely. In the Northern Tradition, it invokes the power of the five deities of the elements, the pre-Vanir goddesses and gods who exist at the primal level of the universe. These deities should be remembered when a pentagram is drawn. In a pentagram, they are invoked in the following order:

Kari — Hler   — Erda   — Loge — Rinda
(Air) — (Water) — (Earth) — (Fire) — (Ice)

The power is drawn into the figure by tracing these points in a deosil (sunwise) direction. A pentagram with runes makes a fine insigil.

You can use any of these runes or sigils singly, or in combinations which you feel appropriate. They are appropriate culturally, and have been proven by centuries of use.

Magical Analysis of Rune Forms

Some of the more complex rune forms contain other, simpler runes. The meanings of these simpler runes assist and explain some of the qualities of the complex runes.

Thorn

Thorn is a powerful protective figure. Its stave form, with an upright bearing a V-shape, is analysed as an Is rune bound together with the <-shaped form of Ken. It combines the fiery power of Ken with the binding nature of Is. The other form of the Thorn rune is the equilateral triangle with one side upright. The triangle is an ideal form for enclosing power. It is the shape of a Vé, a sacred enclosure of the Northern Tradition. In England, London's Westminster Abbey and Houses of Parliament stand on ground which once was a Vé. This was the sacred triangular island of Thorney, a magically-protected place ideal for sacred rituals. In Denmark, the royal sacred Vé at Jellinge was enclosed by a triangle of standing stones. The Valknut, three interlaced triangles, the symbol of Odin, is a form of Thorn rune which invokes the power of three times three.

Gyfu

Gyfu, a rune of linking, is formed from two <-shaped Ken runes: ><. These can be formed both on the horizontal and vertical planes. On the horizontal, they represent the coming-together of people on the human level, whilst on the vertical, they signify the connection between the gods and humanity.

Jera

The Jera rune can take two forms. One is a stave form, whilst the other is two unconnected angular lines. The first analyses as an Is rune upon which an enclosed Ing rune is superimposed. This combines the binding, static power of Is with the fiery, generative quality of Ing. It expresses beautifully the fixing of fertility in the harvest.

Another analysis shows Jera made up of two Thorn runes sharing the middle stave. The thorny triangle faces outwards, protecting the stave from both directions. Jera is the rune of midwinter. Its double Thorn echoes the two-faced god Janus, who guards the winter solstice. He looks back to the old year and forward to the new. Jera's stave form is a in-gathering form of the rune Dag, which rules the midsummer solstice. The open form of Jera can be seen as two <-shaped Ken runes, interpenetrating without touching, the interplay of fire forces, powering the cycle of the year.

Ehwaz

The Ehwaz rune analyses as two mirror-image Lagu runes in contact. This controlled double flow expresses the mobile qualities of the horse rune well.

Figure 34 Jera rune as the harvest garland, representing successful completion.

Man

The Man rune has several analyses. Each analysis of the Man rune tells of contact between two human beings – the male and the female. The first can be seen as two Wyn runes facing one another. This symbolises the joy of togetherness that two humans can experience. Another analysis is two overlapping Lagu runes. Again, male and female qualities flow together in shared human life. The

third interpretation is of two stave-shaped Ken runes, again
in contact with one another. This represents the unification
of the intellect which makes up human society.

Ing

The Ing rune takes two forms. It has an enclosed and an
open form. The enclosed form is lozenge- or diamond-
shaped. In this form, it represents enclosure of power, the
fire within. The most perfect form of the enclosed Ing rune
is the Egyptian Diamond. This is an important figure in
sacred geometry which, according to Masonic tradition,
originated with the surveyors and architects of ancient
Egypt. It is composed of four right-angled Pythagorean
triangles arranged back to back. This makes the Egyptian
Diamond's length 8 units and its width 6 units. Each side
of the diamond is 5 units long. The perimeter measures 20
units and its area is 24 square units. These numbers are
significant in both the Masonic and runic traditions.

In its enclosed form the Ing rune is made of four lines.
In its outgoing form it has eight. The enclosed form can be
divided either way to make two Ken runes. The outgoing
form of the Ing rune is also geometrically significant. It is
a supremely symmetrical figure – like two overlapping Ken
runes or two Ken runes added to the enclosed form of Ing.
This expresses well the expansive power of this form
compared to the in-gathering nature of the enclosed form.
When it is divided in two, the outgoing Ing is made of two
Gyfu runes and four Ken runes. Divided down the middle,
the outgoing Ing rune also makes two 'old form' Sigel
runes. These are all beneficial runes of light and intellect.

The outgoing form of Ing also represents the year. The
line on one side represents the light and the other, the
darkness. The open ends of the rune represent the midwinter solstice, the time at which the day is the shortest and
the night the longest. From there, the days get longer and
the nights correspondingly shorter. At the vernal equinox,
they are the same length. This is the first crossing point of
the Ing rune. From this point on, the light continues to
grow with longer days, and the darkness diminishes with
shorter nights. Then, at the midsummer solstice, the light
is   at   its   highest   point   with   the   longest   day.
Correspondingly, the darkness is at its lowest point with

the shortest night. This is symbolised by the mid-point of the Ing rune. From then on, the light begins to decline again, with shortening days and lengthening nights. At the autumnal equinox, day and night are the same length once again. This is the second crossing point on the Ing rune. After this, the day declines and the night increases until we reach the winter solstice once again.

Dag

The Dag rune can be broken down into two triangular Thorn runes facing one another. The power of protection is turned inwards, an inversion of the Jera rune. The inward Thorns make a barrier that prevents entry, but Dag is the 'door' rune, and so entry is allowed to some. Dag can also be seen as two Ehwaz runes, one upright and the other inverted. Again, this denotes motion and also the stopping of motion. Both interpretations are conditional. In some circumstances, entry or movement is possible, whilst at other times, it is prevented. The final interpretation, as Gyfu between two Is runes, also has this meaning.

Ior

The Ior rune has two analyses. The first is an Is rune upon which a Gyfu is superimposed. This brings static qualities to the magical linking power of Gyfu. The second interpretation is two Nyd runes on the same stave; one being a mirror image of the other. This is a powerful image of binding, corresponding with the binding power of Ior.

Gar

Gar is the only rune with four-fold symmetry. It can be analysed as a Gyfu rune overlapping an enclosed Ing. This joins the talent or gift of the gods with the inner generative fire. It is highly appropriate for a rune of centring and completion.

Bind Runes

One of the most powerful ways of using runes is to combine two or more individual runes to make a single composite sign. These are bind runes. The main reason for making

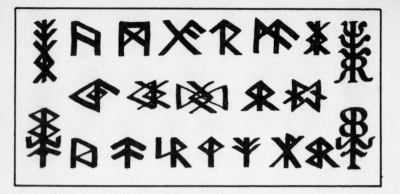

Figure 35 Bind runes: The longer bind runes at each end are straight and cursive versions of each other, invoking protection, power and plenty, and fertility and growth respectively. Top line: *Alu*, the flow of ready power; I am; *Gibu Auja*, bringing good luck; success in legal action; mindpower (hugrune); protection and stability. Second line: love rune (man for woman); love rune (woman for man); eternal lastingness; personal motion; powerful binding. Third line: safe journey; divine energy; rapid action; balanced joy; wealth and security; the gift of joy; easy birth.

them is to create a magical symbol for a particular purpose. Magically, they combine the qualities of the runes of which they are made. Also, when certain runes are used together, they can produce a much stronger effect than one rune alone. These important combinations should be used as bind runes. They embody a special quality, magically empowered to achieve a certain result. Many bind runes have exquisitely beautiful forms, which increases their attraction. Below are some of the more useful combinations of runes. Except where noted, all runes are bound together in the upright position.

Feoh

As a symbol of gain and plenty, Feoh is best connected with the runes which reinforce its power. Bound with Ur, this calls upon the power of healing. Combined with As or Os, it is used magically to gain wealth or success through intellectual means. When joined with Odal, Feoh brings reward through perseverance, whilst Feoh and Dag are used in workings which aim for an increase in wealth. Feoh with Ac or Erda brings plenty.

Ur

Ur bound with Feoh is a rune of healing. When it is bound with Ul, the healing power is increased greatly. With As or Os it combines primal strength with the divine power of intellect. Ur-As and Ur-Os are bind runes which deal with the power of sorcery known as *loegr*. Combined with Rad, Ur brings the strength and ability for making necessary changes. It is a good bind rune for strength during a journey. It can be used on a car to guard against breakdowns. Bound with Stan, Ur brings the power of immovable strength. Ur and Ziu bring immediate power and success to a magical working.

However, when Ur is inverted, it drains away strength. It is used this way round to break or destroy processes harmful to the rune user. For example, bound with Ehwaz or Lagu, Ur reversed helps to prevent unfortunate occurrences.

Thorn

Thorn is a rune of protection and/or attack. Bind runes containing Thorn are mainly used for binding magic. The bind runes which incorporate Thorn with Hagal, Is, Nyd, Ior, Stan or Wolfsangel, slow or disrupt processes already in progress. When bound with Eoh or Ehwaz, Thorn produces a powerfully protective bind rune, bringing the user good luck, whilst success is invoked with Ziu. Reversed Thorn with upright Rad helps us to control the will.

As

Bound with Feoh, As or Os are used magically to gain wealth through intellectual prowess. A bind rune of As or Os with Ur brings the user the power of *loegr*, whilst with Wyn it assists one's creative mental effort. When it is paired with Gyfu, As produces the bind rune *Gibu Auja*. This is one of the most popular bind runes, meaning 'good luck'. When bound with Peorth, As gives the powers of rediscovering hidden knowledge. When both runes are inverted, the bind rune generates forgetfulness. Bound with the hog rune Man, it brings wisdom, whilst with Lagu, academic brilliance is produced. As and Os reinforce

one another, bringing intellectual insight and the power of
poetry and song. With Cweorth, As brings the power of
divine, transforming fire to a magical working. Paired with
Ziu, As brings divine intellectual power to irresistible
strength.

Rad

Generally, Rad tends to accelerate the power of motion in
any other rune. A bind rune of Rad and Ken brings the
power of creativity. Bound with Tyr, Rad makes an
important bind rune for those involved in legal actions. It
will ensure that the litigation will prove successful for the
rune user, so long as he or she is in the right. It cannot assist
injustice. Bound with Ur, Rad is good for strength during
journeys, protecting cars against breakdown and accidents.
With inverted Thorn, Rad enables the magician to keep her
or his will under full control.

Ken

When paired with As, Rad, Wyn, Hagal, Elhaz or Os, Ken
assists in successfully accomplishing creative work. Bound
with Cweorth, the positive aspects of this rune are
enhanced. With Sigel, Ziu or Sol, Ken brings the power of
illumination. It is an ideal bind rune to use when you need
to see clearly. When paired with Nyd, Is, Ior, Stan or
Wolfsangel, Ken's outgoing nature is bound. This is useful
when actions need to be hidden, or motives concealed from
the sight of others. Also, when paired with Odal reversed,
Ken binds one's own activities. This can be used, for
example, in giving up bad habits.

Gyfu

With As, this makes *Gibu Auja*, a most auspicious bind
rune. Another powerful bind rune using Gyfu is made
when it is joined with Wyn, making the bind rune 'gift of
joy'. This is the magic sigil used in the Christian tradition
as the *Chi-Rho* monogram of Christ.

Wyn

Joined to As, Wyn brings creative mental effort. Also, when
paired with Ken or Ziu, Wyn assists all kinds of creative

work. But when it is used reversed, especially with binding runes like Is and Nyd, the result is misery.

Hagal

Hagal and Rad together make a powerful bind rune of return. It is used magically to send back ill wishes to their point of origin. When bound with Ken, it enhances fertility of mind and body. In binding magic, Hagal is used in combination with Is, Nyd, Ior, Stan and Wolfsangel. Delay can be produced by pairing Hagal with inverted Odal. Generally, when bound to inverted runes, Hagal emphasises the negative qualities of those runes. Hagal can be bound with Peorth to produce money by means other than work. The bind rune of Tyr and Hagal is used to bring forth creative, formative powers.

Nyd

Magically, Nyd is used mainly for binding spells. In general, when Nyd is paired with another rune, it brings the power of binding to the other rune's meaning. With similar runes, such as Hagal, Is, Ior, Stan and Wolfsangel, it creates powerful bindings which are difficult to remove.

Is

As with Nyd, Is puts a static binding upon the runes with which it is paired. Again, when paired with Hagal, Nyd, Ior, Stan and Wolfsangel, powerful binding runes are created. The bind rune of Is and Dag is the double axe or *Labrys*. In the Mediterranean region, this is the symbol of the Great Goddess. Her northern tradition equivalent is Nerthus. This symbol of authority gives any working considerable power.

Jera

When Jera is paired with Peorth, it increases the chances of gain. This is most effective with inheritances. Bound with Ur, Sigel, Erda, Ul or Sol, it helps recovery from illness.

Eoh

When Eoh is bound with Thorn upright, it makes a strong bind rune of protection against magical and physical harm.

Also, bound with Sigel and Elhaz, it is a powerful protection against all ills.

Peorth

Bound with Feoh or Hagal, Peorth is said to bring luck in gambling, or unexpected, unearned money from another source. A bind rune made of Peorth with Jera or Odal, is effective in gaining financially from a legacy or inheritance.

Elhaz

Elhaz is the most powerful protective rune, and all bind runes containing it are protective. When it is paired with Thorn upright, the bind rune shields us from all harm. Combined with Eoh, Elhaz wards off magical attack. Bound with Sigel, Elhaz prevents our personal problems from taking over our lives. Wolfsangel and Elhaz together create a magical barrier of awesome power.

Sigel

The power of Sigel empowers the runes with which it is paired. But you should be aware of the danger, as this may accelerate or over-emphasise them. Sigel with Rad or Lagu is an accelerator of events. With Ken, personal enlightenment can be achieved, whilst with Tyr, personal energy is stimulated. Combined with Eoh, Sigel shields against all harm. Balance can be restored with bind runes made of Sigel and Gyfu, Ing or Dag. These bind runes bring a new balance and the right conditions for good health, including recovery from depression. Sigel with Ur, Jera, Man or Ul, can be used in healing when a rapid recovery is needed. We can be shielded from our personal problems by using the bind rune of Sigel and Elhaz. Sigel with Cweorth is a powerful bind rune of rapid transformation.

Tyr

In bind runes, Tyr reinforces the powerful, beneficial aspects of any other rune. With Feoh, Tyr brings personal power and financial success. Bound with Rad, it is effective in legal cases, as long as one is in the right. Combined with Wyn, Tyr brings lasting joy. By binding Hagal and Tyr together, we can gain access to our creative powers, whilst

with Eoh, it channels our *megin* (magical personal önd).
Bound with Peorth, Tyr brings sexual attraction. It is a
powerful love rune. Sigel and Tyr together denote personal
power and physical success. Tyr with the Man rune
inverted is a bind rune for defeating one's opponent in
combat.

Beorc

Beorc bound with Dag brings expansiveness. A bind rune
for fertility and plenty combines Beorc with Erda. Beneficial
growth is brought with Lagu combined with Sigel or Sol,
the power of fruitfulness.

Ehwaz

Ehwaz bound with Rad gives good conditions when
travelling. With Ken, Ehwaz brings the ego under the will's
full control. The bind rune of Ehwaz and Man states 'I am'.
Ehwaz and Ing bring longevity, and Ehwaz with Lagu is
effective in causing confusion and breakdown. Inverted
with Ur, Ehwaz can cause a change of plans, or bring about
an unexpected event.

Man

Man bound with As or Os gives us knowledge and
wisdom, whilst intellectual strength comes from Man and
Lagu. If the Man rune is inverted, it tends to counteract or
cancel the influence of the rune with which it is bound. It
is only used in binding magic.

Lagu

Lagu bound with As brings academic success, whilst with
Tyr, it assists women in asserting their rights. Combined
with Ehwaz or Dag, Lagu brings confusion and the
breaking-up of the present state of things. The Lagu-Man
bind rune brings intellectual strength to current activities.

Ing

Ing bound with another rune brings out the qualities of
transition or completion in that rune. Paired with Ehwaz,
Ing signifies longevity, whilst inverted with Lagu, it is the

bringer of grief and distress. Ing with Dag is a beautiful bind rune denoting durability and longevity. Bound with Gar, Ear or Calc, final completion is denoted. These make an appropriate ending for magical workings.

Odal

Paired with As, Os or Man, Odal brings a visionary ideal to the mind. It enables the user to express his or her will in action. Odal bound with Ur or Peorth brings success through persistence. If you want increased prestige, a bind rune of Odal with Dag will bring it. To delay or interrupt a process, Hagal should be paired with Odal reversed.

Dag

With Feoh, Dag is used to increase wealth. With Bar and Lagu, the growing, expansive qualities of these runes are enhanced. When Dag is paired with Not, Is, Ior or Stan, it tends to reduce their negative, binding, qualities. The bad effects of inverted runes are reduced when paired with Dag. Combined with Is, Dag makes the *Labrys*. This is a symbol of inflexible, authoritarian behaviour. It is powerful in imposing decisions on others. Confusion is brought when Dag is bound with Lagu. Dag and Odal bring an increase in prestige.

Ac

Bound with Lagu, Ac is a powerful bringer of growth.

Os

The bind rune of As and Os brings intellectual insight, increasing our powers of song and poetry. With Feoh, Os is bound to bring wealth through intellectual pursuits. With Ur, one's magical abilities are enhanced. Os and Wyn together help our creative mental effort, especially in the area of speech or writing. Bound with Peorth, Os brings rediscovery of hidden information. It is used with the hog rune Man for wisdom, whilst with Lagu, it produces eloquence. Paired with Ziu, Os allies the divine power of speech to irresistible strength.

Yr

Yr and Gyfu bound bring happiness in marriage or partnership, a compensation for unselfishness. Yr and Dag signifies change from a seemingly good position to a bad one.

Ior

Ior paired with other runes binds their powers. Bind runes of Ior with other binding runes, such as Hagal, Nyd, Is, Stan, Wolfsangel and Man inverted are ideal for hindering, delaying and stopping any process.

Ear

The rune Ear bound to Erda invokes the power of the earth.

Cweorth

Cweorth is a rune of transformation. With other runes of change, it accelerates their progress.

Calc

Bound with As, Calc makes a rune of power. It makes the powerful ending *az*, which occurs in magic words like Erilaz (runemaster), Laukaz (growth) and the rune name Elhaz.

Stan

Stan paired with other runes binds their powers. Bind runes of Stan with other binding runes, such as Hagal, Nyd, Is and Ior are ideal for hindering, delaying and stopping any process. With Ur, Stan is a source of immovable foundation. The bind rune of Wolfsangel and Stan is powerful in magic which aims to trap something.

Gar

This is a powerful rune of completion. Paired with other runes, it anchors their power at a certain place. With Stan, it is useful for magically founding anything.

Wolfsangel

Paired with other runes, Wolfsangel binds their powers.

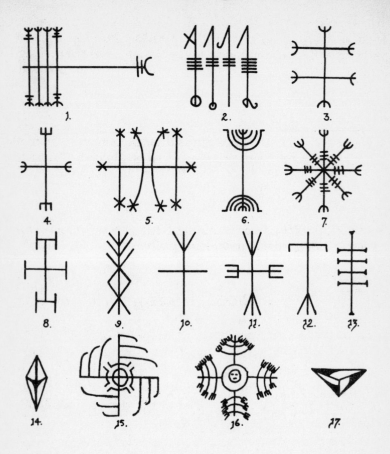

Figure 36 Icelandic, Irish and British magic sigils based on cryptic
runes: 1, Kaupaloki; 2, sleepthorn; 3, strength; 4, against anger; 5,
rowan door protection; 6, strength/courage; 7, irresistibility; 8, Runic
Cross, consecration; 9, power, wealth and protection; 10–13 magical
sigils. 10, Lunnastig Stone, Shetland; 11, Ballywheen, Kerry, Ireland;
12, Monksgrange, Drogheda, Ireland; 13, Maghera, Down, Ireland;
14, Fire Eye, far seeing; 15 Ginfaxi, victory in combat; 16, Angurgapi,
generating uncertainty; 17, Dragon's Eye.

Bind runes of Wolfsangel with the other binding runes,
Hagal, Nyd, Is, Ior and Stan hinder or stop.

Erda

The Mother Earth rune, Erda, bound with the feminine
runes denotes fertility and nurture.

Ul

Combined with other runes of healing, such as Ur and Hagal, Ul makes a powerful bind rune of recovery from illness.

Ziu

Paired with other runes, Ziu enhances and increases their powers. But it is such a powerful rune in its own right that it is rarely found in bind runes. Ziu with Thorn is the bind rune for success.

Sol

Sol's gentle solar power combines with any of the feminine runes to bring peace and plenty.

Runic Triads

Bind runes can be made from more than two runes – there are also many powerful combinations of three runes. Some of the most powerful are key words or names in the runic tradition. In some cases, the name's meaning overrides the meaning of the three runes together. But, most often, the runic kennings and the meaning of the word are in perfect harmony with one another.

Names from beast lore are powerful runic triads. Together, Ur, Lagu and Feoh make the magical word ULF. This means Wolf. It represents the aggressive power of the wolf. Magically, it brings the assistance of a powerful force. Its number is 24. Beorc, As and Rad make BAR, the power of the bear. This also includes the nurturing, protective power of the mother bear, symbolised by the goddess Artio. Its number is 27.

As, Lagu and Ur make the magic word ALU. Literally, this means 'ale', symbolising the mystic 'water of life' – the water of the Gods' primal power. Alu brings good things, changes for the better. It is used to bring divine guardianship to a working, through the power of *loegr* (operative magic). These powers are completely for the user's benefit. Like Bar, it has the number 27.

With Jera and Sigel, or Jera and Ul, Ur makes a bind rune

of potent healing. The bind rune made of As, Feoh and Ing
brings us release from a problem by breaking up the things
that bind us. As, Wyn and Odal (or Os, Wyn and Odal)
draw upon the three-fold power of the Allfather, the gods
Odin, Vili and Vé. These three runes are used to bring our
life into perfect harmony with our will. It gives us the
strength to continue on our chosen path.

As, Sigel and Ken are bound together to make the runic
word ASC. This is the sacred ash tree of the Gods,
Yggdrasil. It gives us the power to survive attacks and to
come unaffected through our troubles. Ziu can be used in
place of Sigel here. Ken, Dag and Sigel are used to bring
illumination, transforming our consciousness. If Ken is
replaced by Cweorth, this makes the runic triad of
transformative enlightenment. Cweorth, Dag and Sigel
bring us new ways of solving problems.

Gyfu, As and Rad come together to make the word GAR.
This is the magical name of the spear of Odin. This bind
rune draws on the magic of Odin's weapon, bringing
beneficial power to our assistance. Its number is 16.
Together, Gyfu, Ing and Ehwaz bring a lasting quality to a
working, whilst Gyfu, Man and Wyn help to heal the rifts
between people. This triad should be used in magic that
aims for a more harmonious future. Gyfu, Wyn and Yr
assist us in achieving stable, unselfish contentment. The
bind rune of Wyn, Odal and Dag makes the word WOD.
This means 'divine inspiration', as in the name Woden
(Odin). Its number is 55. Magically, it allows a bad situation
to be transformed joyfully through inspired action.
Another triad for this is Wyn, Dag and Cweorth.

Combinations of the icy Hagal, Nyd and Is are used to
cause delay and binding. Hagal, Is and Not make the word
HIN, which distances and hinders things from taking their
due course. Its number is 30. Triads of any of these runes
with Ior, Stan or Wolfsangel cause powerful binding and
delaying. Nyd, Stan and Wolfsangel cause capture and
binding. Similarly, Nyd, Is and Lagu is wholly negative.
Spelling the word NIL, it is used to bring about the total
destruction of something. Its number, 42, is one of great
power in the Northern Tradition.

Jera, Feoh and Wyn help us bring together the things
which lead to an abundant, joyful life. Jera, Ur and Sigel
are used to help the process of healing an illness and can

help in solving a problem. The bind rune of Jera, Rad and Hagal is used to neutralise and return another's ill wishes. Jera, Rad and Thorn combine to make the runic power-word JRTh (Jörth) the Earth. This is used to bring about favourable conditions for a project, but it will work only in harmony with 'the way of the world'. It cannot deflect or turn the course of events. Its number is 20. Jera combines with Ken and Ing to make a love charm for a man. Tyr, Ing and Jera can be used by women for the same effect.

Elhaz, Odal and Thorn are runes of powerful protection. When we use them, they defend us against any bad consequences which might result from our working. The bind rune of Peorth, As and Rad gives us access to hidden or forgotten knowledge. It helps us to see important things we may have overlooked. Sigel, Odal and Lagu make the name of the solar goddess Sól, indicating the brilliant energy of the Sun. This has the same effect as the single late rune, Sol. It helps us to have the inner strength and stability to cope well with changes happening now. Its number is 60.

A bind rune of great power is made of Sigel, Tyr and Rad. This can help us greatly in any conflict, especially justified legal actions. Sigel, Elhaz and Rad are the runes of protection in physical combat, as used by warriors in ancient days. Tyr, Yr and Rad together make the name of the god of strength and success, Tyr. When we use this, however, we should remember that Tyr's success is through self-sacrifice for the greater good. This bind rune will benefit the collective, rather than the individual. Bound together, Ehwaz, As and Man give us the power to use our knowledge successfully. It allows wise judgements that bring beneficial results. Ehwaz, Ing and As are used to bring us into closer union with the mystic secrets of life. Ing, Nyd and Gyfu make the word ING. This invokes the god Ingva-Frey, the power of generation. In this form, its number is 28. Ing, Lagu and Elhaz together are the runes of protection to be called when holy water is sprinkled over someone about to enter combat.

Odal, Nyd and Dag combine to make ÖND. This is the vital breath, the universal soul of all things. It helps us to overcome apparently major problems. By coming into harmony with our circumstances, we transcend them. Its number is 58. Used with Rad inverted, Dag and Lagu are

Figure 37 Runic-inscribed Celtic cross by Gaut Björnsson, Ballaugh, Isle of Man, in the form of the rune Sol.

used to bring confusion and disruption. Dag, Ehwaz and Lagu have the same effect. Odal, Thorn and Rad make the name Othr. This is the name of one of the divine lovers of the goddess Freyja. It brings balance between stability and motion, giving us the power to explore areas outside those which are accepted as 'normal' or 'conventional'.

Runic Names of Power

Runic words of power are composed of a number of runes. Each rune resonates with the aspect of önd that it represents. Certain combinations are important. These are the Names of Power, which come mainly from Old Norse and Anglo-Saxon early runic languages. When we use them, we access the power that the name symbolises as well as the combined power of the individual runes. We also access the word's numerological equivalent. Below are the most potent runic Names of Power, with their meaning and numerological value. They can be used wherever appropriate, where they will enhance any magical process or working. (See Chapter 5 for a detailed discussion of runes and numerology.)

Name of Power	Meaning	Number	Goddess, giant equivalent
Ar	honour, respect	9	
Gar	spear	16	Afi
Auja	good luck	22	Ing
Ulf	wolf	24	
Asc	ash-tree	26	Kari
Bar	bear	27	
Alu	holy drink	27	
Vé	sacred place	27	
Hrafn	raven	29	
Lathu	a summons	30	
Alag	on-lay	36	Frey, Vor
Hrusa	land	36	
Hugin	thought	39	
Salu	health	42	Thiazi
Iorth	the Earth	42	
Gothi	priest	44	
Wihaz	sanctified	45	Mani, Bragi
Svin	sacred hog	45	
Alraun	root-image	46	
Burin	carving tool	46	
Nethan	to boldly go	46	
Ymir	primal giant	47	Bor, Aegir
Asatrú	faith in the gods	48	
Gandr	wand power	50	Bil
Laukaz	growth	50	
Vitki	magician	52	Thjalfi
Gungnir	spear of Odin	52	Erda
Eard	native soil	52	
Wihyan	to sanctify	53	Tiwaz, Hela
Munin	memory	53	
Hael	an omen	53	
Ehwe	transmission	55	Ull, Nerthus
Wod	divine inspiration	55	
Wexan	to grow	56	
Önd	vital breath	57	Gialp
Gibu Auja	bring good luck	60	Sól, Nudd
Asgard	home of the gods	60	
Mattr	personal force	63	
Medu	mead (sacred drink)	65	
Athele	noble	66	

Name of Power	Meaning	Number	Goddess, giant equivalent
Megin	personal magic power	67	
Erilaz	runemaster	69	Harbard, Veratyr, Skuld, Ostara
Sond	a message	73	
Ofreskr	second-sighted	75	
Framsynn	far-sighted	77	Borvo
Örlog	destiny	79	
Anmod	single-minded	81	
Haigalaz	sacred potency	80	
Ungandiz	magically protected	81	
Mell	sacred hammer	81	
Audhumla	primal cow	87	Gunlod
Wodiz	divine frenzy	87	
Midgard	middle Earth	88	
Bifrost	rainbow bridge	91	
Valhalla	hall of the gods	92	Forseti
Aurgelmir	primal being	94	Wilbet, Gwydion
Othroerir	cauldron of inspiration	94	
Mjöllnir	Thor's hammer	123	

Postscript

The Rúnfalaich

Since they were given to the human race, the runes have been in continuous magical use. In former days they were used by scribes, diviners, wise men and women for everything from fortune telling to memorial inscriptions. But however they were employed, their basic religious and magical meaning was still present within them. For all of this time, rune lore has survived, preserved in ancient writings, on runestones and in folk tradition, magical formulae, heraldry, vernacular architecture, folk art and hereditary magical practice. Throughout the centuries rune users have been part of the corporate experience of runecraft. This links us all together, wherever they were or are. We are all participators in the Rúnfalaich, the fellowship of rune users throughout space and time.

Today, there is a greater awareness than ever of the runes, even in places where runes never reached in ancient times. There is an interest and understanding which is expanding year by year. The runes contain a dynamism that exists now, an eternal and present reality which is an inspiration. By using the runes now, we can hear the runemasters and runemistresses of old speaking directly to us. Today, we can make our own individual discovery of the living presence of the runes in the past and in the present. Rune magic provides us with a means of turning things to our advantage and, in the spirit of service, to the advantage of our fellow human beings.

Figure 38 The goddess Frigg, queen of heaven.

Appendices

Appendix 1:
Runic Correspondences

Each rune has a tree, herb, colour, polarity, element and
deity. These correspondences are used in advanced rune
magic.

Rune	Tree(s)	Herb	Colour	Polarity	Element	Deity	Symbolic meaning
Feoh	elder	nettle	light red	female	fire/earth	Frey/Freyja	the primal cow, Audhumla
Ur	Birch	Iceland moss	dark green	male	earth	Thor/Urd	horns of the ox
Thorn	oak/thorn	houseleek	bright red	male	fire	Thor	the thorn, hammer of Thor
As	ash	fly agaric	dark blue	male	air	Odin/Eostre	the ash Yggdrasil
Rad	oak	mugwort	bright red	male	air	Ing/Nerthus	wheel under cart
Ken	pine	cowslip	light red	female	fire	Heimdall / Freyja/Frey	fire of the torch / primal fire of Muspellheim
Gyfu	ash/elm	heartsease	deep blue	m/f	air	Gefn	sacred mark
Wyn	ash	flax	yellow	male	earth	Odin/Frigg	wind vane, flag
Hagal	ash/yew	bryony	light blue	female	ice	Urd/Heimdall	structural beams, the world, hailstone, serpent
Nyd	beech/rowan	snakeroot	black	female	fire	Skuld	fire-bow and block
Is	alder	henbane	black	female	ice	Verdandi	icicle, primal ice of Niflheim
Jera	oak	rosemary	light blue	male/female	earth	Frey/Freyja	sacred marriage heaven/earth
Eoh	yew/poplar	bryony	dark blue	male	all	Ullr	vertical column of the Yew tree

Rune	Tree(s)	Herb	Colour	Polarity	Element	Deity	Symbolic meaning
Peorth	beech/aspen	aconite	black	female	water	Frigg	the womb, a dice cup
Elhaz	yew/service	sedge	gold	male/female	air	Heimdall	the elk, the flying swan, open hand
Sigel	juniper/bay	mistletoe	white	male	air	Balder	the holy solar wheel
Tyr	oak	aconite	bright red	male	air	Tyr	the vault of the heavens over the cosmic pillar
Beorc	birch	lady's mantle	dark green	female	earth	Nerthus/Holda	breasts of the Earth Mother Goddess
Ehwaz	oak/ash	ragwort	white	male/female	earth	Frey/Freyja	two poles bound
Man	holly	madder	deep red	male/female	air	Heimdall/Odin/Frigg	marriage of earth/heaven
Lagu	osier	leek	deep green	female	water	Njord/Nerthus	sea wave, waterfall
Ing	apple	selfheal	yellow	male/female	water/earth	Ing (Frey)	the genitals
Odal	hawthorn	clover	deep yellow	male	earth	Odin	enclosed estate, land property
Dag	spruce	clary	light blue	male	fire/air	Heimdall	balance (night, day)
Ac	oak	hemp	light green	male	fire	Thor	mark tree, boundary oak

Rune	Tree(s)	Herb	Colour	Polarity	Element	Deity	Symbolic meaning
Os	ash	'magic mushroom'	dark blue	male	air	Odin	mouth, speech eloquence etc.
Yr	yew	bryony/ mandrake	gold	male/ female	all	Odin/Frigg	yew tree, bow, midpoint
Ior	linden/ivy	kelp	black	female	water	Njord	Jörmungand, the world serpent
Ear	yew	hemlock	brown	female	earth	Hela	earth-grave
Cweorth	bay/beech	rue	tawny	female	fire	Loge	funeral pyre
Calc	maple/rowan	yarrow	white	female	earth	Norns	grail-cup
Stan	witch hazel/ blackthorn	Iceland moss	grey	male	earth	Nerthus	sacred stone
Gar	ash/spindle	garlic	dark blue	male	all	Odin	spear of Odin
Wolfsangel	yew	wolfsbane	blood-red	female	earth	Vidar	wolf-hook
Erda	whitebeam/ elder/birch	mint	brown	female	earth	Erda	garden
Ul	buckthorn	thistle	tawny	male	air	Valdh	turning-point
Ziu	oak	aconite	orange-red	male	air/fire	Ziu	thunderbolt
Sol	juniper	sunflower	gold	female	fire	Sól	sun disc

Appendix 2:
Attributes of the Northern Deities

Each Northern goddess and god represents a certain collection of powers and attributes, which can be contacted and used in rune magic. Below are the main powers and qualities attributed to these deities.

Aegir	god of the stormy sea
Baldr	sun god who is killed and resurrected
Bragi	god of poetry and boasting
Eír	goddess of healing and medicine
Erda	primal earth goddess (Allmother)
Fjolnir	minor god of wisdom and learning
Forseti	axe god of justice
Frey	fertility god (also Fro, Freyr and Ingvé-Frey)
Freyja	fertility-huntress goddess, free sexuality (also Vanadis)
Frigg	goddess of settled civilisation, married sexuality. Queen of Heaven
Gefn	goddess of gift-giving
Gefjon	goddess of unmarried women
Gersemi	goddess of beauty, Freyja's daughter (see also Hnossi)
Heimdall	watcher and guardian god (see Rig)
Hela	goddess of underworld and the dead
Hermod	messenger of the gods, son of Odin
Hler	primal water god
Hlín	goddess of compassion
Hnossi	goddess of beauty, Freyja's daughter (see also Gersemi)
Iduna	goddess of eternal life
Ing	fertility god (see Frey)
Kari	primal air deity
Lofn	goddess of secret love affairs
Loge	primal fire god
Loki	trickster god
Mani	moon deity
Mimir	god of waters beneath the earth, the unconscious
Nehallennia	great mother of sea and vegetation
Nerthus	mother earth goddess (see Erda)

Njord	stiller-of-storms god
Oberon	High Lord of Elves and Men
Odin	'Allfather' spirit god of the runes, inspiration, shamanism, magic and war
Phol	god of male fertility (aspect of Balder)
Ran	goddess of death for those who perish at sea
Rig	god of society's order (see Heimdall)
Rinda	primal goddess of the frozen earth
Sif	consort of Thor
Skadi	scathing goddess of wintertime destruction
Skuld	third Norn or 'Weird Sister', the future
Snotra	goddess of women's gentle wisdom
Sól	sun goddess
Sjöfn	goddess of love
Syn	guardian goddess of doorways
Tîwaz	god of war and victory (also Tyr)
Thor	hammer god of thunder, agriculture and craftsmanship
Tyr	see Tîwaz
Ullr	winter god of archery, skiing and yew magic (also Uller and Ulli)
Urd	first Norn or 'Weird Sister', the past
Vali	archer god, assimilated with St Valentine
Var	goddess of awareness
Vanadis	by-name of Freyja
Vé	Odin's brother, holiness
Verdandi	second Norn or 'Weird Sister', the present
Vidar	son of Odin, slayer of the Fenris Wolf
Vili	Odin's brother, the will
Vor	witness goddess
Walburga	lunar goddess
Waldh	forest god of healing
Woden	by-name of Odin
Ziu	sky god

Appendix 3:
Runic Half-Months

During the year, each Elder Futhark rune rules a half-month. These times of year are especially powerful for magic connected with that rune. Below are the beginning dates of each runic half-month. (Times are local apparent time, averaged to the nearest hour):

Rune	Times of day	Strongest point	Half-month begins
Feoh	12.30–13.30	13.00	29 June 03.00
Ur	13.30–14.30	14.00	14 July 08.00
Thorn	14.30–15.30	15.00	29 July 14.00
As	15.30–16.30	16.00	13 August 19.00
Rad	16.30–17.30	17.00	29 August 00.00
Ken	17.30–18.30	18.00	13 September 06.00
Gyfu	18.30–19.30	19.00	28 September 11.00
Wyn	19.30–20.30	20.00	13 October 16.00
Hagal	20.30–21.30	21.00	28 October 22.00
Nyd	21.30–22.30	22.00	13 November 03.00
Is	22.30–23.30	23.00	28 November 08.00
Jera	23.30–00.30	00.00	13 December 14.00
Eoh	00.30–01.30	01.00	28 December 19.00
Peorth	01.30–02.30	02.00	13 January 01.00
Elhaz	02.30–03.30	03.00	28 January 05.00
Sigel	03.30–04.30	04.00	12 February 10.00
Tyr	04.30–05.30	05.00	27 February 16.00
Beorc	05.30–06.30	06.00	14 March 21.00
Ehwaz	06.30–07.30	07.00	30 March 02.00
Man	07.30–08.30	08.00	14 April 07.00
Lagu	08.30–09.30	09.00	29 April 12.00
Ing	09.30–10.30	10.00	14 May 18.00
Odal	10.30–11.30	11.00	29 May 23.00
Dag	11.30–12.30	12.00	14 June 04.00

Appendix 4:
The Northern Tradition Planetary Hours

The planetary deities of the Northern Tradition rule certain hours. Magically, these hours are best for operations related to the deities.

	Sunday	Monday	Tuesday	Wednesday	Thursday	Friday	Saturday
00.00–01.00	Thor	Frigg	Loki	Sól	Mani	Tyr	Odin
01.00–02.00	Tyr	Odin	Thor	Frigg	Loki	Sól	Mani
02.00–03.00	Sól	Mani	Tyr	Odin	Thor	Frigg	Loki
03.00–04.00	Frigg	Loki	Sól	Mani	Tyr	Odin	Thor
04.00–05.00	Odin	Thor	Frigg	Loki	Sól	Mani	Tyr
05.00–06.00	Mani	Tyr	Odin	Thor	Frigg	Loki	Sól
06.00–07.00	Loki	Sól	Mani	Tyr	Odin	Thor	Frigg
07.00–08.00	Thor	Frigg	Loki	Sól	Mani	Tyr	Odin
08.00–09.00	Tyr	Odin	Thor	Frigg	Loki	Sól	Mani
09.00–10.00	Sól	Mani	Tyr	Odin	Thor	Frigg	Loki
10.00–11.00	Frigg	Loki	Sól	Mani	Tyr	Odin	Thor
11.00–12.00	Odin	Thor	Frigg	Loki	Sól	Mani	Tyr
12.00–13.00	Sól	Mani	Tyr	Odin	Thor	Frigg	Loki
13.00–14.00	Frigg	Loki	Sól	Mani	Tyr	Odin	Thor
14.00–15.00	Odin	Thor	Frigg	Loki	Sól	Mani	Tyr
15.00–16.00	Mani	Tyr	Odin	Thor	Frigg	Loki	Sól
16.00–17.00	Loki	Sól	Mani	Tyr	Odin	Thor	Frigg
17.00–18.00	Thor	Frigg	Loki	Sól	Mani	Tyr	Odin
18.00–19.00	Tyr	Odin	Thor	Frigg	Loki	Sól	Mani
19.00–20.00	Sól	Mani	Tyr	Odin	Thor	Frigg	Loki
20.00–21.00	Frigg	Loki	Sól	Mani	Tyr	Odin	Thor
21.00–22.00	Odin	Thor	Frigg	Loki	Sól	Mani	Tyr
22.00–23.00	Mani	Tyr	Odin	Thor	Frigg	Loki	Sól
23.00–24.00	Loki	Sól	Mani	Tyr	Odin	Thor	Frigg

Appendix 5:
The Eight Tides of the Day

Tides	English	Anglo-Saxon	Welsh	Ruling Runes
4.30–7.30	Morntide	Morgan	Bore	Tyr, Beorc, Eh
7.30–10.30	Undernoon	Daeg Mael	Anterth	Man, Lagu, Ing
10.30–13.30	Noontide	Mid Daeg	Nawn	Odal, Dag, Feoh
13.30–16.30	Undorne	Ofanverthr Dagr	Echwydd	Ur, Thorn, As
16.30–19.30	Eventide	Midaften	Gwechwydd	Rad, Ken, Gyfu
19.30–22.30	Nighttide	Ondverth Nott	Ucher	Wyn, Hagal, Nyd
22.30–1.30	Midnight	Mid Niht	Dewaint	Is, Jare, Eoh
1.30–4.30	Uht	Ofanverth Nott	Pylgeint	Peorth, Elhaz, Sigel

Appendix 6:
Zodiac/Runic Correspondences

Zodiac sign	Ruling planet	Deity	Day	Stone	Animal	Rune
Aries	Mars	Tyr	Tuesday	Diamond	Sheep	Eh
Taurus	Venus	Frigg	Friday	Sapphire	Bull	Ing
Gemini	Mercury	Odin	Wednesday	Emerald	Twin Ravens	Dag
Cancer	Moon	Mani	Monday	Agate	Crab	Ur
Leo	Sun	Sól	Sunday	Ruby	Lion	As
Virgo	Mercury	Odin	Wednesday	Sardonyx	Cat	Cen
Libra	Venus	Frigg	Friday	Chrysolite	Serpent	Wyn
Scorpio	Mars/Pluto	Tyr	Tuesday	Opal	Scorpion	Nyd
Sagittarius	Jupiter	Thor	Thursday	Topaz	Aurochs	Jera
Capricorn	Saturn	Thor	Thursday	Turquoise	Goat	Peorth
Aquarius	Saturn/Uranus	Loki	Saturday	Amethyst	Eagle	Sigel
Pisces	Jupiter/Neptune	Thor	Thursday	Bloodstone	Fish	Beorc

Appendix 7:
The Palaces of the Gods

The twelve palaces of the gods, listed in *Grimnismál*, have the following correspondences:

Palace	Zodiac Sign	Deity	Dates	Runes	Rune completely within sign
Bilskirnir	Aries	Thor	March 21–April 20	Beorc/Eh/Man	Eh	30 March–14 April
Thrymheim	Taurus	Skadi	April 21–May 20	Man/Lagu/Ing	Lagu	29 April–14 May
Folkvang	Gemini	Freyja	May 21–June 20	Ing/Odal/Dag	Odal	29 May–14 June
Himminbjorg	Cancer	Heimdall	June 21–July 20	Dag/Feoh/Ur	Feoh	29 June–14 July
Breidablikk	Leo	Balder	July 21–August 21	Ur/Thorn/As	Thorn	29 July–13 August
Sokkvabekk	Virgo	Saga	August 22–September 22	As/Rad/Cen	Rad	29 August–13 September
Glitnir	Libra	Forseti	September 23–October 22	Cen/Gyfu/Wyn	Gyfu	28 September–13 October
Gladsheim	Scorpio	Odin	October 23–November 22	Wyn/Hagal/Nyd	Hagal	28 October–13 November
Ydalir	Sagittarius	Ullr	November 23–December 20	Nyd/Is/Jara	Is	28 November–13 December
Landvidi	Capricorn	Vidar	December 21–January 19	Jara/Eoh/Peorth	Eoh	28 December–13 January
Valaskjálf	Aquarius	Vali	January 20–February 18	Peorth/Elhaz/Sigel	Elhaz	28 January–12 February
Noatun	Pisces	Njord	February 19–March 20	Sigel/Tyr/Beorc	Tyr	27 February–14 March

Glossary

The following list gives the exact definitions of technical terms used in rune magic and other Northern Tradition work. The abbreviations below give the original language where the words originated.

Key:

AS	Anglo-Saxon
EA	East Anglian
E	Traditional English
EC	Ecclesiastical
G	Gaelic
I	Irish
N	Old Norse
S	Scots

Aesir	the goddesses and gods of the Teutonic pantheon (N)
Aett	one of the eight directions; a place; homestead; family (N)
Airt	Aett (q.v.) (S)
álag	on-lay (q.v.) (N)
Alfödr	Allfather, 'the oldest of the gods' (N)
álfreka	to desecrate, literally, to drive away the elves (N)
Asa	a god of the Aesir (N)
Asatrú	name given to the religion revering the Aesir (N)
Burin	Tool for carving runes, etc. (I)
Call	magical incantation (EA)

Croomstick	staff with hooked end, used physically or magically (EA)
Cunning Man	man with knowledge of the use of spells, herbs, traditional medicine and magic (E)
Dominical Letter	letter used as a number in the seven-day week cycle (EC)
Feisefín	the Ogham wheel known as Fionn's Wheel, Window or Shield (I)
Ferridge	a gingerbread biscuit or cake, bearing appropriate symbolic designs, in this case, runes (EA)
Galdr	call (q.v.)(N)
Gandr	magic wand, also the power emanating from one; blast (q.v.)(N)
Golden Number	year-number in the 19-year cycle of Sun and Moon (E)
Hamfarir	travelling around in an assumed shape or form different from one's usual natural form (N)
Hamingja	mutable magic energy, through which shape shifting and other magical skills are accomplished, sometimes personalised as a guardian angel or spirit (N)
Hamr	body shape or image (N)
Harrow	an outdoor altar, usually stone (AS)
Hlutr	a small portable image of a deity (N)
Hugr	the cognitive-perceptive faculty (N)
Insigil	runic 'star' drawn inside a circle (E)
Ka!	'So be it!', 'So mote it be!' (EA)
Landvaettir	guardian earth sprites (N)
Lík	the physical body (Lich) (N)
Lindorm	dragon-like ribbon pattern containing runes (N)
Loegr	(invasive sorcery commanding spirits) operative magic (N)
Megin	a personal force, distinct from physical power or strength, the possession of which assures success and good fortune
Mete Wand	measuring stick (E)
Minni	the faculty of reflection, the mind (N)
Nawn	Noontide (W)
Nithstong	Niding Pole for cursing an enemy (N)

Nowl	the navel of the body, or the sacred *omphalos* of a place (EA)
ódhr	the faculty of inspiration (N)
ófreskr	second-sighted, one with vision of events in the spirit world (N)
Ogham	the ancient British and Irish tree alphabet (I)
Önd	vital breath or universal soul (N)
Öndvegissulur	main pillars of a wooden temple, the most sacred part, into which the Reginnaglar (sacred nails) were hammered (N)
On-lay	a spell or incantation pronounced on a place (N)
Sál	the 'shade', after-death image (N)
Sele	time of day, year or season (EA)
Stall	an indoor altar (E)
Tein'éigin	need-fire (G)
Tide	a defined span of time (e.g. the eight Tides of the day) (E)
Transvolution	the processes and effects of 'the way things happen' (modern technical term)
Vanir	the pre-agricultural goddesses and gods of organic life (N)
Vé	sacred enclosure (N)
Vébond	posts and rope enclosing a Vé (N)
Völva	a wise woman (N)
Warlock	man with the power of binding spirits using runes, calls and knot-magic (from Old Norse *vardlokkur*)
Wyrd	the web of causal and effective processes in the world (AS)
Yarthkin	harmful earth sprite (EA)

Further Reading and Select Bibliography

The area covered by rune magic and related subjects has a large literature. These are the major relevant works, which will help readers to extend their lines of enquiry.

Agrell, Sigurd: *Semantik Mysteriereligion och nordisk Runmagi*. Bonniers, Stockholm, 1931.

——: *Lapptrumor och Runmagi*. C.W.K. Glerup, Lund, 1934.

Anderson, Mary: *Colour Therapy*. Aquarian, London, 1990.

Arntz, Helmut: *Handbuch der Runenkunde*. Niemeyer, Haale a.d. Saale, 1944.

Ayres, James: *British Folk Art*. Thames and Hudson, London, 1977.

Aswynn, Freya: *Leaves of Yggdrasil*. Privately published, London, 1988.

Baeksted, A.: *Mâlruner og troldruner: Runemagiske studier*. Politikens Forlag, Copenhagen, 1952.

Baker, Margaret: *Folklore and Customs in Rural England*. David and Charles, Newton Abbot, 1974.

Barley, N.F.: *Old English Colour Classification: Where do Matters Stand? Anglo-Saxon England*, vol 3, p.15–28, 1972.

Barratt, William: *Deathbed Visions*. Methuen, London, 1926.

Barrett, Clive: *The Norse Tarot*. Aquarian, Wellingborough, 1989.

——: *The Viking Gods*. Aquarian, Wellingborough, 1989.

Bates, Brian: *The Way of Wyrd*. Berkley, New York, 1983.

Bernheimer, Richard: *Wild Men in the Middle Ages*. University Press, Harvard, 1952.

Besant, Annie: *Man and His Bodies*. Theosophical, London, 1911.

Blacker, Carmen, & Loewe, Michael (eds.): *Ancient Cosmologies*. RKP, London, 1975.

Blum, Ralph: *The Book of Runes*. Eddison-Sadd, London, 1982.

Bonwick, James: *Irish Druids and the Old Religions*. Dorset, New York, 1986.

Branston, B.: *The Lost Gods of England*. Thames and Hudson, London, 1957.

Brennan, J.H.: *Astral Doorways*. Aquarian, Wellingborough, 1986.

Bromwich, R.: *Trioedd Ynys Prydein*. University of Cardiff Press, Cardiff, 1979.

Brøndsted, Johannes: *The Vikings*. Penguin, Harmondsworth, 1965.

Brown, A. (ed.): *Early English and Old Norse Studies*. Methuen, London, 1963.

Burton, Richard F.: *Ultima Thule*. London, 1875.

Campbell, J.G.: *Superstitions of the Highlands and Islands of Scotland*. Edinburgh, 1900.

Chadwick, H.M.: *The Cult of Othin*. Cambridge University Press, 1899.

——: *The Heroic Age*. Cambridge University Press, London, 1912.

Chaney, William A.: *The Cult of Kingship in Anglo-Saxon England*. University of California Press, Berkeley, 1970.

Cockayne, O: *Leechdoms, Wortcunning and Starcraft*. 3 vols. Rolls Series, London, 1864.

Cosijn, P.J.: *Het Burgundische Runenopschrift van Charnay. Taalkundige Bijdragen*. Haarlem, 1877.

Coxhead, Nona: *Mindpower*. Mandala, London, 1987.

Clark, Anthony: *The Aquarian Rune Pack*. Aquarian, Wellingborough, 1987.

Dahlberg, Erik: *Suecia Antiqua et Hodierna*. Stockholm, 1661–78.

Dent, A: *Lost Beasts of Britain*. Harrap, London, 1964.

Devereux, Paul: *Places of Power: Secret Energies at Ancient Sites*. Blandford, London, 1990.

——: Steele, John, & Kubrin, David: *Earthmind*. Harper and Row, New York, 1989.

Dickens, Bruce: *Runic and Heroic Poems*. Cambridge University Press, Cambridge, 1915.

Ebers, Edith, & Wollenich, Franz: *Felsbilder der Alpen*. Hallein, 1982.

Eliade, Mircea: *Shamanism*. Princeton University Press, Princeton, 1964.

——: *The Myth of Eternal Return, or, Cosmos and History*. Princeton University Press, Princeton, 1971.

Elliott, Ralph W.V.: *Runes: An Introduction*. Manchester University Press, Manchester, 1959.

Ellis, Hilda R.: *The Road to Hel*. Cambridge University Press, Cambridge, 1943.

Elworthy, Frederick Thomas: *The Evil Eye*. John Murray, London, 1895.

Evans-Wentz, W.Y.: *The Fairy Faith in Celtic Countries*, Oxford University Press, Oxford, 1911.

Fillipetti, Herva, & Trotereau, Janine: *Symboles et pratiques rituelles dans la maison paysanne traditionelle*. Paris, 1978.

Flowers, Stephen: *Sigurdr, Rebirth and Initiation*. The Rune-Gild, Austin, 1985.

——: *Runes and Magic: Magical Formulaic Elements in the Older Runic Tradition*. Lang, New York, 1986.

——: *The Galdrabók: An Icelandic Grimoire*. Samuel Weiser, York Beach, 1989.

Fox, Oliver: *Astral Projection*. University Books, New York, 1962.

Gimbutas, Marija: *The Goddesses and Gods of Old Europe*. Thames and Hudson, London, 1982.

Gjerset, K.: *History of Iceland*. Macmillan, London, 1924.

Golther, Wolfgang: *Handbuch der germanischen Mythologie*. Leipzig, 1895.

Gorsleben, Rudolf J.: *Die Hoch-Zeit der Menschheit*. Köhler and Amerlang, Leipzig, 1930.

Graf, Heinz-Joachim: *Die Runennamen als sprachliche Belege zur Ausdeutung germanischer Sinnbilder. Germanien*, 1941, pp. 254–9.

Grattan, J.H.G., & Singer, C.: *Anglo-Saxon Magic and Medicine*. Oxford University Press, Oxford, 1952.

Graves, Robert: *The White Goddess*. Faber, London, 1961.

Green, C.: *Out-of-the-Body Experiences*. Institute of Psychophysical Research, Oxford, 1968.

Grimm, Jacob: *Teutonic Mythology*. Dover, New York, 1966.

Grönbech, Vilhelm: *The Culture of the Teutons*. Oxford University Press, London, 1931.

Guillaume, J.Y.: *Les Runes et les Etoiles*. Narbonne, 1983.

Haigh, D.H.: *The Runic Monuments of Northumbria*. Sheffield, 1870.

Halifax, Joan: *Shamanic Voices. The Shaman as seer, poet and healer.* Dutton, New York, 1979.

Henderson, G.: *Survivals in Belief among the Celts.* Glasgow, 1911.

Herrmann, H.A.: *Ein unbekannter Runenstabkalender. Germanien,* 1939, p. 266–7.

Herrmann, Paul: *Das altgermanische Priesterwesen.* Diderichs, Jena, 1929.

Hesse, Hermann: *The Glass Bead Game.* Cape, London, 1970.

Hickes, G.: *Linguarum Vett. Septentrionalium Thesaurus, 1703–05.* Scolar Press, London, 1970.

Hodgkin, R.H.: *A History of the Anglo-Saxons.* Oxford University Press, Oxford, 1939.

Holmberg, Axel: *Skandinaviens Hällristningar.* Stockholm, 1848.

Homeyer, C.G.: *Die Haus- und Hofmarken.* Berlin, 1870.

Houston, Jean: *The Possible Human.* Tarcher, Los Angeles, 1982.

Howard, Michael: *The Runes and Other Magical Alphabets.* Aquarian, Wellingborough, 1978.

——: *The Wisdom of the Runes.* Rider, London, 1985.

——: *Understanding Runes.* Aquarian, London, 1990.

Huxley, F.: *The Way of the Sacred.* Thames and Hudson, London, 1974.

Jacobsen, Lis & Moltke, E.: *Danmarks Runeindskrifter.* Copenhagen, 1942.

Jankuhn, H.: *Die Ausgraben in Haithabu.* Deutsches Ahnenerbe, Berlin, 1943.

Jansen, Sven B.: *Runes of Sweden.* Bedminster, New York, 1962.

Jensen, K. Frank: *Magiske Runer.* Sphinx, Copenhagen, 1991.

——: *The Prophetic Cards – a catalog of cards for fortune-telling.* Oroboros, Roskilde, 1985.

Jung, C.G.: *The Collected Works* (20 vols.). Routledge and Kegan Paul, London, 1978–89.

Jung, Erich: *Germanische Götter und Helden in Christlicher Zeit.* Berlin, 1939.

Kermode, P.: *Manx Crosses.* Methuen, London, 1907.

Kilner, Walter J.: *The Human Atmosphere.* Dutton, London, 1911.

Klimo, Jon: *Chanelling: Investigations on receiving information from paranormal sources.* Aquarian, Wellingborough, 1988.

Krause, Wolfgang: *Runen.* De Gruyter, Berlin, 1970.

Larsen, S.: *The Shaman's Doorway.* Harper and Row, New York, 1976.

LeShan, Lawrence: *How to Meditate.* Aquarian, Wellingborough, 1989.

Lewis, I.M.: *Ecstatic Religion.* Penguin, Harmondsworth, 1971.

Lindenschmit, L.: *Die Altherthümer unserer heidnischen vorzeit.* Mainz, 1874–7.

Lindqvist, Sune: *Gotlands Bildsteine* (vols I & II), Kungl. Vitterhets Historie Och Antikvitets Akadamien, Stockholm, 1941–2.

Lommel, A. *Shamanism.* McGraw-Hill, New York, 1967.

Lovelock, James: *Gaia: A New Look at Life on Earth.* Oxford University Press, London, 1979.

Macalister, R.A. Stewart: *The Secret Languages of Ireland.* Cambridge University Press, Cambridge, 1937.

MacCulloch, J.A.: *The Religion of the Ancient Celts.* Edinburgh, 1911.

——: *The Celtic and Scandinavian Religions.* London, 1948.

Magnusson, Finnur: *Runamo og Runerne.* Copenhagen, 1841.

Martin, Anthony: *Understanding Astral Projection.* Aquarian, Wellingborough, 1990.

Maslow, Abraham: *The Farther Reaches of Human Nature.* Penguin, Harmondsworth, 1973.

Masters, R.E.L., & Houston, J.: *The Varieties of Psychedelic Experience.* Harper and Row, New York, 1966.

Matthews, John (ed.): *A Celtic Reader.* Aquarian, London, 1991.

Mayr, Rolf: *Hausmarken von Kobern. Germanien,* 1934, p. 101–9.

Michell, John: *The Earth Spirit.* Thames and Hudson, London, 1974.

——: *Simulacra.* Thames and Hudson, London, 1979.

——: *Spontaneous Images and Acheropites. Fortean Times 30,* 1979.

Mogk, E.: *Germanische Religionsgeschichte und Mythologie.* Schikowski, Berlin, 1927.

Moltke, Erik: *Runes and Their Origin: Denmark and Elsewhere.* Viking Society for Northern Research, Copenhagen, 1984.

Nichols, Ross: *The Book of Druidry.* Aquarian, London, 1990.

Odle, Chris: *Practical Visualization*. Aquarian, Wellingborough, 1990.

Olrik, Axel: *Ragnarök: Die Sagen vom Weltuntergang*. Berlin, 1922.

Olsen, M.: *Farms and Fanes of Ancient Norway*. Bokcentralen, Oslo, 1928.

—— (ed.): *Norges innskrifter med de yngre runer*. Bokcentralen, Oslo, 1944.

Osborne, Marijane, & Langland, Stella: *Rune Games*. Routledge and Kegan Paul, London, 1982.

Page, R.I.: *An Introduction to English Runes*. Methuen, London, 1973.

Pennick, Nigel: *Ogham and Runic: Magical Writing of Old Britain and Northern Europe*. Fenris-Wolf, Bar Hill, 1978.

——: *The Ancient Science of Geomancy*. Thames and Hudson, London, 1979.

——: *Runestaves and Oghams*. Runestaff, Bar Hill, 1986.

——: *Lost Lands and Sunken Cities*. Fortean Tomes, London, 1987.

——: *Einst War Uns Die Erde Heilig*. Felicitas-Hübner Verlag, Dehringhausen, 1987.

——: *Games of the Gods*. Century, London, 1988.

——: *Practical Magic in the Northern Tradition*. Aquarian, Wellingborough, 1989.

——: *Das Runen Orakel*. Droemer Knaur, München, 1990.

——: *Runic Astrology*. Aquarian, Wellingborough, 1990.

——: *Mazes and Labyrinths*. Hale, London, 1990.

——: *The Origin of Ogam and Runestaves*, in *Celtic Secrets*, ed. Donald L. Cyr, Stonehenge Viewpoint, Santa Barbara, 1990.

——: *The Secret Lore of Runes and Other Ancient Alphabets*, Rider, London, 1991.

Petter, Nikolaas: *Klare Onderrichtinge der Vortrefflijcke Worstel-Kunst*. Amsterdam, 1674.

Philippson, E.A.: *Germanisches Heidentum bei den Angelsachsen*. Tauchnitz, Leipzig, 1929.

Rees, Alwyn, & Rees, Brinley: *Celtic Heritage*. Thames and Hudson, London, 1967.

Rendel, Peter: *Understanding the Chakras*. Aquarian, Wellingborough, 1990.

Reuter, Otto Sigfrid: *Germanische Himmelskunde*. Köhler and Amerlang, Jena, 1934.

Roberts, Anthony: *Geomythics*. *The Ley Hunter* 88, 1980.

Rosen, Sven, & Rickard, Bob: *The Runamo Runes. Fortean Times* 35, 1981.

Ross, Anne: *Druids, Gods and Heroes of Celtic Mythology.* Routledge and Kegan Paul, London, 1986.

——: *The Pagan Celts.* Routledge and Kegan Paul, London, 1986.

Rothenberg, J. (ed.): *Technicians of the Sacred.* Doubleday, New York, 1968.

Schneider, K.: *Die Germanischen Runennamen, Versuch einer Gesamtdeutung.* Athenaeum, Meisenheim, 1956.

Schramm, P.: *Herrschaftszeichen und Staatssymbolik.* Stuttgart, 1954.

Shippey, T.A.: *Poems of Wisdom and Learning in Old English.* Cambridge University Press, Cambridge, 1976.

Smith, Susy: *The Enigma of Out of the Body Travel.* Helix, London, 1965.

Spiesberger, Karl: *Runenmagie.* Schikowski, Berlin, 1955.

Slauson, Irv: *The Religion of Odin: A Handbook.* Asatrú Free Church Committee, Red Wing, 1978.

Stanley, E.G.: *The Search for Anglo-Saxon Paganism.* Brewer, Cambridge, 1975.

Stephens, George: *The Old-Northern Runic Monuments of Scandinavia and England.* London, 1866.

Storms, G.: *Anglo-Saxon Magic.* Nijhoff, Den Haag, 1948.

Strachan, Francoise: *Natural Magic.* Golden Hands, London, 1974.

Stretton, Clement E.: *Tectonic Art. Ancient Trade Guilds and Companies.* Melton Mowbray Times Co, Melton Mowbray, 1909.

Stromback, Dag: *Sejd.* Geber, Stockholm, 1935.

Syversen, Earl: *Norse Runic Inscriptions.* Vine Hill Press, Sebastopol, 1979.

Taylor, I.: *Greeks and Goths: A Study on the Runes.* London, 1879.

Thorsson, Edred: *Futhark: A Handbook of Rune Magic.* Samuel Weiser, York Beach, 1984.

——: *Runelore: A Handbook of Esoteric Runology.* Weiser, York Beach, 1987.

——: *At the Well of Wyrd: A Handbook of Runic Divination.* Weiser, York Beach, 1988.

——: *Rune Might: Secret Practices of German Rune Magicians.* Llewellyn, St Paul, 1988.

Tolkien, J.R.R.: *Tree and Leaf*. George Allen & Unwin, London, 1964.

Turville-Petre, E.O.G.: *Myth and Religion of the North*. Holt, Rinehart and Winston, New York, 1964.

Tyson, Donald: *The Power of the Runes*. Llewellyn, St Paul, 1988.

Vigfusson, G. (ed.): *Icelandic Sagas* (4 vols.), London, 1887–94.

von List, Guido: *Das Geheimnis der Runen*. Guido von List Gesellschaft, Wien, 1912.

von Reichenbach, Karl: *The Odic Force*. University Books, New York, 1968.

von Zaborsky, Oskar: *Urväter-Erbe in deutsches Volkskunst*. Deutscher Ahnenerbe, Leipzig, 1936.

Walker, Barbara G.: *The Woman's Encyclopedia of Myths and Secrets*. Harper and Row, San Francisco, 1983.

——: *The Woman's Dictionary of Symbols and Sacred Objects*. Harper and Row, San Francisco, 1988.

Walker, Benjamin: *Beyond the Body*. Routledge and Kegan Paul, London, 1974.

Wardle, Thorolf: *Runelore*. Deutschgläubige Gemeinschaft, Braunschweig, 1983.

——: *The Runenames*. Deutschgläubige Gemeinschaft, Braunschweig, 1984.

Weber, Edmund: *Runenkunde*. Berlin, 1941.

Westergaard, Kai-Erik: *Skrifttegen og Symboler*. Oslo, 1981.

Willis, Paul E.: *Profane Culture*. Thames & Hudson, London, 1978.

Willis, Tony: *The Runic Workbook*. Aquarian, Wellingborough, 1986.

Wirth, Hermann: *Die Heilige Urschrift der Menschheit*. Köhler and Amerlang, Leipzig, 1934.

Wood-Martin, W.G.: *Traces of the Elder Faiths of Ireland*. London, 1902.

Worsae, J.J.A.: *Runamo og Braavalleslaget*, Copenhagen, 1844.

Zaehner, R.C.: *Mysticism, Sacred and Profane*. Oxford University Press, Oxford, 1957.

Zeller, Otto: *Der Ursprung der Buchstabenschrift und das Runenalphabet*. Biblio, Osnabrück, 1977.

Index